MERGERS &
ACQUISITIONS

Real people...

MERGERS & ACQUISITIONS

A Practical Guide for
Private Companies and their UK
and Overseas Advisers

Consultant Editor:
Jonathan Reuvid

KOGAN PAGE

London and Philadelphia

Publisher's note

Every possible effort has been made to ensure that the information contained in this book is accurate at the time of going to press, and the publishers and authors cannot accept responsibility for any errors or omissions, however caused. No responsibility for loss or damage occasioned to any person acting, or refraining from action, as a result of the material in this publication can be accepted by the editor, the publisher or any of the authors.

First published in Great Britain and the United States in 2007 by Kogan Page Limited
Reprinted 2007
First published in paperback in 2008

Kogan Page Limited
120 Pentonville Road
London N1 9JN
United Kingdom
www.koganpage.com

Kogan Page US
525 South 4th Street, #241
Philadelphia PA 19147
USA

© Jonathan Reuvid, the individual contributors and Kogan Page Limited, 2007

The right of Jonathan Reuvid and the individual contributors to be identified as the authors of this work has been asserted by them in accordance with the Copyright, Designs and Patents Act 1988.

ISBN 978 0 7494 5269 8

British Library Cataloguing-in-Publication Data

A CIP record for this book is available from the British Library.

Library of Congress Cataloging-in-Publication Data

Mergers and acquisitions : a practical guide for private companies and their UK and overseas advisers / [edited by] Jonathan Reuvid.

     p. cm.

  Includes bibliographical references and index.

  ISBN 978-0-7494-5269-8 (pbk.)

  1. Consolidation and merger of corporations--Finance. 2. Consolidation and merger of corporations--Management. 3. Private companies--Finance. I. Reuvid, Jonathan.

  HG4028.M4M453 2008

  658.1'62--dc22

                       2008018080

Typeset by Saxon Graphics Ltd, Derby
Printed and bound in Great Britain by Cambridge University Press

Contents

Notes on contributors

Adrian Alexander is a corporate finance partner with Mazars LLP, the international accountancy and business advisory firm. Based in the Brighton office, he acts for owner-managed businesses, supporting them through major transactions, and is active in all the main corporate finance disciplines: sales, M&A, raising finance and investigation work.

Mazars acts for some of the fastest-growing entrepreneurial companies in the UK, offering a complete range of accountancy and business advisory services including audit and assurance, tax advisory and compliance, corporate recovery and insolvency, consulting, forensic and investigations, corporate finance and financial services for private individuals.

Simon Arthur is a partner in the corporate and commercial services team at Horsey Lightly Flynn solicitors, Newbury. He specializes in corporate transactional matters with a particular emphasis on mergers and acquisitions, equity raisings, corporate restructurings and non-contentious employment matters.

Horsey Lightly Flynn is a partner-led practice which can trace its London origins back to 1891. Through a number of strategic mergers and new partnerships, it now serves a growing list of 'blue chip' corporations, smaller commercial businesses and private clients, nationally and internationally from offices in London, Newbury and Bournemouth.

Steven Conybeare is a corporate solicitor who has specialized in corporate advisory work for small and medium-sized companies for over 12 years. As well as acting on a range of corporate finance transactions, he has also been a non-executive director and company secretary of a number of smaller companies, giving him a great insight into the concerns, the pressures and the requirements faced by directors and investors.

Conybeare Solicitors is an independent corporate law firm, specializing in company and commercial law. The firm has a dynamic approach to providing solutions based on its technical expertise and business experience.

Peter Gray began his career in corporate finance with Minter Ellison, a leading Australian law firm, where he qualified as a lawyer before joining the corporate finance group of Clifford Chance in London in 1989. After completing an MBA, Peter joined Cavendish Corporate Finance in 1994 and was appointed a director in 1997. He is a frequent lecturer and author on the subject of mergers and acquisitions.

Cavendish Corporate Finance Limited specializes in selling businesses. Working across a broad range of sectors, Cavendish's clients include private companies, financial institutions and fully listed public companies. Cavendish acts only on behalf of vendors with typical transactions falling broadly within the £10 million to £150 million value range.

Peter Guinn is a chartered accountant and chartered tax adviser. He is a partner at Alliotts Corporate Finance involved in acquisitions, equity and debt fund raising and restructuring for SME businesses both in the UK and overseas through Alliott Group, an international network of independent accountants and lawyers.

Alliotts Corporate Finance is a division of Alliotts Chartered Accountants, a firm of dynamic chartered accountants and business advisers with offices in London, Harrow and Guildford. Represented worldwide via the Alliott Group network, the firm acts for both UK and overseas companies, providing a hands-on service to the SME sector.

Stephen Harris has spent more than 20 years in the business advisory sector helping owner-managed businesses, covering equity and debt raises as well as advising on acquisitions and disposals, including those from recovery positions. He is a Director in Mazars' national corporate finance team.

Catherine Hemsworth is a Senior Associate in the Corporate Group at Pinsent Masons. She works on a wide range of private equity transactions, including acquisitions and disposals, joint ventures, institutional investments, group reorganizations, MBOs, MBIs and start-ups. She has also worked in a number of public offers of shares for unlisted public companies.

Edward Hoare is a Corporate Partner in the London office of international law firm Faegre & Benson LLP. He represents buyers and sellers on a variety of UK private company share and asset-based transactions, typically involving amounts in the £5 million to £100 million price range. His experience includes venture capital investments and MBOs.

Oliver Hoffman is a Corporate Finance Partner based at the Leeds office of Mazars LLP. With 13 years' corporate finance experience gained working at Mazars and previously two 'Big Four' firms, he advises a wide range of clients on acquisitions, disposals, fund raising and corporate strategy. Oliver's speciality is MBOs, and in his four years at Mazars he has helped eight clients to buy businesses through MBOs and five vendors to sell their businesses to MBO teams.

Geoff Howles is a specialist in corporate finance with 30 years' experience of working in the City of London and in industry. He set up Howles & Company in 1996 where he works as an independent consultant specializing in acquisitions and mergers, strategic planning and change management.

Howles & Company are acquisition and merger consultants authorized and regulated by the Financial Services Authority. The firm specializes in project management of deals, deal evaluation and support, strategic planning and change management. It offers practical, comprehensive advice and help, with a committed, personal service.

The **Hurst & Company LLP** tax team, which – inter alia – advises clients in the area of mergers and acquisitions, has collaborated in writing the firm's chapter. David Nolan (a recent addition to the Hurst tax team with eight years' experience in tax) and Sarah Salton (four years at Hurst, three of those in tax) are responsible for the content and it has been edited by Rachel Murphy, David Finn and Andy Culpin.

Nick Jennings is an Associate in the London office of international law firm Faegre & Benson LLP. He specializes in M&A, corporate restructuring, corporate finance and corporate counselling.

Norrie Johnston is founder and Managing Director of Executive Online Ltd. He has provided interim management services since 1997 and is the current chairman of the Institute of Management Consultancy Managers special interest group. He is a sales and marketing-oriented director, with wide hands-on experience in the successful management of dot.com, telecom, technology and technical services businesses in home and international markets. In his earlier career, Norrie held marketing and sales directorships in the engineering sector, involving residential periods in the United States and Pakistan.

Richard Jones is Principal at Punter Southall Transaction Services, a division of Punter Southall & Co Limited. He is a qualified actuary with nine years' experience advising corporate entities on pension and investment issues. Richard is the lead consultant for an investment company with several pension schemes with over US $3 billion in assets. Richard has also worked for a variety of corporate clients and been involved in a number of international mergers and acquisitions.

Alan Kelly is a partner in MacRoberts' Corporate Group and is highly experienced in Scottish corporate transactions including acquisitions, disposals, start-ups, joint ventures, MBOs and private equity investments.

In addition to advising on a broad range of corporate law matters, Alan has presented at numerous seminars on a range of corporate law topics, and as well as experience as a non-executive director, is one of the trainers on the IoD's director training programme.

David Massey has 20 years' City experience as fund manager, broker, analyst and corporate financier, mostly working with small companies. He is also the former Managing Editor of the AFX News financial news service, and the author of *The Investors' Guide to New Issues* published in 1995. He now works with Athanor Capital Partners.

Athanor Capital Partners is a corporate finance boutique, a member of the London Stock Exchange and a member of Ofex (now PLUS Markets) and advises smaller companies on AIM admissions and M&A work.

Kevin McCarthy is a partner at Mishcon de Reya, specializing in corporate finance and M&A with particular expertise in private equity-related transactions, acting for both management and equity finance providers. Kevin advises on IPOs, equity issues and joint ventures for both private and public companies.

Mishcon de Reya is a mid-sized London law firm offering a diverse range of legal services for businesses and individuals. The firm's foundation is its dynamic range of corporate clients that seek effective advice through close collaboration. The firm delivers tailored legal and commercial solutions to businesses of all sizes, both domestic and international.

Andrew Millington is a Corporate Finance Partner with Mazars, the international accountancy and advisory firm, where he is in charge of UK Corporate Finance. He has more than 15 years' experience and has led many M&A and MBO transactions for companies of varying size in a wide range of industry sectors. Prior to joining Mazars, Andrew was an investment director at Barclays Private Equity, and previously a senior manager in Corporate Finance at Coopers & Lybrand.

Gideon Nellen has extensive corporate and commercial law experience, particularly in transactions such as M&A, venture capital, management buy-outs, restructurings and financings. After his articles with Clifford Turners (now Clifford Chance) he worked at Freshfields and at Herbert Smith in their corporate departments.

In 1992 Gideon founded NELLEN as a niche Central London law firm specializing in corporate transactions for a wide variety of SMEs, from IT and media companies to management consultancies and brand companies. NELLEN also advises on a range of commercial contracts.

Daniel O'Connell joined Forsyte Kerman in 1987 and became a partner in the Company Commercial Department in 1992. He is a founding partner of Kerman & Co, the successor company to Forsyte Saunders Kerman. Daniel has broad experience in company and commercial matters and deals primarily with acquisitions and disposals of companies and businesses.

Kerman & Co is predominantly a commercial practice dealing with the commercial transactions of corporate and high net worth individual clients. The firm also has a substantial private client practice which advises on trusts, probate and tax planning.

Alan Pratten is managing director of the Mergers, Acquisitions & Disposals Practice at Heath Lambert group. He has extensive experience with major multinational organizations and in advising on deals in the M&A arena. Alan is a founder of and author to the British Venture Capital Association Insurance Services.

Heath Lambert is a dominant force in the M&A market, working with over 50 of the leading European investment houses, accountants and law firms. It operates from London, Hamburg, Paris and, through Arcadia Inc., New Jersey and Atlanta. The team produces the British Venture Capital Association's Technical Guidance notes on insurance matters.

Dave Rebbettes is a Director of BCMS and is a regular speaker at over 70 venues across Europe and the USA annually, providing an experienced insight into how the sale price of private companies can be maximized by looking beyond traditional valuation methods. His experience has helped guide BCMS to become a leading private mergers and acquisitions company in Europe.

Peter Reilly is Managing Director of Aquila Financial Limited. Before forming Aquila Financial in 2002, Peter's career encompassed a number of finance and commercial roles in the Inland Revenue, BP plc, BG plc and Enterprise Oil plc. In 1999 he was appointed Head of Investor Relations at Enterprise Oil, and remained in the role until the takeover by Shell in 2002.

Aquila Financial provides strategic financial communications and public relations advice. The firm brings together a blend of financial communications, journalism, public relations and hands-on City experience. Within an intense global competition for investment opportunities, financing, investor attention and market share, Aquila can help its clients to communicate their aims and ambitions effectively.

Paul Rivers-Latham has lived and worked in Italy, Singapore, the United States and the UK. He has worked with venture-backed technology companies for over 20 years, and is a partner and Director of Technology at Cobalt, a transatlantic corporate advisor to TMT companies.

David Stanning has spent the past 30 years developing the company/commercial arm of B P Collins, having spent the previous three years learning the art of plain-speaking and dealing with one of Sydney's premier law firms.

With 20 partners, B P Collins has developed over 40 years into a significant all-round firm in the West London/Thames Valley area, where it focuses on building long-term relationships, delivering valued advice to corporate and private clients promptly, pragmatically and hopefully with a sense of humour.

David Stevenson is a Partner in the Corporate Group of Pinsent Masons and is a private and public company M&A specialist.

Pinsent Masons is a full service international law firm, distinguished by its depth of knowledge, experience and commitment to specialist market sectors. The firm, which ranks in the UK top 15 and the Global 100 of law firms, has over 260 partners and a total legal team of around 900 worldwide.

Dr Mike Sweeting so enjoyed his first degree that he chose to do another one straightaway. As a result, he claims that a good knowledge of modern poetry is indispensable to M&A. He first lectured at the age of 21 and published at 22, then changed his mind and has spent his entire working life marketing companies.

Acquisitions International (AI) is the market leader in 'headhunting' the right company to buy. The company has a unique research centre near Newbury employing over 90 staff, from which it has worked worldwide for clients from 12 countries. AI works for trade buyers, MBI teams and private equity clients.

Duncan Taylor joined Nelsons in 1993 and heads the Business Services Department. He has practised exclusively in the area of company and commercial law since qualification, concentrating on corporate transactional work since joining Nelsons. This comprises company and company business sales and purchases, MBOs/MBIs, corporate structuring and reorganization work and secured lending.

Nelsons is one of the largest and strongest law firms in the East Midlands, with over 240 staff at offices in Derby, Leicester and Nottingham. Its Business Services Department provides advice in all commercial areas through its corporate, commercial, construction, commercial property and employment teams.

James Turner is a director in the Leeds office of PKF (UK) LLP, accountants and business advisers, and heads the national mergers and acquisitions team. James joined the firm in 1989 and has over 10 years' experience in corporate finance. As well as M&A transactions, James has also been involved in a number of MBO/MBI and fund raising assignments.

PKF (UK) LLP is one of the UK's leading firms of accountants and business advisers which focuses on developing private and public companies. The UK firm employs 1,600 staff and has 22 offices across the UK. M&A assignments are handled by the UK corporate finance team which comprises more than 60 staff.

Philip Wild was admitted as a solicitor in 1984 after articles at Macdonald Stacey, where he remained as an Assistant, before becoming a Partner in Kidd Rapinet on the merger of the two firms in 1987. He specializes in company and commercial law and intellectual property law. He has particular experience in M&A, company secretarial and insolvency work, the drafting of commercial agreements, contracts of employment, and IT and software licensing work.

Kidd Rapinet is a modern law firm which has grown rapidly by amalgamation with other firms, each of which has brought its own style, personality and, most importantly, people to help build the Kidd Rapinet of today. The firm operates from a number of locations in London and the south-east of England.

David Wilkinson is a corporate partner at Field Fisher Waterhouse, a law form with offices in London and Manchester. It is part of the European Legal Alliance which has offices in 25 European cities.

David has a proactive and commercial approach. He advises clients ranging from entrepreneurs to UK and multinational companies, on a wide range of corporate transactions including acquisitions, disposals and joint ventures.

Peter Wood is a Corporate Partner at Pinsent Masons, specializing in private equity transactions, including acquisitions and disposals, MBOs, MBIs, institutional buy-outs and development capital transactions. He also has experience of public company work and has been involved in rights issues, placings and recommended takeovers.

Lisa Wright is the head of Zephus Ltd, a provider of M&A data and a subsidiary of Bureau van Dijk Electronic Publishing (BvDEP), which publishes ZEPHYR. She is responsible for the business in terms of research, development and liaison with the global sales team. Lisa joined Zephus in 2001 to manage the transition of its business from a free to fee-paying service and to seek new revenue streams. She was involved in the instigation of the discussions with BvDEP which led to its acquisition of Zephus. Lisa is a graduate of Manchester Metropolitan University with a postgraduate certificate in business administration at the University of Salford. Prior to joining Zephus, Lisa had spent seven years in sales in the company information and M&A data arena.

BvDEP is one of Europe's leading electronic publishers of business information, best known for its range of international company information products which include OSIRIS, FAME, AMADEUS, ZEPHYR and BANKSCOPE.

Introduction

Mergers and acquisitions activity, referred to universally by its M&A acronym, carries a cachet of mystique and glamour by reason of the headlines and business press comment which international mega-deals attract. In the first six months of 2006, M&A worldwide reached the highest half-year volume on record, including the exceptional period of the dot.com boom. The estimated deal value for the period was US $1,930 billion (£1,055 billion). Financial reporting is focused on the deals in global equity capital markets for which the top 10 investment banks are the dominant advisers. In these markets, the front-runner Goldman Sachs with a 12.1 per cent share signed off on 113 deals in the first half of 2006, with an average value of US $388 million, and earned many millions in fees for its services. The industry sectors that generated the largest shares of total global value for the period were finance (14 per cent), telecoms (12 per cent), utilities and energy (10 per cent), real estate or property (7 per cent) and healthcare (6 per cent). Interestingly in Europe, despite the vast funds available to spend on deals, loans made to private equity groups to finance buy-out deals declined for the first time since the first half of 2002, by 16 per cent from 2005.

All of this high-profile activity is far removed from the more modest M&A activity of mid-market public companies and private companies in the SME sector, for which this book has been written. However, the principles of structuring M&A transactions are closely similar whatever the size of deal or company involved, as many of the contributors point out in their texts. Nor is the basic legal documentation vastly different, although there are many more hoops for public companies to pass through in order to satisfy stock exchange requirements or possible referrals to competition regulators.

One distinction that is largely ignored in the chapters of the book, but which readers may wish to bear in mind, is the difference between an acquisition and a merger. Put simply, an acquisition is a transaction where one company buys either the shares or the assets of another company, by issuing its own new shares, cash, debt or a mixture of these forms of consideration. A merger transaction is where both parties agree to combine their businesses, and for this purpose form a new company that issues shares which replace the shares of both businesses.

Depending upon the relative proportions of the issued capital in the new company that the two parties wish to achieve, a part of the consideration may be satisfied by the issue of debt or by cash that the holding company borrows for the purpose. Although the term 'merger' may give the impression that the deal is a combination of equals, whereas 'takeover' has a negative connotation for the management and shareholders of the company acquired, the practical effect may be little different. In most cases, one party to the merger transaction receives a clear majority of the equity and control of the board. There is no escaping the truth that in nearly all M&A transactions there is a 'predator' and a 'victim', whatever euphemisms may be used to describe the deal.

For this reason alone, it is essential that the directors and shareholders of acquiring companies and their targets have a clear understanding of the ventures on which they are embarking, how to structure them, how to identify and approach potential partners, how to carry out the purchase or sale negotiations, and how to appoint and make the best use of advisers. Shareholders and directors will also need to develop their knowledge of the complex legal documentation and processes involved, as well as the taxation implications for their companies and themselves, and employment and insurance issues. Several contributors have included case studies to illustrate the pitfalls and the unsatisfactory outcomes that may occur where the legal processes are not carried out thoroughly.

The various contributors to this book are all professionals in their fields with wide experience of M&As, and we hope readers will find the advice and enlightenment that they need to develop the appropriate M&A strategies for their companies. In some cases flotation may be preferred to M&A, and the opening and closing chapters refer to flotation strategy and the equally complex preparation that will be required to pursue this alternative.

Jonathan Reuvid

Part One

M&A as a business strategy

Growth curve, plateau or peak? An entrepreneur's guide to growth

Stephen Harris, Mazars

What does growth mean?

Whether you're an entrepreneur with an idea or the CEO of a global public company, chances are that you talk about growing your company. But when you talk about growing an embryonic business and growing a multinational, are you really talking about the same thing? After all, growth means different things to different people. Even its metrics are diverse. It can refer to sales, profits, market share, industry reputation or standing within the community – or all of these.

Children grow (and grow up), but not at the same rate, or to the same capacity. A business is no different. Younger businesses often grow in short spurts, increasing simple measures such as sales or profits. More mature businesses expand. They broaden their services and market their experience, as well as products and services, to their customers.

That's why you can't talk about growth as a straight line. Detours, sidesteps and pauses come with the territory. That's no bad thing. The plateaus that occur between growth spurts allow space for reflection and direction (or re-direction). But plateaus are also fraught with danger. Some of the danger is external: these are spaces where competitors lurk, ready to overtake your business. The danger is also internal: inactivity can lead to a loss of momentum, and ultimately retreat.

In terms of access to finance, there are broadly five growth stages in a company's lifespan: inception, organic growth, purchased, lifestyle, and beyond IPO (see the enterprise growth model). Each has its own characteristics, risks, potential financial sources and success criteria, as illustrated in Figure 1.1.1.

Business beginnings

Inception is where it all starts. You have the good idea or the cutting-edge technology and the conviction that you're not only different from, but better than, the competition. But you'll need something more to be successful: customer demand. Developing a product in the hope you'll find a niche where it will sell is a high-risk strategy. Instead, you need to be clear about where the demand is coming from, and ensure your solution will meet it.

Small, incremental achievements mean a lot during the inception phase because every day has a very clear purpose – even if that purpose is basic survival. Intensity is the hallmark of inception. Because everything is a new challenge, each win feels like a personal victory. And although you're putting in hard work for small numbers, you can be proud that your own efforts have propelled you there. Yet this intensity has its drawbacks. You're trying to be different, yet deliver a product or service that people want. You're new and fresh, the product is bright and shiny, but evolution is easier than revolution.

Enterprise growth model

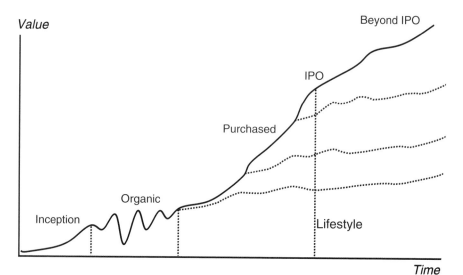

Figure 1.1.1 The enterprise growth model

Matching money and action can be tricky. Most business activity is hand-to-mouth, typified by clear milestones: 'When customer A pays, then I'll pay supplier B.' In fact, risk feels different in the inception stage than it ever will again. Entrepreneurs tend to assess risk much lower than other people, a consequence of the total belief in what they're doing. Although entrepreneurs are driven by the belief that the business will be a success, every setback, however minor, comes as a personal blow. People outside the business will view it more dispassionately.

At this stage, the primary risk is non-acceptance of the business because of price, product or service, or customer satisfaction. Get these basics right and you have a business. Get them wrong and you're guaranteed certain and rapid failure. In any case, you'll need finance at a stage when potential sources of funding are limited. Financiers often profess their undying support for small business communities but that won't stop them looking at every opportunity with the dispassionate view of the investing outsider rather than with the unshakeable enthusiasm of the entrepreneur.

At this stage, the cheapest source of finance is your own. It will be the one you are directed to first: 'Why don't you work for nothing, use your savings and borrow more against the house?' Alternatively, you could approach friends and family. Occasionally, people aren't sure what they're giving the money for and they're less than pleased when they don't get it back. But some of the most successful businesses in the world started this way. Bill Gates, then a second-year student, started his Microsoft career in his friend's garage, turning an existing computer language into a form that could be understood by a machine. It took two years to achieve US $22,000 of revenue, by which time Gates had seven employees all working on the same beliefs.

Or take the father of the golden arches. Ray Kroc mortgaged his home and invested his life savings to become the exclusive distributor of a milkshake maker. Hearing about the McDonald's hamburger stand in California running eight mixers at a time, he pitched the idea of opening up several restaurants to the brothers Dick and Mac McDonald, convinced that he could sell eight of his mixers to each and every one.

Business angels are savvy investors who back businesses with their own money. They are like friends but with expertise in a specific business segment. They can be invaluable to businesses looking for a step up, but be warned: they will expect (and often demand) a close working relationship. They'll scrutinize your business plan. They'll want to understand how they will get the investment back – and when. The question you should ask is what you want from them.

If friends and angels can't help, banks might – but they are likely to seek personal guarantees. The Small Firms Loan Guarantee Scheme allows a proportion of the lending to be underwritten by the government, but you'll still need a robust business case.

Despite its reputation, the 'venture' in venture capital doesn't automatically embrace high risk. Venture capitalists will need to be convinced that you'll make them money – and they'll expect a sizeable slice of your business. Some venture firms specialize in early-stage businesses but they're selective about the nature and type of business they'll invest in, and the level of return they seek on their investment.

At least in this phase, the badges of success are easy to identify: sales, positive cashflow, a healthy bank balance, and a sense that today is better than yesterday all count.

Inception plateau

There is little plateau effect during the inception phase because every day tends to deliver its own win-or-lose scenarios. But the familiarity of the daily battle can generate its own problems in the longer term. With sales levels just high enough to allow for personal financial satisfaction, the entrepreneur is happy to achieve the same level. As a result, the business wins new customers but the 'big' breakthrough is always around the corner.

It could be that the business loses out on price or service or has to make special efforts to meet expectations. Meanwhile, the bank, customers and suppliers are effectively imposing their own limits on it.

Organic growth

So the business is growing. By now, you'll be winning new business – and even shedding 'old' customers who no longer fit. During the organic stage, you'll be adding new products and services that complement your core offerings, as well as increasing the number of people who deliver them. Ad hoc arrangements will no longer work, and the increased demands generate a need for infrastructure.

Systemization devolves functions to different people and departments, often relocated into larger premises. During this phase, too, you could well bring in high-level people to share the vision and drive the business forward. So the business grows – but not necessarily uniformly. Sales increase, as do gross margins as economies of scale begin to kick in. But so do overheads, putting profitability and cashflow under pressure.

To make things worse, overheads typically require paying monthly. Your customers may not be so accommodating. Meanwhile, because they rely on credit ratings that show the business still to be in the inception phase, suppliers may be imposing credit limits.

By this time, the business has gained a momentum of its own, consuming resources in increasing quantities. So what are the hallmarks of the organic growth phase? It's tempting to say it's more of the same as that in the inception phase. But the business will also be undergoing changes. For one thing, it will change the product matrix, seeing repeat business (more of the same products to the same customers), complementary products (new products to existing customers), and customer growth (existing products to new customers). It might also look to diversify, selling new products to new customers, which can lead to greater use of resources and sometimes severe dips in performance.

The chief risk during this phase is complacency. Having survived the inception phase, entrepreneurs often believe they're over the worst and can at last concentrate on making money. Often, they overestimate the permanence of the footprint they've gained in the market. There are no easy ways to grow a business, and tactical planning and risk mitigation strategies are key to successful growth.

But there are other risks, too – which change with business cycles and vary according to the type of business. One is new product risk. Not only is it time-consuming, but customers will view existing products in the light of new performance. Likewise the risk of service failure. It's easy to promise service standards but do you have the infrastructure to deliver? And you need to be sure that your new customers deliver their end of the bargain. In other words, can you manage credit risks and debt collection?

The good news is that it can be easier to access finance in this phase. Seeing a business get past the initial phases can give a business angel confidence that it has the basics in place – and the business can point to difficulties it has met and overcome. Similarly, with a track record and potentially valuable assets, the business becomes more attractive to banks.

Businesses that show signs of growth will be increasingly attractive to venture capitalists seeking to grow and exit businesses relatively quickly. The venture capitalist will want to invest loan capital, acquire equity, and be in a position to effect change if things go wrong. The business, in turn, gets support in winning customers and gravitas in negotiations with suppliers.

Now, too, you may have the option of asset-based lending, which increases as your business expands. This form of finance is useful in sell-and-forget businesses but is hard to use in contract businesses where delivery is based on future performance.

So what does success look like in this phase? Success should be measured in reference to a clear plan – what was the business trying to achieve and what has it actually achieved? Increased sales and margins count. So do repeat business, customer recommendations and a reputation within the local business community and the sector.

Organic plateau

It is often at the organic stage that the business becomes a 'lifestyle', with a consequent loss of momentum and drive. Although the business keeps going and the entrepreneur's salary increases in line with improved profitability, the business starts to focus on product features rather than mapping out strategic goals.

Purchased growth

Purchased growth covers a whole range of activities, from poaching teams of people from competitors to outright acquisition of a business. The idea of acquisition is that it accelerates the business model, giving it greater impetus than organic growth. Because acquisition gives the business something it cannot get quickly or incrementally, the hallmark of this stage is step change. It might be a joint venture – an agreement that gives both parties something they want that the other has. It can work, for instance, when it matches a strong product on one side with strong distribution on the other, but it's often seen as a way of merely sharing risk, with neither party fully committed.

In some cases, for instance where there is strong demand for products, a straightforward distribution deal might be better. The issue is often that your product is new to the market and needs to attract sufficient demand and margin to make the distributor commit resources.

Purchased growth can give the business access to new territories, though you should be aware that your competitors may have avoided them for good reasons. You should also be aware that customs and regulations differ, as do product standards, sales techniques and customer expectations (think of US cars in the UK).

Acquisition targets can include both complementary and competitive businesses – complementary when they give you something you need, and competitive if they stop someone else having what you want, from a skilled workforce to additional market share.

The risks in this phase are significant, but they can be contained with planning and due diligence. The primary risk is integration: after the paperwork is completed, the new arrangements have to work and people who were not party to the negotiation have to work together. The same goes for systems and expectations: different businesses will have grown in different ways, and different people will have different expectations. A consistent culture is laudable, but a wholly consistent culture will be impossible. Add regional diversity and the risk becomes even higher, because culture and customs are overlaid with national pride, laws and regulations.

Ensuring that there is 'financial glue' that keeps all parties focused should be part of the mix. People will do things well if they want to, acceptably if they have to, and not at all if they don't need to.

At this stage the business will have access to a wider range of funding sources than ever before. With solid past performance, banks will be willing to lend based on past and projected profitability, both of the company and of target businesses. With asset-based debt, specialist lenders will consider property, machinery and debt positions in a loan package, allowing the existing owners to maintain their full value in the company. At the same time, private equity houses will consider investing in the business for expansion.

By now, the business will have a stronger infrastructure, with decision making in line with formal strategic planning. With the stakes raised on risks and rewards, you can see success in terms of larger numbers, spread ownership and formal incentive schemes, and diverse control. At the same time, the supply chain has become more complex – probably moving cross-border and with multiple sourcing strategies.

Purchased plateau

This means the entrepreneur is no longer alone. Even if he or she retains majority ownership, day-to-day control will be long gone. The plateau at this stage can appear to be regression to the organic phase, with incremental activity. The business has reached a stage where management are comfortable, financiers are comfortable and a period of consolidation is acceptable.

If the owners are under no pressure to achieve capital gains and earnings are at acceptable levels, the business can look at other areas of 'growth', including employee participation, skills development, corporate citizenship, and environmental and fair trade principles.

Beyond IPO

Whole books have been written on the processes and benefits of initial public offerings (IPOs). In the context of growing businesses, managers need to consider going public unless they plan to make the business itself a target for purchased growth. There are other reasons, too. Listing will increase the ownership base, raise additional capital to grow the business further through acquisition, and create an exit strategy that will allow the existing owners to achieve a partial sale of their shares. The fact that it will likely be recognized as a major player will allow the business access to business opportunities that weren't available before.

Both the business and its management will be on public display. Although entry onto the market can be a means of raising additional funds, managers still need a clear plan for what they plan to do with it. Investors will have bought shares in the expectation of bigger returns, and will expect management to invest appropriately.

On the other hand, being a public company may provide new and improved banking arrangements. The status of the company and interest in it may provide a further platform for growth. A growing shareholder base and rising share price will demonstrate that the company is growing – a far cry from the aspirations of an entrepreneur and the shared beliefs of a handful of colleagues and friends. Well-planned and executed strategies in a growing business should ensure the best value for the shareholders.

Being public does not prevent the company being a takeover target, which makes a plateau effect at this level dangerous. Yours may be viewed as a company without ideas and ripe for new management. Effective communication is still essential, and the message needs to have an even broader appeal than before.

Lifestyle?

The plateau effect can be positive if you use it as a valuable period for self-assessment and consolidation, rather than self-congratulation and lethargy. When self-congratulation sets in, the business becomes a 'lifestyle' business, and one where higher risks start creeping into the business model.

Businesses that have entered the lifestyle phase lose their competitive edge. Although they continue performing for several years, during that time investment may decline. Management drive dwindles and those managers still hungry for success will leave. Lose your A team, and you'll have no one to run your business in future. Even if customer loyalty remains high, the market won't stagnate just because your business has. Other businesses will start viewing the customer base as easy pickings that can be targeted with new solutions and products.

Once these symptoms start to appear, the entrepreneur will likely get involved in the business again. But by now, the business will have moved on. Second-tier management may have moved on as well. And even the options to sell the business may result in depressed values as buyers detect a less than hyper-motivated team.

Alternatives to flotation: accessing capital and exit strategies

Kevin McCarthy, Mishcon de Reya

Why do companies float?

The reasons that an unlisted company might choose to float are many and varied. For each company with different individual circumstances there will be different drivers and aspirations, and a different sense of why flotation might appear an attractive option. Therefore, before evaluating the alternatives to flotation, it is important to understand the principal reasons and perceived advantages of coming to the market. These might include all, or some of, the following:

- *Access to capital:* Listing on a stock exchange affords a company access to external equity capital which would not otherwise be available. The levels of capital potentially available through flotation can be significant, and if capable of being tapped, can afford a source of funds sufficient to support even the most aggressive of growth strategies. This was demonstrated in the recent demutualization and flotation of Standard Life as a means of enabling the company to support and grow its business and to take advantage of market opportunities.
- *Exit strategies/liquidity of stock:* Listing provides a market for a company's shares, thereby offering shareholders a means to realize the value of their holdings. In practice, such liquidity is often the principal rationale for a company coming to market. The existing shareholders in a company may have

reached the point where they are seeking an exit strategy in relation to the whole, or part only, of their shareholding. The public markets for company shares afford a potential exit by creating an externally valued, publicly traded market for such shares.

■ *Brand recognition:* Beyond the initial press coverage which accompanies a flotation, there is a general perception that a listed company enjoys a higher brand profile and therefore greater public awareness of the company and its products. This is unlikely to be the principal reason behind an initial public offering (IPO), but can be an attractive consequential benefit.

■ *Employee participation in ownership:* Through the use of employee share schemes, and the transparent value that public markets afford to such shareholdings, a flotation can engender a sense of ownership in the company among employees, and as a result, foster long-term commitment to the business.

■ *Efficiencies resulting from regulatory requirements:* As a result of the various regulatory impositions including, in particular, the disclosure requirements incumbent upon a listed company, listing often leads to improved internal processes and controls, which can in turn lead to more defined management structures and greater operating efficiencies in the company.

Each of these reasons (and this is by no means an exhaustive list), or a combination of them, might provide the impetus for a company to seek a listing. However, for a lawyer advising a corporate client considering flotation, it is essential to drill down further in order to understand the underlying reasons for the proposed float. It may indeed be that bringing the company to the market is the most appropriate course of action, but in certain circumstances, more appropriate alternatives may be available.

Accessing capital

Whether an enterprise is planning to grow by seizing acquisition opportunities or by developing organically, expansion will require an injection of capital to support and sustain the growth strategy. The source of such financing or the method by which it is to be obtained will be an important factor in shaping a company's programme for development, and there is no doubt that a flotation, for example on the London Stock Exchange (LSE), can provide a valuable financing resource. Early 2006 represented an impressive period for raising capital through IPOs on the LSE. In the first seven months of the year, £17.8 billion was raised (exceeding the £17.4 billion raised by IPOs during the whole of 2000).

However, there may be more appropriate means of raising capital than an IPO. To name but a few common obstacles, the process may be too expensive, problematic issues might be raised through due diligence, the management team may not be ready for life in a publicly quoted company, the company might not yet have realized its full potential as a private entity (and therefore a later float might unlock more value), or the markets themselves might be unfavourable at a given point in time.

What alternatives might, therefore, be available in order to access capital?

Venture capital/private equity

Private equity financing is a medium to long-term source of financing by investors in return for an equity stake in what are perceived as high-growth unquoted companies. The British private equity industry is the largest and most developed in Europe, and worldwide is second only to the United States. It is a multi-billion pound industry, and the pool of cash available for investment is growing at a phenomenal rate. The British Venture Capital Association (BVCA) reports that in excess of £27 billion of funds were raised in 2005 (more than double the previous year). And that money is being spent : investments reached £11 billion in 2005, up 21 per cent from £9.7 billion in 2004. The UK is home to private equity funds of all shapes and sizes, be they captives or independents, niche industry participants, or funds having a particular geographical focus or target investment range.

In some circumstances the term 'private equity' is used to refer to the leveraged buy-out market, but elsewhere, and in particular across continental Europe, the term 'venture capital' is used synonymously with private equity. Whatever the definitions, private equity/venture capital is essentially capital provided by outside investors for the financing of new, growing or struggling businesses, the investee company generally being perceived as a high-risk investment offering the potential for high returns.

Many, but by no means all, of the companies sourcing private equity/venture capital are companies which are start-up, entrepreneurial and small-to-medium-sized enterprises. Fund providers will look for a well-researched, documented and supported business plan and a strong management team. If a company is judged to be a suitable candidate for equity investment, the fund will provide a slice of equity finance which will then be supplemented by various tranches of preferred equity and debt. Depending on the nature and size of the equity investment, this debt element will be more or less highly leveraged, and will itself be of various types and denominations – PIK, mezzanine, high-yield, senior bank debt, and so on (of which some are secured, and some are not).

The main advantage of equity finance is that a significant sum of money is committed to the company, and with it comes a wealth of expertise and business savvy gained from the provider's experience with previous ventures. Being associated with a private equity fund may also, of itself, enable a company to secure further funding from other sources. Although equity finance is usually from a single source, at the higher end of the scale consortium bids are becoming more the norm, as was seen in 2006 with a US $33 billion bid by KKR/Bain/Merrill Lynch for HCA.

In some respects, private equity funding can be seen as cheap money as, unlike a loan, there is no requirement to pay interest. However, the equity of the founders is diluted, and usually in favour of a single and influential shareholder. Private equity investors will seek to exert significant control on the investee company, working debt hard, driving efficiencies in the business and steering a route to profitable growth. Ultimately, the fund will realize its initial investment and take its profit in priority to founder shareholders. Securing private equity finance can be a complex and time-consuming process. The management of the company will need to devote time to compiling a history of the company's profitability as well as a full, detailed business plan with financial forecasts which they will be required to update (and deliver against) on an ongoing basis. Furthermore, the management will be asked to warrant the key information on the company to the acquiring provider.

Despite these difficulties, private equity/venture capital has proven to be a popular and successful alternative to public listing in raising capital for growth. On balance, owner/managers tend to consider a diluted position in a faster-growing, more successful business as an acceptable trade-off for this type of investment. Of course, it may simply serve to defer the issue, since a common exit strategy for equity providers is in fact to float their portfolio companies on the public markets.

Debt finance

Debt financing is another alternative source of capital in the absence of, or in combination with, equity finance. Facilities exist to cater for almost any amount of money, either through high-street banks or offered by a syndicate of banks and other financial institutions.

The simplest method of debt financing is by way of loan. The applicable interest rate on that loan will reflect the level of risk that the lender is willing to accept, and it may vary from company to company depending on financial status, credit rating and financial history. Loans are commonly secured by way of fixed and floating charges on the assets of the company and/or guaranteed by a third party.

Secured debt is the cheapest to obtain because it is relatively low-risk for a lender. It is also the most widely available, and a variety of debt financing structures have emerged over the years as lenders have become increasingly sophisticated and imaginative in developing new products.

It is important for a company to achieve a proper balance between its debt and equity so that the company is not left too highly geared. Too much debt, and a company will be exposed to fluctuations in cashflow and/or adverse changes in its trading conditions, which would affect its ability to meet the repayment obligations. Significant or repeated breaches of such obligations would result in both damage to the company's credit rating and additional charges or penalties being imposed on it for default.

The principal advantage of debt financing over equity financing is that it allows the shareholders of the company to retain undiluted ownership and control of the company. On satisfaction of the repayment of the loan, the lender has no further claim on the business. Therefore, the relative merits of equity financing and debt financing are reflected in this trade-off of ownership and control on the one hand as against cost of capital on the other.

Debt financing can be more accessible than equity finance since, from the perspective of a lender, it carries less risk. In the event of the company's insolvency the secured lender will have priority over the general creditors of the company in the distribution of the company's assets, and will have priority over equity holders.

In summary, debt financing can be a useful alternative to public listing in circumstances where an owner/manager wishes to retain control of a company and does not wish to incur the expense and invest the time required to secure a private equity investor or to float a company on a public stock exchange.

Private placing and/or pre-emptive offers

A private placing, although not an exact term, usually means an issue of new shares to a restricted group of persons, such as institutions or high net worth private investors rather than the general public. A company may carry out a private placing either directly with investors or with the help of a broker. A private placing memorandum is prepared by the company, including a description of the terms of the offering, the company's business, risks attached to the company and other material terms, and the target placees are then invited to subscribe under the terms of the offer.

Strict limits apply to the number and value of shares that are the subject of a private placing, and the company must be mindful of the complicated financial promotion provisions contained in the Financial Services and Markets Act 2000 and the rules regarding prospectuses which came into effect in July 2005 by virtue of the Prospectus Directive. This complicated regulatory framework imposes significant restrictions upon what, and to whom, securities may be offered and the terms and format in which such may be done.

A rights issue (or open offer) is a method by which a company offers its existing shareholders the right to buy newly issued shares or other securities in proportion to the shares that are already held by them. The shares issued pursuant to a rights issue are usually to be subscribed in cash at a discount to the market price. Strictly speaking, it is only a rights issue when the right to subscribe itself is capable of being sold by the shareholder.

While both private placings and rights issues are available to publicly quoted companies, they are equally a means of accessing capital for unquoted companies. The mechanics of both these routes can be complicated but the lower costs involved, relative to a flotation, make them attractive alternatives. Obviously, the pool of funds which may be available by these means will be less than if the company were to access the publicly traded capital markets, but this may be sufficient for a company's present purposes. Moreover, the process certainly affords the company more control over the diversification of its shareholder base.

Exit strategies

There comes a point in the lifecycle of most companies when the founder shareholders wish to realize some or all of their shareholding and extract a return for their investment and efforts over the years. Floating the company on the public equity capital markets can (subject to regulatory lock-in restrictions) certainly provide one means of exiting, but again, alternatives are available. These can include the following.

Trade sale to third party

A trade sale is the sale of the share capital of the company or the business and assets of the company to a strategic investor, being an entity within the same sector. A trade sale normally provides an immediate and complete exit for the existing share-holders, and a trade purchaser may be prepared to pay a premium for the shares or assets in order to achieve strategic aims (for example, entry into a specific market, expansion of its market share or the creation of business synergies).

A trade sale is, therefore, in certain circumstances a viable alternative to IPO in order to achieve an exit, and is usually cheaper and on the whole more straight-forward (although when a trade sale is conducted by auction it can become signifi-cantly more expensive and complicated). Management of a company contemplating a partial trade sale may be hesitant because of the unknown nature of any new owner, and may be concerned that the new owner may not be compatible with the existing management culture. In such circumstances the management may be persuaded to launch a management buy-out (MBO). If, on the other hand, a total exit is proposed, such concerns might be of less importance.

Management buy-out

An MBO can provide a means of exit for owner/managers. In the process of an MBO, management (usually backed by equity financing from a private equity provider) acquires control of the business from the current owners. Where the management are owner/managers of the business this provides a means of unlocking an often substantial proportion of their shareholding. An MBO does not, of course, provide a complete exit. The private equity provider will be reliant upon the management team remaining in place for a period following investment.

A typical structure sees management retain a minority stake in the company, with incentives built into the ongoing shareholder arrangements designed to encourage strong performance in the initial period following the buy-out. Clearly, however, where owner/managers are able to attract external equity investment an MBO can provide an attractive means of liquidating stock while retaining an interest in the ongoing management and future performance of the business.

Sales of minority interest (trade or venture capital)

A partial exit may be achieved by the sale of a minority interest in a company to either another company or an institution such as a venture capitalist. As in the case of a full trade sale, the consideration paid by the purchaser would be taxable in the hands of the selling shareholder(s), and it is important to consider how best to structure such a proposed sale.

The market for this type of sale is fairly restricted since the target company is privately held and its shares cannot easily be valued or traded. Such non-liquid stock – and a stake giving no management control – might be a disincentive for purchasers, although of course the purchase might afford a wider strategic opportunity.

It is not uncommon to see a corporate strategy for growth based on bolt-on acquisitions, either as a means of expanding a company's presence in a given sector or as a means of reaching into new sectors or geographies. Therefore, a well-run privately owned business, where the owner/managers are seeking a partial exit, may well be able to find a willing buyer in order to effect such an exit.

Share buy-back

There are many reasons why a company might wish to effect a buy-back of its own shares, and the commercial reasons underlying such a purchase might differ between a public listed company and a private company. However, one of the principal reasons for a share buy-back is in order to return cash (or other assets) to the company's shareholders.

A typical private company scenario is where one or more owner/shareholders wish to exit the company but in circumstances where the remaining shareholders are either unable or unwilling to purchase those shares. In order to effect a buy-back, a company will usually be required to have sufficient available profits. In certain circumstances a private limited company is permitted to purchase its shares out of capital. Provided that the shares to be repurchased are fully paid up, and that a buy-back is permitted by its articles of association, the company can make a payment out of capital in order to repurchase the shares, subject to compliance with various statutory requirements. Statutory declarations as to the solvency of the company are required to be given by the company directors, and in certain circumstances, notice of the proposed buy-back must be served on the company's creditors. Once repurchased by the company, the shares are cancelled.

For any individual shareholder proposing to exit by this route there are important tax consequences to be considered. Depending upon how the buy-back is structured, the receipts may be taxable in the hands of the exiting shareholder as either income or capital (or both), and careful tax planning should be undertaken in advance of implementing such a scheme.

Conclusion

Exactly which alternatives to flotation are available to a company will very much depend on the rationale underpinning the proposal to float. Just as the process of coming to market can be expensive and time-consuming for a company, so can be the available alternatives. A company considering the next step in its strategic development should consider all options available and its current stage of development before deciding which is the most appropriate course of action.

Selling a private company

Dave Rebbettes, BCMS Corporate

Introduction

Selling a private company is fundamentally not just an accounting or legal matter. First and foremost, it is a sales and marketing matter. That changes in traditional thinking are required is certain. Absence of success using traditional methods makes that argument loud and clear. It is essential to bring proactive marketing principles back to the fore.

BCMS is involved in the process of taking around 120 companies to market every year. Its clients come from a vast array of industries. Whether you are a service company or a manufacturer, large or small, the principles discussed will work for you.

Why sell?

This may seem a strange question, but analysing your objectives is important from the outset. The deal will need to be constructed in a way that will maximize your objectives. If your objectives are not clear, then neither will be your planning. The motto of IBM comes to mind: 'He who aims at nothing is bound to hit it.'

Typically, owners choose to sell for one or more of the following reasons.

BCMS CORPORATE

Selling a company? Think differently!

BCMS Corporate specialise in the sale and acquisition of privately owned companies with turnovers exceeding £1 million.

As one of Europe's leading specialists, BCMS have developed a very effective system to identify the most appropriate purchasers. Covering all industry sectors, over 2,500 delgate attended our free seminars in 2006 leading to more than 800 meeting with us privately to discuss their company's future. In fact, BCMS sell more privately owned business in the UK than anyone else.

Call **01635 299616** for more information or log onto **www.bcmscorporate.com**

BCMS Corporate - a refreshingly different approach.

Change in lifestyle

Maybe after many years in the business you have reached a point where you desire to do something different with your life. It is normal for people to radically alter their goals in life every decade, so don't be surprised if your objectives are changing.

Entrepreneurs versus managers

Owners are usually entrepreneurs, who by nature are creative, full of ideas and naturally energetic. For them, starting a business was the most natural thing in the world. However, as the business has developed they have found themselves increasingly stifled by managerial responsibilities, such as employment legislation, personnel issues, health and safety matters and new EU regulations. They feel that the fun has gone from the business, and 20 years on they look for a disposal as a sensible way to exit and start a new chapter in life.

Time

It is not unusual for owners to take the view that now is the right point to exit the business, because it makes huge demands on their time, leaving them little to enjoy other activities. The business has become all-consuming. Many areas of life suffer when this problem arises.

Business lifecycle

There comes a time when it is appropriate that a sales is sought for both shareholders and the company. Many companies grow well in their early years (see Figure 1.3.1). In due course sales can start to plateau (point (a) in Figure 1.3.1). It is often disproportionately difficult and expensive to break out of this plateau or ceiling. A significant investment is now usually required. This may be an investment in increased exports, new product development or restructuring of the company.

If this investment is made, then the cycle will repeat itself (point (b) in the figure). Without investment the lifecycle will tend to decay (point (c) in the figure). For many it now becomes a matter of inclination: 'Ten years ago we would have invested unhesitatingly, but today it is not appropriate.' Perhaps to start investing in the company, to borrow heavily or to plough all profits back in for many years is not an option that you are prepared to consider. At this point both the company and shareholders usually benefit from a sale.

Whether your objective is to liberate your time, reinvest in a new venture, release family wealth or emigrate, your goals must be considered carefully if the deal is to be constructed appropriately.

Key factors that influence a successful sale

Misaligned thinking and action at the early stages of considering a sale can account for many failures. Being determined to address the following four issues will have a major influence on success.

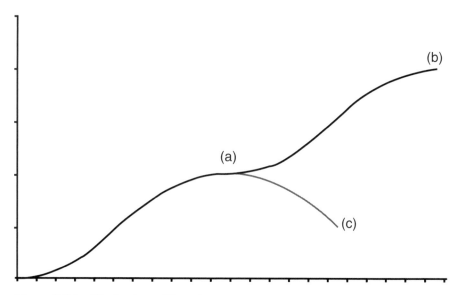

Figure 1.3.1 The business lifecycle

Avoid passivity at all costs

The best purchasers are often not considering an acquisition. Buying a company may not be on the agenda. The only way to find such buyers is through an active search. On the other hand venture capitalists and large plcs looking to sustain share values are always on the hunt, but rarely pay a premium. Passive selling will only ever locate such buyers.

Selling products successfully involves active enquiry generation. Why should selling a business be any different? BCMS has developed a vast database of tens of millions of companies. Using this unique global resource, it actively contacts (on average) 200–300 prospective buyers just to locate two to three good ones. There is no short cut.

Additionally, a search should not be restricted to the UK. Overseas buyers seeking access to the UK will often buy small to medium-sized companies, and a strategic acquisition may well attract a premium.

Research

There is a large team at BCMS dedicated to this early research and identification of potential buyers. With all of this commitment it still takes four weeks to complete this element of a project. Failure to find hundreds of good prospects will almost certainly result in 'no sale'. Interestingly, the more companies you approach the luckier you get. Approaching no more than 12 competitors by mail is virtually certain to fail.

It is also essential to think laterally, to look beyond the obvious. For example, consider the sale of a small company specializing in the installation of demountable office and industrial partitioning. Traditionally, the majority of contacts would be with larger competitive partitioning companies. As implied earlier, the average number of larger companies in the UK may be no more than 12. In this example our partitioning company sells to building contractors, specifiers, local authorities and architects. The question to ask is, 'What other products and services do these buyers specify?' These complementary products would include suspended ceilings, raised access flooring, lighting, building control systems, access control systems, industrial flooring, security systems, fire alarms, structured voice and data cabling and HVAC (heating, ventilation and air-conditioning) systems, to name but a few. Other manufacturers and installers of the above products could be prospective purchasers. In addition to this, searching for competitive and complementary companies outside the UK is essential. Globalization is a significant reason why a premium may be paid.

BCMS usually identifies between 200 and 300 prospective purchasers, visiting the website of each company in order to validate the appropriateness of the research. If the potential purchaser does not have a website, a telephone call is made to confirm that the research is valid.

Bidder competition

There is one factor that influences saleability more than any other, and that is bidder competition. Having a choice of buyers, in effect 'creating a market', is the single most important issue that a vendor can address.

Not only must you find a choice of buyers, you must also find a choice of strategically motivated, financially strong buyers. It is essential that this matter is not compromised. Therefore, you will have to contact many potential purchasers and this will dramatically influence the sale. Failure to address this will result in a poor deal for you. BCMS contacts directly (by telephone initially) an average of more than 200 prospective purchasers per vendor.

Bidder competition influences three things:

- the speed of the deal;
- the price achieved;
- the terms of the deal.

It is fair to say that whoever establishes choice has the greatest control over the negotiation. Without choice it will nearly always be the vendor who concedes first. Lack of choice means that terms will be dictated to you, and stress is increased. With choice you have far greater influence over the terms.

Future potential

The number one reason behind any acquisition is quality of client base. The second motive for purchase is good potential for growth. When you sell a company you do not sell its historic performance, or its current performance. What you should sell is how the company will look in three years under new ownership. When the purchaser has applied its resources, its finances, its sales activity and brought its client base to bear on your products and services, what will the company look like? A number one acquisition dictum is, 'Try to pay for a company's past, consider the present but only buy the future.'

Negotiating skill is essential, and in BCMS's experience, there is a consistent difference between the highest and lowest bids of around 270 per cent. This differential is the result of the motivation of the buyer and the benefits that it can bring to the business, which invariably differ from buyer to buyer.

The more you consider this issue, the more obvious it becomes that simply basing value on multiples of past performance is inappropriate.

The 270 per cent rule

It is worth repeating that if you negotiate well with a choice of strategically motivated buyers, you will almost certainly receive a diverse range of bids. On average, BCMS approaches between 200 and 300 prospective purchasers to sell just one company. It takes approximately five months to vet and qualify this first list down to no more than six or eight. These prospects will be asked to submit a competitive bid. (Chapter 3.5 lays out a proven process for securing competitive bids.)

If valuation was truly rooted in relatively standard multiples of adjusted average profit, then all bids would be relatively similar. There would never be a 270 per cent differential. All buyers would use similar logic, figures and multiples. The bids would be much closer together.

Why, therefore, is one buyer prepared to pay 270 per cent more than another? The answer is simple. One company is buying for a very different reason from another. The reality is that motives of purchasers ultimately determine value rather than multiples of profit, and this in turn means that it is almost impossible to value a business. It is not too difficult to evaluate a walk-away price or even an aspirational price, but not a sale price. There is no 'correct price'; a company is always worth what anyone is prepared to pay for it.

In addition, each buyer will apply different variables. A complementary product or service supplier will benefit from being able to cross-sell to both sets of clients. An overseas company will gain access to a new market. A competitor may make huge savings in production, at the same time eliminate a competitor, and release some downward pressure on price. All of these perceived benefits will influence price.

Additionally, a company that generates cash or enjoys guaranteed income streams might be seen as a purchase with lower perceived risk. This will also have a significant influence over the price that a buyer is prepared to pay.

One important message that the BCMS negotiation director keeps in mind is always to negotiate from what at first glance appears to be an unreasonable position. Selling a company on the basis of future growth rather than past performance seems unreasonable. A buyer might well argue, 'Why should we pay a premium price when it is our actions that generate this future growth?' That is a fair question. The seller's defence is to have a choice of buyers. As already stated, having a choice of buyers is the single most influential issue that affects a company's value and saleability. Incidentally, when the managing director of the acquiring company wants to sell his/her business in 10 years time he/she too will have an equal right to be unreasonable.

If a prospective buyer is not prepared to see value in future growth, somebody else probably will. In addition, remember that neither party alone brings the ingredients for this future growth; both buyer and seller contribute, and therefore both should benefit.

Good preparation

Somebody controls every negotiation, and if it is not you, it will be the buyer. The factor that gives greatest control is to have a choice of buyers. Being well prepared for the coming negotiations is a second important factor. Key areas of preparation through which BCMS leads its clients include:

- *Considered communication.* There are many ways to protect confidentiality, an issue that must be considered early on in the process. When do you tell staff? What do you say to them? It is far wiser to talk about raising investment for the future growth of the business, than raising finance for the retirement of the shareholders. In fact the language that is used throughout the process and negotiations is very important. In reality, confidentiality is a far greater perceived than actual problem. Staff or major clients almost never jump ship when hearing the news (planned or unplanned) of a possible sale. Indeed, new owners could well mean great opportunities for staff. Nevertheless, confidentiality should be taken seriously and communications plans must be made.
- *Documentation.* In order to guide its clients, BCMS uses a 78-point checklist of documents and information that need to be prepared. The critical documents are the brief, the prospectus, the step change business plan and the schedule of benefits.
- *First impressions.* Arguably this is a minor point, but it is often so easy to put right that it is worth considering. How does the property look to a third party? When was the floor last swept? How long have the 50 rotting pallets been leaning against the front of the building? First impressions can be of disproportionate importance. People will assume (rightly or wrongly) that a tidy operation represents a tidy business.

  How about your staff? Do they deal with customers and prospects in a polite and professional manner? A buyer may well call in with a fictitious enquiry in order to get a feel for the company's manner.
- *Objectives.* What are your objectives? Why do you want to sell? What are your price aspirations? When do you want to exit? All of these issues will influence the type of buyer that is approached and the nature of the deal. Each sale will need to be constructed to meet your objectives in the most tax-efficient way. If your objectives are not clear, nor will be your planning.

- *Negotiation training.* Almost every BCMS client chooses to endure its infamous 'dry run' meeting. In this dummy run negotiation, efforts are made to identify and prepare for all difficult questions and negotiating traps. (The negotiating process is discussed in a separate chapter in Part Three of the book.)
- *Removing skeletons from the closet.* Tax evasion, phantom employees, contractors versus employees, unresolved litigation, product warranty problems and so on: these (though rare) can occasionally be deal killers, or at the very least affect the price, and will need to be considered prior to taking a company to market.

The project brief

This document will form both the objective and plan for all that that follows. Resist any inclination to skip this part of the project. Although you already know all there is to know about your own business, what you write down you tend to review. This is a healthy and sometimes illuminating process.

BCMS clients often reveal their surprise after the project brief. After the brief, they regularly place more value on their own business. The key elements of the brief are:

- *administration*: key contact points, confidential telephone numbers and so on;
- *company history and background:* milestones in the company's history;
- *company structure:* key staff, property, shareholders, vulnerabilities;
- *product and service information:* activities, benefits, unique selling propositions (USPs), future product development, patents, accreditations, suppliers;
- *sales and market information:* customers, sectors, vulnerabilities, reputation, competition, sales activity, geographical coverage;
- *the future prospects:* potential for growth, market conditions, sales planning, capacity, gains for the buyer;
- *financial and other:* statutory accounts, management accounts, trading cycles, skeletons in the cupboard, adjustments to earnings, cash position, the nature of the deal;
- *the potential purchaser:* geographic location, current activity, nature of clients, areas of synergy;
- *miscellaneous:* professional advisers, confidentiality, companies to avoid and so on.

The full BCMS briefing form can be downloaded from www.bcmscorporate.com.

Among other things, the brief will be used to produce the prospectus or information memorandum. BCMS does not conform to traditional thinking when it comes to the prospectus. A typical prospectus consists of 80, 90 or even 100 pages of detailed information, but BCMS maintains that a traditional style prospectus gives away too much information far too early. Typically, the prospectus will be produced and then a gap-year student will be asked to locate 10 or 12 competitors to whom it will be mailed.

Most professionals produce the prospectus in order to try and sell a company. This objective is wrong. The prospectus should never be designed to sell a company, but to sell a meeting – a meeting at which the option of entering into negotiations will be considered. The typical prospectus is feature-rich and devoid of benefits for the seller.

When producing this document, it is essential to think *benefits*. The focus should be on the buyer and not the company for sale. People only invest in benefits. Benefits make people buy – they are the all-important and typically absent payload.

A good prospectus should be no more than 15–20 pages and should include a disclaimer, administrative information, company history, shareholder information, reasons for sale, products and service information, future potential, key benefits of the acquisition, sales information, financial summary and a proposal summary.

The profile of the purchaser

A critical part of the initial brief is to consider the profile of the ideal purchaser. It is necessary to paint an identikit picture of the acquirer. Key questions to consider will be:

■ *Where will the buyer be located geographically?* It is important to recognize that the buyer of your business may well be an overseas company. An overseas buyer may well pay a premium to gain access to your market. After all, consider its alternatives:

 – It could appoint agents and distributors in this country. However, the Institute of Export confirms that 12 out of 13 export partners fail in the short term, primarily because they do not invest enough in selling.

 – The buyer could develop and grow organically in this country: develop the product, secure an office, recruit the right staff and gather a strong client base. However, this route is 'littered with corpses'. It is shockingly expensive and less than 3 per cent of companies globalize in this way. By far the most successful route to internationalization is to grow by acquisition.

■ *What products and services will the buyer be selling?* Don't forget that a premium price may be forthcoming from a complementary company rather than a head-to-head competitor. Your products can sell to its clients and vice versa.

 Customers who buy your products or services probably buy many other products and services. What are they? What products fit alongside your own?

■ *What do your buyer's clients look like?* It is likely that there will be a high degree of commonality between your customers and those of your buyers. The same buyers, decision makers and specifiers that it sells to will also be your customers.

■ *Is your buyer financially strong?* Interestingly and with almost no exceptions, MBOs are bad news for the vendor. In almost every case the managers cannot finance the acquisition and are forced to borrow money. However, the lender will never lend a premium over and above the short-term return on investment (ROI). It is now the lender who will determine value and not the buyer.

The ideal buyer will be financially strong. It will need good access to funds. If it relies too heavily on borrowed money, then the lender will have too great an influence on the price that is paid.

At the end of this process you will have assembled a reasonable picture of the ideal purchaser. However, a word of caution. In many cases, the best buyer does not conform to the ideal profile. Indeed, if you restrict your search for a buyer to the obvious at the expense of opportunism, then you could lose good opportunities. It is vital at this stage to think laterally and creatively.

Don't forget that the best purchaser for you may well not be looking to buy. It might be successful, profitable and growing without the need to purchase your company. An acquisition may well not be on the agenda. It will now become tempting to cut corners, but to do so will invoke great penalties. This may surprise you, but statistically, opportunistic acquisitions are more likely to be successful than those planned well in advance. We are, in effect, giving the acquirer a finite time in order to create a 'scarcity value'.

Such an opportunity may not recur for many years, and a premium price may well be more forthcoming from a complementary company than from a competitive company.

(Management of the negotiation process is discussed in detail in Chapter 3.5 to which this chapter is the prequel.)

Acquisition target strategies

Mike Sweeting, Acquisitions International

It is a sad fact that 60 per cent of the companies that go on the acquisition trail in the UK in any given year achieve nothing. Of the remaining 40 per cent, 63 per cent will regret the purchase they made (sources: PWC, Harvard Business School, Acquisitions International). Besides the myriad of sector-specific or project-specific issues, one glaring factor stands out. Most companies identify the wrong acquisition targets in the first place!

The structure of the marketplace lends itself to failure for four reasons:

- too few targets;
- inappropriate targets;
- lack of creativity;
- lack of forward planning.

These four factors crop up time and time again. Many large corporate buyers make all four mistakes concurrently. Let us look at the issues and their remedies one by one.

The need to increase the number of targets

It is no surprise that so many deals do not get done when we look at the impracti-cably small shopping list that companies work from. The average British buyer looking for purchases only looked at eight companies last year. The average for the decade is 10 companies looked at, per acquirer per annum. Incidentally, this figure means anywhere in the world, so the company trying to do six deals worldwide may have only looked at eight candidates. This is manifestly too few to achieve the two goals of identification: choice and comparison.

Choice

Always get scared when buyers get romantic. 'There is only one firm for me,' they coo. This is manifestly untrue, although it must be conceded that in multinational, billion-plus deals the number of candidates does suddenly decrease, and that there may be a reduced field or fewer ways of achieving the required goal.

In the normal M&A world that we inhabit there are always more companies available to buy than you currently know about. There are always alternative ways of achieving the same ends. Maybe you could buy two complementary but slightly different firms rather than the one obvious one that everyone else is bidding on as well. Maybe you could enter into a joint venture, then buy. Maybe you could just buy the best (or the worst) division. Maybe you can cherry pick from brands or revenue streams. Maybe a firm in another country is better.

Comparison

Buying companies is a bit like headhunting a chief executive. Of course you do have the option of only interviewing one or two of your chairperson's cronies and picking the one who is available right now, but most professionally minded firms would not follow that course of action First there would be a long list, then a short list, then several consecutive interviews, and so on. The goal is obviously twofold: to match the person to the company's strategy and to achieve meaningful comparison of candidates in that context.

When buying companies it is so easy to throw this best practice out of the window in the excitement of the 'hunt'. Although we noted that the average shopping list last year was eight targets, it is rare that they are examined concurrently or in any true comparative fashion. The acquisitive firm gets excited in January and looks at two or three that its auditor put its way. After the initial excitement these candidates looked pretty boring or overly expensive. Several further things rapidly come to the fore:

■ Those who own companies smaller than your own are usually pretty eccentric.
■ You are at the mercy of what the accountants and brokers are trying to shift. (Why should you be the one to be offered the best companies first?)
■ It is all much more time-consuming than you originally thought.

As a result nothing more is looked at until June or July. By this time you are pretty fed up with your advisers because they have nothing more to offer you, and by now you are essentially doing the hunting yourself. As a result it becomes easy to just look at a competitor or two, or a supplier or two. You will naturally stay in your comfort zone unless you make a major resolution to do the contrary. By September everyone is really scraping the barrel. In other words the chairperson has been sent out to talk to 'contacts'. Meanwhile your auditor has contacted two or three brokers to see if they have anything. The result is three more companies to look at before Christmas.

The above may be a bit exaggerated, but not much. Typically the goalposts have been moved at least twice and the targets have never been looked at thoroughly together. There has been no attempt to establish a true 'scientific sample' of what *should* be bought. All the emphasis has been on what *could* be bought. As an aside, company brokers (of which there are around 350 in the UK) love this kind of acquirer. The broker can trot out any dog of a company and the increasingly frustrated acquirer is more and more likely to look at it.

No wonder the integration figures look so awful. No wonder only 40 per cent of those who go on the acquisition trail make a purchase in the year they started looking. In fact the average time for making a corporate purchase is *over two years* from decision to signing of sale purchase agreement. What is really amazing is that this figure includes the very speedy deals like distress sales and purchases from the administrator that only take weeks. How many years must some deals take, for the average to still be so long?

The need to improve appropriateness of targets

As already implied, the first thing to suffer in the above context is the quality of the businesses on offer. There are usually about 40,000 businesses for sale in the UK at any one time. Many of these are very small: post offices, family hotels, shops, restaurants and so on. Most of the remainder are what might be termed 'boring'. They are contractors in the construction industry, printers, steel stockholders, subcontract engineers and agricultural firms.

So every year there is a substantial mismatch between what is on offer and what is required. Acquisitions International (AI) is often contacted by buyers in the mistaken belief that it is yet another broker. One gentleman called recently and asked, 'Do you have any medical electronics companies with net profits over half a million, tried and tested products, evergreen contracts and located in the south-west?' It was easy to deduce why he wanted such a firm, but it had to gently pointed out to him that if AI had such a jewel and he was an appropriate buyer, it would already have been offered to him!

Here is another relevant statistic. Only 7 per cent of done deals in Europe each year involve a buyer that was known to be buying and a seller that was known to be selling. This doesn't mean that it was general knowledge; it means that it was known in the world of M&A professional services. In other words, most of those who actually buy companies had not declared themselves to be on the acquisition trail, and most of the companies sold have not been officially on the market at all.

There is a final factor that leaches the best firms away from you. The way the market is working right now means that private equity and venture capital usually pay around 10 per cent more than a trade buyer. A trade buyer pays around 10 per cent more for a company than a MBI team. A MBO team often has peanuts to offer compared with any of these types of purchaser. Consequently, if you are identifying companies to buy using anyone whose business it is to sell companies (this might be a merchant bank, boutique, corporate accountant or broker), then your place in the pecking order will be defined by the above.

In summary, you will not even be offered what advisers have, unless you can match the prices they can obtain (often more easily) from others. This is why the rest of this chapter focuses on developing strategies on how to escape from this pattern. Basically, if the normal pond in which to fish is small and very muddy, how can a big lake be found that has not been over-fished? Read on.

The need to be more creative in target identification

So often acquisitive companies sit down with their advisers at the beginning of a search and are asked the same tired old questions. 'Who are your competitors? Who are your suppliers?' From these and other scintillating questions a list of what I call the 'usual suspects' is produced. It is neither a long list nor a short list. Most of the work (if any) has been done by the client, not the adviser. Here are some alternatives deriving from 17 years of seeking to do things more laterally and more effectively.

Complementary companies will always deliver more than competitive companies. They need to share at least one common characteristic if you are an experienced acquirer, all except one if you are new to the acquisition game. The obvious variables are:

- shared client base;
- shared supplier base;
- shared geographical coverage;
- shared method of doing business;
- shared type of activity;
- shared technology.

This will allow you to create several 'subsets' of companies. Your reasons for buying firms from each subset may differ. The payback time will almost certainly differ. The 'bang for your buck' will also be different. The outcome of this wider search will be that the prices of companies in each subset will also differ wildly. All of a sudden the whole thing opens up. Your budget may go much further now than you first envisaged. You will also find that you are now dealing with companies that are not all subject to exactly the same market conditions as either your own company or each other.

About 10 per cent of AI's shopping list in each AI project consists of companies that are on the edge of the target profile. A disproportionate 30 per cent of its deals come from this 'outer' group. These are companies that turn out to be great. But you wouldn't have otherwise found them, because you would have been unable to describe what they look like to either your own staff or an adviser! When you have been scientific in developing a large, robust target list, *then* you can afford to cast around and be opportunistic, but not before.

No database is complete or completely accurate. There are always companies that have already moved into your ideal zone without mentioning it to the wider market. There are always other companies that are about to become ideal, or in the process of doing so. If you are too narrow you will miss all these firms. Fortunately this is exactly what your competitors *will* do. In some industries everyone goes after the same tired old suspects. Be different. There are many more companies out there to buy than you think. Be creative. Think laterally.

For instance, about 10 years ago AI was asked to find a joint venture (JV) partner, with a view to eventual purchase, in India for a client in Ulster. The client makes the world's leading hairbrush for women. Every distributor and manufacturer we approached in India was interested in a deal due to the client's reputation – as long as it was not their time, money or other resources that were used! Some wished to sell a lot of the client's goods at Indian prices, others wanted to sell a smaller amount at a massive mark-up. Neither approach would deliver the relevant strategic impact. Within our research group we asked a simple question. What was really needed? Answer: commitment, land for development, an ability to handle Indian bureaucracy and a similar manufacturing process. As a result we approached all 40 paintbrush manufacturers in India. Our rationale was that they had a cash cow that was dying, very similar machinery and everything else but a client base!

Thirty-seven companies had a good laugh at AI's expense. Three had put aside large sums of money for diversification. The successful firm put in £1.5 million upfront. The conditions for the JV included a year's trial run of inter-trading. The partner became our client's most successful distributor ever – in four months! The moral of the story is to look not at the things that separate you from complementary businesses, but at the things that can make both firms fly.

There are also usually a number of human factors that make a deal either a lot of fun or a real bind. There is nothing wrong with including these as criteria. What is terribly foolish is to make such factors central to the deal. Some time ago, there was a scramble to do a deal in the British Virgin Islands, when the best company to buy was actually in Barnsley. I once tracked US inward investment into Ireland. Strangely enough there was a direct correlation between that investment and two other factors. One was the proximity of golf courses, the other was the closeness to good fishing on the River Shannon! These are not 'bad' things as a bonus, but so often cause acquirers to make a poorer commercial decision. If two targets are very similar and the price is relatively similar too, then the golf or the company castle is icing on the cake. Too often these things are the cake itself. I greatly admire the way that Huntsman Chemicals managed to resist the lure of ICI's stately homes and golf courses. It concentrated on buying the things it was good at, like boring old process plants.

Of course, there is a law of diminishing returns. AI used to go 35 per cent wide in the early days, but learnt the hard way this was overdoing things. Nonetheless, it is always better to have too many companies in the kitty and be able to kick most out. The alternative is having too few and getting stuck, as is so clearly the norm. Keep the odd ones and the 'miscellaneous' ones to start with, but be ruthless in your later comparisons. It is now time to look at how to do this without alienating the best firms.

The need for forward planning

As a rule of thumb, the more that is put in pre-deal, the fewer integration problems there will be post-deal. It's a bit like marriage! If AI thought that cutting corners would deliver as effectively as doing the whole demanding process, it would probably cut corners. *But it is never worth it.* What is recommended to you involves substantial upfront labour, but the goal is to substantially reduce the *overall* work and to ensure a lasting success. Every day that is put into research will save you six days later on. Every day put into early vetting of targets will save you five days later on.

As a result AI has taken the route of substantial investment in business data. This is because we have to. No single database is truly accurate. No single database is truly comprehensive. No single database is truly up to date. The best answer we have yet found is to collate *all* the different sources of information concerning each company being researched as a target. Some of those will coincidentally be already for sale or will have recently failed to sell. This is not irrelevant information and could become useful – if the company fits your requirements in the first place. So much of M&A is based upon trying to convince an inappropriate buyer to purchase an inappropriate seller just because one is on the acquisition trail and the other is for sale.

As a tip, never stick to just what that company's own world says about it. If that firm is an exporter, obtain data from other countries about it, particularly countries where the firm already does business. The best information on Mexican companies isn't going to be in Mexico. Go to the State of Texas. Its Mexican data will be excellent, because it has to be. The Dutch are a trading nation, so you will find that Netherlands-derived data is usually excellent. US and UK firms often try to 'massage' their credit ratings in Anglophone credit check systems. They have probably not tried to do this with data from Holland or France. Check several credit agencies, reflecting different markets, different perspectives, different scoring methods.

Conclusion

■ Larger acquisition shopping lists give you:
  – room for manoeuvre;
  – more room to negotiate;
  – the power to say 'no' more often;
  – speedier deals because you have leverage.
■ More varied targets give you:
  – companies in each market subset available at different prices;
  – potential for hassle-free diversification;
  – the ability to buy hard-to-come-by skills when you buy the company;
  – less vulnerability to market changes;

- less exposure to changes in legislation or regulation.
- Creativity gives you:
  - companies your competitor does not know about;
  - companies no one else is bidding on;
  - a higher chance of faster return on investment.
- Forward planning gives you:
  - less likelihood the deal will collapse;
  - alternatives if it does fold;
  - more time spent on the real issues;
  - much less stress because deadlines can really be met.

the **team** for **growing businesses**

The challenges of management buy-outs

David Stanning, B P Collins

Management buy-outs (MBOs) typically occur in one of two situations: first, when part of a business that is regarded as 'non-core' is sold by 'the group' to a management team, and second, when an entire business is sold in order to provide an exit route for the existing shareholders, often the founder and his/her family. In either case, there is usually a presumption on the part of the seller that, because this is an in-house deal, it will all be very straightforward and thus quick, easy and inexpensive!

This chapter focuses on the second situation, the sale of an entire business, and will attempt to provide some insight into the challenges that often arise in the context of an MBO, particularly if they are unforeseen and thus unplanned.

An MBO is seen as the preferred exit route in variety of circumstances, but particularly when the outside market is tough, with few likely trade buyers, or where there is an unusual business such that the specialist knowledge of the management team is anticipated to produce a higher price than a trade sale. Less usual is the situation where 'patron' owners see an MBO as their opportunity to reward their team. The common theme in all of these is succession, with the owner/founder looking to extract fair value from a lifetime's work. It is something of an art to balance the different expectations of the parties in this context.

Talk of an MBO can conjure up images of passing on the ownership of a company in an atmosphere akin to that of a cosy family get-together, but sometimes, as we all know only too well, family parties can develop into less than comfortable gatherings, after which relationships are infinitely worse than before. It can be the same with ill-planned, or ill-judged, MBOs where, in extreme cases, well-meaning but patronizing owners make a meal of handing on, almost gifting as they see it, to their 'fortunate' employees the company or business that they have painstakingly built up over the years.

But even without the emotional hang-ups, MBOs can set their own challenges, arising from the lack of arm's length negotiations and the fact that, on many occasions, this is a new step up in risk and responsibility for the MBO team. Invariably the transaction gives rise to some interesting dynamics, not only because the team will be buying from their current boss but also because they will also be needing to establish their own pecking order, a process where individual perceptions can throw up remarkable variations!

MBO OR EBO?

An important opening move is to establish the extent to which a proposed transaction is in fact an MBO. Many supposed MBOs are in practice EBOs, employee buy-outs, where the new team has less knowledge of the business than might have been thought, and even less experience of management generally. Particular points to address initially include assessing the following:

- *The strength of the MBO team:* will they need outside help to boost their combined experiences? Who is the leader? Committees rarely prove to be effective decision makers when the going gets tough. Objective appraisal rather than British tact must be the order of the day here.
- *The depth of their knowledge about the business.* 'You don't know what you don't know' can be a trite but true summary of the MBO team's position, so the MBO team should be taken through the standard due diligence enquiries to discover where their knowledge gaps occur. While the MBO team may not be unduly concerned, those financing them surely will be.

How much, and how?

Another 'first step' must be to sort out price and then finance – how much, from whom and by when? In terms of price, difficulties can arise at both ends of the scale. If the price is set apparently on the high side, the MBO team may feel that they are paying over the odds for a business that some or all of them have helped to build up (that is, they are buying their own goodwill in the business), and if the price is set too low, our friends at HM Revenue & Customs may suggest that these are employees standing to gain by reason of their employment and thus that they should be taxed on any 'gift' element in the price.

As we all know, valuing private limited companies is very much an art not a science, with a number of different valuation methodologies available to 'assist' in this exercise. All that can fairly be said on this subject is that there is clearly scope for debate and argument that a business is not worth as much without its management team (who should therefore pay less for the business). So, once again, an early point on which to reach agreement, perhaps with the intervention of the third-party funder who clearly has an interest in paying as little as possible, is the price. It is always easier to leave the arguing to a third party and to avoid the charge of being an ungrateful employee!

An olive branch to be offered to a seller who believes the price to be too low could be a 'non-embarrassment' clause, providing that if the company is on-sold again within a relatively short period, the original seller stands to receive part of any gain over the MBO price.

In terms of raising finance, the MBO team must be encouraged to produce a proper business plan showing the anticipated requirements of the business for funds, not only for the purchase of the business but also for future working capital needs. This will dictate the likely source of such finance and the appropriate split between debt and equity. Too much of the latter could result in too little for the MBO team; too much of the former could mean the business is dragged under by the weight of repayments. An experienced corporate finance adviser will help the MBO team to decide between the various sources of finance, which may include a loan-back from the seller(s), investment by 'business angels' (of whom there is a growing number with an increasingly sophisticated understanding of the entrepreneur/investor relationship) or so-called 'vulture capitalists', or even banks, some of which are now showing a refreshingly flexible approach to providing funds for MBOs.

Whatever the source of external funds, the MBO team will themselves be required to invest their own money in significant amounts, if only to prove to themselves and others that they really mean business. For some, this can involve remortgaging the family home, with the attendant concerns and anxieties that such a move brings with it.

Fiduciary duty and other conflicts

These preliminary issues must be sorted out before the legal process kicks in, and during all of this the MBO team will still be engaged full-time in working for the business and its current owner. This of itself gives rise to another challenge unique to MBOs, namely that of conflicting loyalties, and in the case of MBO team members who are directors of the target company, potential breaches of fiduciary duty, a heavily legalistic expression and concept that can bring headaches to a few in the context of an MBO.

In its broadest sense, fiduciary duty obliges directors to put the interests of the company and its shareholders ahead of their own, sometimes a difficult task in the context of an MBO. Perhaps all that need be said here is that the issue of fiduciary duty should not be overlooked. Provided there is transparency on all sides, and no secret profits either anticipated or made, there should be no problem.

Silence is golden

Another issue of practical concern is confidentiality. Who should be told about the possible MBO and when? Anxious to avoid concerns and disappointment should the transaction fail, many take the line that no one outside the immediate party should be told anything until there is a 'done deal', but this is more difficult to achieve than might be imagined, with the potential for secret meetings, passworded communications, and unexplained decisions for those outside of the magic circle. Again, this aspect calls for a common-sense approach appropriate for the particular circumstances.

The MBO team will also have to assess how to handle other employees who are not part of the MBO team and who may resent being left out.

The possibility of the transaction falling through raises another concern for the seller, namely the prospect of a disappointed and, worse, disenchanted management team. Obviously much will depend on the reasons for the failure, but if the breakdown occurs because of perceived intransigence, or a change of heart, on the seller's part, then the seller should be prepared for the backlash in the form of demotivation or, worse still, resignations. The image of jilted brides comes to mind.

Warranties: to be, or not to be?

Another fertile source for debate in MBOs is the time-honoured issue of warranties. 'Patron' sellers will, rightly or wrongly, take the view that they are passing over the business at a discounted price, and further that the MBO team probably know as much, if not more, about it than they do. So the warranties initially on offer will relate to their ownership of the shares and not a lot more. In this situation, the presence of an outside investor can provide the white knight for the MBO team, because that investor will certainly require detailed and extensive warranties much more in line with those expected, and given, in a third-party sale. The difficulty for the MBO team arises when they find themselves between a rock and a hard place, in that neither seller nor funder will shift position. This is yet another occasion for the experienced (and silver-tongued!) lawyer to persuade the various parties to give and accept warranties appropriate for the particular case, failing which the transaction will break down, with unhappy consequences for all.

Relationships

Another essential document in the context of an MBO is the shareholders/investors agreement, governing the relationship between the team and the outside investors, if such there are, and also, most importantly, the relationships within the MBO team and the inevitable 'what ifs?' that all too often make an unwelcome appearance in business life.

Clearly it is important to establish proper checks and balances for the investors so that they have the necessary restraints to protect their investment, but it is equally important for there to be a mechanism in place whereby the MBO team can replace those investors if for some reason the relationship breaks down. There is little more frustrating for an ambitious MBO team than conservative investors whose lack of understanding of the business is matched by their lack of business sense and imagination. In particular, the MBO team needs to understand the 'Armageddon' provisions in such an agreement: what can the investors do if things start to go wrong?

It is equally vital that, at the outset of an MBO, the team has addressed the obvious issues in terms of the relationship between themselves, such as:

- their respective management and employment roles and terms;
- their ultimate game plan;
- how additional finance should be raised;
- when and what the exit route might be, collectively and individually;
- disagreement between them on any material issue;
- death or critical illness;
- underperformance;
- share sales and transfers;
- terms of employment.

Without an effective agreement covering these and other issues, the MBO team could sooner or later find itself at odds, and then in disarray, with the result that the team becomes a rudderless yacht, loses way and eventually founders. The shareholders' agreement must provide for certainty in such situations, with a quick and decisive outcome to enable the venture to proceed with the least loss of time and energy.

Fair play

A final aspect not to be overlooked is the matter of post-sale restraints, both on the original seller and on any member of the MBO team who decides, for whatever reason, to move on earlier than anticipated. Restrictive covenants are notoriously difficult to enforce unless carefully drafted and appropriate to the particular context. Usually there will be little room for argument in the context of the original buy-out, but other MBO members, and in particular the investors, will want to ensure that there is no scope for their investment being damaged by competition from an early leaver.

Conclusion

In the author's experience, working on an MBO tends to be more time-consuming and demanding because of the number of relationships and issues that have to be dealt with, often in parallel, in terms of seller/buyer, MBO team internally, MBO team/investor, and MBO team/bank. It is, in general terms, a mistake to underestimate the challenges here and to assume that, because the principal parties know each other, it will all be easier than a third-party sale. That might be the case in a country where plain speaking is the order of the day, but here in Britain, we have the charming but occasionally frustrating trait of avoiding saying what we really think for fear of upsetting people. So issues that could and should be resolved earlier get put on the back burner for another time, occasionally with the result that, when a difficult issue is at last raised, it is seen as a deal-breaker whereas when the transaction started out, it was just another point to be discussed. One day we will all learn to speak up, and speak early.

That said, there are many positives along the way of an MBO, in particular seeing the team having the chance to develop as a management team with the opportunity to have a meaningful say in their own destiny, and with a bit of good luck and good advice, to make a significant sum of money along the way. MBOs will doubtless remain, and rightly so, a preferred exit route for many who have no other obvious succession route.

The meteoric rise of the MBO

Oliver Hoffman, Mazars

Management buy-outs (MBOs) have become an established feature of the corporate landscape over the last 25 years. The concept itself is simple. Who better to buy a business than the people who manage it? The reality is more complicated, and a whole industry of corporate finance advisers, corporate lawyers, bankers and venture capitalists (VCs) has been spawned to help management teams (and the shareholders from whom they buy their businesses) through the buy-out process.

This chapter highlights the most common scenarios in which an MBO occurs, and identifies the type of businesses that make good buy-out opportunities (as well as those that don't). Additionally, a look at the trends seen in the MBO marketplace in the last few years may point towards the future of the MBO.

Backdrop

In a nutshell, an MBO is the purchase of a business from its shareholders by the current management, usually with funds provided by a bank and/or third-party equity providers. MBOs are still a relatively new concept in the UK. Prior to 1981 it was illegal under company law for a company's shares to be purchased with borrowed money secured on the assets of the company itself. When this restriction was removed, the UK was able to follow the lead set by the United States in the 1970s and the MBO as we know it today was born.

Statistics from the Centre for Management Buy-Out Research show that there were over 600 reported MBOs in the UK in 2005, with a combined value well in excess of £20 billion. The actual number of MBOs is likely to be much higher as many transactions, particularly those involving smaller and family-owned companies, are not always publicly reported.

Why have MBOs become so popular?

The MBO has become such a phenomenon for three main reasons:

■ It gives a business owner an alternative to selling to a trade buyer. Smaller businesses in particular are often difficult to sell, as they can be below the radar and interest level of larger acquirers. The option of a sale to the management team therefore opens up another avenue of possibility to the owner.

While there is sometimes a financial downside for a vendor in a sale to management (as management teams don't have as deep pockets as some trade buyers), the upsides can be beneficial. With a sale to management the owner can sell without having to disclose potentially sensitive information to someone in the trade. Also confidentiality surrounding sale discussions can be better protected than when a business is being marketed to a wider audience. MBO sales are also attractive to paternalistic vendors who want to see the business continue under private ownership by the management rather than being subsumed within a larger organization where the company's identity and culture may be lost.

It is not at all uncommon (although it may seem rather cruel) for management teams to be regarded by vendors as a fallback position: someone to sell the business to if nobody else wants to buy it. The MBO is an exit planning insurance policy!

■ A plentiful supply of capital has helped. Pension fund managers and wealthy individuals alike saw the returns made by those that invested in some of the early MBOs, and have allocated large amounts of cash to be invested in this market. The banks too have seen that there is profit to be made in lending to companies going through a buy-out, and have set up specialist 'leveraged finance' teams to provide finance to this market.

■ Management teams have been lured by the prospect of making life-changing amounts of money as well as taking control of their own destiny. This money-making opportunity comes from financial leverage. In most cases, a management team buys all or most of the shares in the company with a relatively small amount of their own money. The bulk of the money is provided by third parties (banks and/or equity investors). Over the next four to five years they use the profits generated by the business itself to pay off the banks and investors. What they are left with is a business with little or no debt that can be sold, potentially making a very large profit for themselves. Tens of thousands of pounds are often turned into multi-millions for successful management teams.

Sounds too good to be true, doesn't it? Well, MBOs are not without their downsides. If a business veers off-plan and fails to deliver the profits required to pay off its borrowings, the outcome can be devastating. Surveys have estimated that up to a third of businesses that go through a buy-out fail in their first few years with administration/receivership often a consequence. Most advisers operating in the MBO arena will argue that the majority of MBOs that go wrong do so because the MBO team overpaid for the business and burdened it with too much debt. Hindsight is a wonderful thing.

Of higher risk than an MBO is a management buy-in (MBI). The principles of an MBI are the same as that of an MBO with the exception that the managers buying the business do not currently work for the company they are buying. MBIs are particularly common in circumstances where the incumbent management team does not have the strength and depth to mount an MBO bid itself. These are higher risk than MBOs as there is greater potential for problems in the business to be hidden by vendors and only unearthed once the company has been acquired.

The most common types of MBO

Most buy-outs fall into one of the two categories below.

Privately owned and family businesses

The vast majority of MBOs are spawned as a consequence of vendor retirement planning or shareholders simply wanting to cash in their chips. The opportunity to orchestrate an MBO is often given by vendors to their management teams on soft terms (or at least, terms that they perceive to be soft) as a 'thank-you' for management's contribution to the success of the business. What may be a lower price than can be achieved by a sale on the open market is offset by non-financial benefits to the vendor such as ease of sale and preservation of company identity post-sale. Also, 'better the devil you know than the devil you don't'.

Disposal of a non-core subsidiary

Usually as a consequence of a change in strategic direction or following a merger, large groups often find themselves sitting on a business no longer deemed to be core. A sale to an MBO team in this circumstance is often looked upon as a convenient way of exiting from a business, which can be relatively quick and often remain under wraps until it completes.

Poor-performing businesses where significant staff reductions are necessary to turn the business around often find themselves in the hands of management teams, as the group cannot risk the backlash to other group companies of a staff restructuring under group ownership. This is often a good opportunity for a management team to buy a business relatively cheaply, as it is removing a problem for the group board.

Sales to MBO teams of non-core businesses are also commonly found in circumstances where a group becomes financially stretched and looks to sell a subsidiary to pay off some debt.

Characteristics of a business suitable for a buy-out

Some businesses are more suited for an MBO than others. Although not prerequisites, here follow some of the key characteristics of a business ripe for an MBO.

Strong management team

Businesses do not run themselves. While it is very easy to focus on how profitable a business is and the opportunities available in the market it operates in, bankers and VCs principally back the management team that runs a business rather than the business itself. A broad management team with a proven track record and a strong leader is the ideal. Often gaps in the team are plugged with new blood from outside the business at the instigation of the financiers.

Mature/stable business with a track record

Businesses operating in mature markets are usually more predictable than those in changing or rapidly growing markets. Banks like predictability and are more inclined to lend to businesses where the future is clear than to those where it is not. Understandably banks want to be as certain as they can that the business they lend to will consistently generate the level of cash required to pay back their interest and capital. To do so, they usually look to the past as a pointer to the future.

A stable business that has demonstrated a consistent performance in a mature market is ideal for a bank, and can often support a higher level of debt than a rapidly growing business.

Where difficulties can lie

Technology or R&D-based businesses where the value rests in potential future performance rather than current performance are usually unsuited to an MBO approach, as it is difficult to convince lenders of the ability of the company to repay the borrowings with little track record of success.

One of the biggest considerations for funders, particularly in backing MBOs of smaller privately owned and family businesses, is how much of the success of the business is dependent on the vendors leaving the company (who often are those that have set up the business). Funders will be unwilling to lend if they believe the key customer and supplier relationships will walk out of the door with the vendor.

Regardless of to whom they look to sell their businesses, business owners with an intention to sell should plan carefully for a handover of key relationships in the years prior to sale to help them position their business best for sale.

Recent trends in the MBO marketplace

The importance of vendor finance

Changing attitudes of those that fund MBOs have led to changes in the way MBOs are put together and structured. The most notable development seen in the last five years is the increased role played by vendors in helping management teams, particularly in smaller businesses, achieve an MBO. In the 1980s and 1990s, it was commonplace for banks to provide 60 per cent to 70 per cent of the finance for an MBO, with the balance coming from a VC.

In the early 2000s, many VCs saw greater profits to be made by financing larger transactions, and moved away from smaller MBOs (those with a purchase price of below £5 million). Management teams were unable to meet the price aspiration of vendors with bank borrowings alone, and asked the vendors to fill the gap left by VCs by deferring payment of some of the purchase price, typically for two to three years. This 'debt plus deferred' structure has now become commonplace, and has virtually replaced 'debt plus venture capital' at the smaller end of the market.

The secondary buy-out

Having moved away from the smaller deals market but with massive funds provided by investors, VC providers are awash with cash seeking a home. As Corporate UK has become a well-fished pond for MBOs in recent years, VCs have been prompted to invest in businesses already under VC ownership. These situations, commonly known as 'secondary buy-outs', typically involve one VC buying a business from another, enabling the first to crystallize its profit and return funds to its investors. Often new management teams are introduced as the first team cashes in its stake along with the outgoing VC.

A move away from MBIs

Having looked retrospectively at where they have made money and where they have lost it, the funding markets have moved away from financing MBIs in the last few years. This has lead to the 'BIMBO' – short for buy-in management buy-out – a hybrid of an MBO and an MBI where an MBI team or individual lead the purchase of the business supported by the existing managers of that company. The perceived risk of this type of transaction for funders is lower, as the inclusion of the existing management reduces the likelihood of problems arising within the business after purchase that were not previously identified.

A view of the future

The MBO market is likely to become increasingly polarized, with a divide forming between large and small deals. With VCs focusing on progressively larger deals, and bigger and bigger funds being raised for investment by them each year, secondary buy-outs will soon become the norm for larger deals in the same way that debt plus deferred has become the norm at the lower end.

The appetite for MBOs from management teams, vendors and the financial community alike shows no signs of abating. While it will undoubtedly continue to reinvent itself, it is a fair bet that the MBO will be with us for at least the next 25 years.

Grooming a business for sale

Peter Gray, Cavendish Corporate Finance

Introduction

It will never be possible to maximize the proceeds of a company sale unless time is taken before the sale commences to prepare the business for sale. A grooming exercise, which can take place over a few months or even years before a sale exercise, aims to enhance the attractiveness and value of the business to potential purchasers. This is achieved by measures such as:

- positioning the company to maximize value;
- strengthening the company's second-tier management;
- improving margins via cost reductions or selective price increases;
- reviewing the company's accounting policies;
- widening the company's customer and supplier base.

A review of the business to determine appropriate pre-sale grooming measures should cover the following areas.

Positioning

At an early stage, consideration should be given to the types of potential purchaser that might be interested in the company and the valuation which they may attribute to the company. Based on that evaluation, an attempt should be made to maximize

Recent Transactions

Cavendish advised on 15 deals in the first 9 months of 2006 with an enterprise value in excess of £520m

2006

IT Consulting Business

has been acquired by

UK Listed Software and Services Company and TechMark Market Member

---

Whittard of Chelsea plc

has been acquired by

Baugur Group

U-POL Products Limited

has been acquired by

ABN AMRO Capital

Language Line Limited

has been acquired by

Language Line Inc

YORK NOVENCO Group

has been acquired by

Dania Capital

Hale Hamilton

has been acquired by

Circor International Inc

Alphason Designs Limited

has been acquired by

Armour Group plc

Brecon Pharmaceuticals

has been acquired by

AmerisourceBergen

The commercial property division of Countrywide plc trading as Palmer Snell Fulfords and Douglas Duff

has been acquired by

Erinaceous Group plc

AC Electrical

has been acquired by

Wolseley plc

Xit2

has been acquired by

Macdonald Dettwiler Associates

SENAD Group

has been acquired by

Undisclosed

GET Group

is being acquired by

Schneider Electric SA

Greetings Direct

has been acquired by

Flying Brands plc

Noble Denton

has been acquired by

Ferncliff and Hitec Vision

For more information contact:

Cavendish Corporate Finance Limited
40 Portland Place, London W1B 1NB

Tel: 020 7908 6000
Email: info@cavendish.com
www.cavendish.com
www.mergers.net

Authorised and regulated by the Financial Services Authority

Unrivalled expertise in selling businesses

the attractiveness of the company to that category of purchasers. One of the best examples of positioning in UK M&A history was the Seattle Coffee Company which, knowing that Starbucks would at some stage wish to enter the UK market, replicated completely the Starbucks model with a view to being acquired by Starbucks when it did make a decision to enter the UK market. When the inevitable happened, Starbucks acquired Seattle for approximately £1 million per unit.

Financial matters

Margins review

A business may historically have priced its products with its long-term future in mind, and in particular, to deter potential entrants. In a situation where a business enjoys some degree of market power, research could be undertaken to see whether a period of higher prices could be sustained in the lead-up to a sale to enhance profitability.

Review of costs

A review should be undertaken to identify all costs that would not be incurred by an incoming purchaser. While a purchaser will generally not be prepared to give the vendor 100 per cent of the value attributable to these cost savings, in a competitive auction involving other acquirers who would benefit from the same cost savings, and in order to win the deal, a purchaser will need to cede some of the value to the vendor.

In addition, a vendor should conduct a purge on costs, to eliminate excessive and unnecessary costs. If a purchaser is paying the vendor 10 times earnings, every £1 of cost savings will translate into £10 of value.

Finally, research and development expenditure and advertising costs should be reviewed to ensure that they are primarily focused on producing shorter-term results that will have a near-term rather than a longer-term impact on profits.

Strategic/operational matters

Improving earnings quality

One of the most significant ways in which a company can enhance its value and attractiveness to purchasers is by improving its quality of earnings and risk profile. Smaller companies tend to have a higher risk profile because they rely on a small number of customers. In some cases, they may also be over-reliant on one or two suppliers.

A company whose largest customer accounts for less than 10 per cent of its revenues will be viewed much more favourably than one whose largest customer represents over 50 per cent of its revenue base. In the latter case, loss of the major customer is likely to result in the company experiencing severe financial difficulty. In the lead-up to a sale, a company should therefore make every effort to widen its client base, even if this may mean restricting business volumes with the key customer.

Assets review

When a business has assets which may not be required or fully valued by a purchaser, such as surplus property and investments, removal before a sale exercise commences should be considered. In addition, working capital should be reduced to the minimum level required to generate the company's profit stream. Policies concerning stockholding levels, debtors and creditors should therefore be reviewed at an early stage to ensure that there is no 'fat' in working capital. If the company is sold with excess stocks, or excess levels of debtors as a result of poor credit collection, the vendor is in effect gifting the surplus to the purchaser. Any such surplus should be eliminated and the resultant cash either stripped out or (preferably from a tax perspective) added to the purchase price.

Any hidden or undervalued assets of the business should also be identified. If the value of the property assets is understated in the company's balance sheet relative to their market value, they should be revalued independently prior to a sale.

Tax review

All PAYE, VAT and corporate tax matters should be up to date. Tax allowances, if appropriate, should be maximized, and tax computations agreed with HM Revenue & Customs. Any tax losses available to be carried forward should be identified.

Pension schemes

Final salary schemes can give rise to enormous valuation issues on a sale. Where such a scheme exists an attempt should be made to resolve these issues prior to a sale. This may involve commuting the final salary scheme into a defined contribution scheme.

Management review

The quality of the company's management team will generally be of paramount importance to a purchaser, especially where the owner/managers are proposing to leave the business at the time of, or shortly after, a sale. It is important to be able to convince the purchaser that there is competent second-tier management available to assume executive control of the business. This will involve devolution of management control by the owners in the lead-up to a sale. Where second-line management are taking executive decisions, this should be documented. For evidentiary purposes, it may help to recognize their input formally by:

- minuting management meetings;
- issuing formal job descriptions;
- considering job titles and reviewing organizational structures.

Purchasers attach considerable weight to job titles. For that reason, promotion of senior management to the board of directors in advance of a sale will make it easier to convince a purchaser that there will be a self-sufficient management team in place following the departure of the vendor(s). It might also help for the owner/managers to take an extended holiday before the sale to show the purchaser that the business can operate effectively in their absence.

Obtaining the buy-in of senior management to a sale process is extremely important. This may involve putting in place a management incentive scheme which vests on the sale of the company, preferably with a deferred element to assist with management retention. Also, to ensure that there is not a mass exodus of senior management following a sale, most purchasers will wish to see key management secured with service contracts.

Staffing review

Any redundancies made once negotiations with a third party have commenced will normally be treated as unfair dismissal by an industrial tribunal. Accordingly, staffing levels should be reviewed before the sale exercise starts. Staff who would not be required by a purchaser might be employed elsewhere in a group or directly by the proprietor, as appropriate.

Accounting policies review

With a sale exercise in mind, a review should be undertaken of the following accounting policies, with a view to maximizing stated earnings:

- Recognition of profit, particularly for contract-related businesses.
- Depreciation policies, for both tangible and intangible assets.
- Provisions: excessive provisions against stock or even debtors is one of the most commonly used techniques to reduce tax. In the lead-up to a sale, excess provisions should be released to boost both profits and asset values, preferably over more than one accounting period.
- Valuations of properties and investments.
- Research and development – this may play a large part in the purchaser's interest in a private company. Small companies are frequently bought for their innovative skills and product development capabilities. Where all research and development has been written off in the past, this should be identified and highlighted.
- Accounting treatment of any rent-free lease agreements.

Accounting systems

It is essential for the vendor to start preparing monthly management accounts if it has not already do so. During a sale process, it is vital to have up-to-date information on the current trading performance of the company, and purchasers will be looking for the vendor to warrant a recent set of management accounts.

It is equally important for the company to produce budgets. At a minimum, a purchaser will be looking for profit projections for both the current and the following financial year. If the company has not had a history of producing budgets (and preferably beating them), any projections produced specifically for the sale exercise may lack credibility.

Review of business plan and strategy

In the lead-up to a sale, every strategic decision a company makes should take account of the likely impact of that decision on the attractiveness of the business to a potential purchaser. An obvious example might be a decision to extend the lease in the company's head office in the lead-up to a sale. It may be that a purchaser would wish to integrate the vendor's business (with its own), in which case a long-term lease might be a 'poison pill'.

Legal review

A legal audit should be carried out in conjunction with legal advisers and should, at a minimum, ensure that:

- All leases and title deeds are located and reviewed.
- Trading contracts are examined to ensure that no change of control restrictions or prohibitions apply. Such provisions are potential poison pills for a purchaser, and should be resisted to the extent possible.
- Intellectual property rights are registered.
- Shareholder agreements and articles are examined to review provisions relating to a sale.
- Companies House filings are up to date, as are board minutes and other statutory documents.
- Any outstanding litigation is cleared up. Even if it is covered by insurance, major litigation can be a deterrent to a purchaser.
- To the extent possible, the ownership structure of the company is simplified. This may involve buying in minority or joint venture interests. Purchasers value simplicity, and complex ownership structures can diminish the attractiveness of a business.

Other matters

Environmental audit

Potential environmental liabilities will be a major area of concern for any purchaser. Depending on the nature of the business, it may therefore be appropriate for the vendor to conduct an environmental audit prior to the sale to enable the identification and remediation of any potential problems at an early stage. If a purchaser finds major environmental issues during the course of the due diligence, this can have major timing implications, if not endanger the deal.

Public relations

Potential purchasers are much more amenable to a company they have heard of than one whose name they do not recognize. It is often advisable therefore to raise the company's profile prior to a sale, by conducting a public relations (PR) campaign directed not at the company's customer base but at potential buyers of the business. Examples of profile PR of this nature include obtaining editorial coverage on the company in trade or financial publications.

Vendor due diligence

Vendor due diligence involves the proprietor instructing accountants to prepare a due diligence report on the business in advance of a sale exercise being undertaken. The report is then given to potential purchasers who have expressed serious interest in the company for use in finalizing their offers for the business.

The main advantage of vendor due diligence is to flush out financial, tax and other issues relating to the business at the outset of the sale process. As a result, the chances of the deal collapsing once heads of agreement have been reached, or an agreed bidder chosen, are significantly reduced. If the report is prepared properly, it is unlikely that any material issues will arise from the purchaser's due diligence that had not already been identified in the vendor due diligence report.

Conclusion

The more prepared the business is prior to the commencement of the sale process, the greater will be the proceeds of sale. However, it is important not to groom a business for sale in an over-zealous fashion, or attempt to boost profits in artificial ways which will be exposed during due diligence. This will backfire on the vendor and may destroy a relationship of trust established between the vendor and the purchaser. It is also necessary to commence the grooming process long before the sale process gets under way, principally because the impact of the steps taken to enhance profits will take some time to flow through to the company's accounts.

Part Two

Funding considerations

Overview

Peter Wood and Catherine Hemsworth, Pinsent Masons

Introduction

Once a decision has been taken by a company to pursue acquisitions as part of its business strategy, and an appropriate target has been identified, or once a decision has been made to acquire a company by way of a management buy-out, it is obviously crucial that the acquisition can be funded. Without being able to raise the necessary funding, the acquisition strategy of a trade buyer will hit a brick wall, with potentially damaging consequences for the long-term future of the company, or with management unable to realize their ambition to own the company for which they work.

It could be that the trade buyer is sitting on a sufficiently large cash pile to fund the acquisition, cash which it has perhaps generated from a previous disposal of a non-core business, or which it has already raised from its shareholders specifically for this purpose. However, if this is not the case, the trade buyer will need to consider carefully the various funding options available to it.

For a private equity-backed MBO, the funding structure will inevitably differ from that for a trade buyer, and other considerations will apply, which again will need to be tackled at the outset to ensure there is a viable transaction for which appropriate funding can be obtained. Both of these structures are considered in this chapter.

Equity and debt funding permutations

For a trade buyer, acquisitions are typically funded through bank debt or through funds raised from shareholders by the issue of further shares, or a combination of the two. There are a number of factors, covered in more detail in this part of the book, that will influence how the funding is structured, such as tax, the buyer's gearing (the ratio of debt to equity), and its ability to service additional bank debt and interest balanced against the increase in the shareholder base and possible dilution of existing shareholder interests. New shareholders will also be expecting a return on their investment in the form of future dividends. With the recent climate of low interest rates, debt funding has been particularly attractive.

A significant advantage of private equity transactions relates to how the transactions are usually funded. That is, private equity transactions can be structured so that management are 'locked in' and fully incentivized to make the business successful. This is because management will usually have the smallest investment but the potential to make the biggest gain if the company is successful. Structuring of private equity deals is considered in more detail in this part of the book, but typically the private equity house would provide up to 50 per cent of the total funding required, with the bank providing the balance. Management will also be asked to make a small cash investment. Again, the climate of low interest rates has meant that banks have been keen to provide debt funding on private equity transactions as they can potentially generate a higher return than through other more traditional forms of financing. On a private equity transaction, detailed financial modelling will be carried out to determine the split between debt and equity funding. Banks expect to see companies with strong cash generation to enable the debt to be serviced, and look for a strong asset base in order to secure their funding.

Private equity and VC investment perspectives

The past 10–15 years or so has seen the rapid rise in the UK of private equity-backed transactions. Private equity is now a very sophisticated and developed industry in the UK, and plays a major role in the UK economy. It is estimated that around 20 per cent of the private-sector workforce work for a company which has been backed by private equity. A number of the UK's leading companies are backed by private equity, and private equity-backed companies have an impressive record of performance when measured against their quoted company counterparts. It is estimated that the value of UK management buy-out market in 2005 had increased to a record £25 billion (source: Centre for Management Buy-Out Research), for a number of reasons, but largely as a result of the ready availability of bank debt and the fact that private equity funds are flush with record of amounts of capital following very successful fundraisings. As a result private equity houses, and the companies they back, have become an important part of the M&A landscape in the UK.

Private equity houses typically look to back companies with strong growth prospects and a strong management team, which can also support the appropriate funding structure. Private equity houses will also want to know that there are good prospects for them to be able to exit their investment in accordance with their preferred investment timeline. Some of these issues are examined in more detail later in this part of the book. Sectors that seem to work well for private equity-backed transactions include financial services, leisure, logistics, business services, media, healthcare, specialist manufacturing, telecoms and IT services. Less promising for attracting private equity investment are low-growth companies, loss-making companies/'turnaround' situations, one-product businesses, particularly where there are low barriers to entry, and businesses the success of which is solely dependent on the presence in the organization of a certain individual. Markets that are fragmented and ripe for consolidation are also particularly attractive for private equity houses, such as business services, healthcare and insurance broking to name but a few.

Assuming a business is suitable for acquisition by a private equity-backed company, it will be important from the MBO team's perspective that it selects the right private equity partner to work with, which should be more than just about providing the money. While the size of the business, and the level of funding required, will largely dictate which private equity houses would be appropriate, management should also consider factors such as the private equity house's sector experience, what it can bring to the table strategically, what level of controls it is likely to insist on, how 'hands on' it will be and who will be its representative on the board. The private equity house and the management team will be partners in the business together for potentially several years, so it is important that the fit is right at the outset.

Mezzanine and other debt finance

Recent deal structures have reflected greater liquidity in the debt market and competition among lenders to secure deals. For example, it is increasingly common to see different tranches of financing and for the repayment profile to be structured, with repayment tranches being loaded to the back end of the term. This allows companies a little more headroom at the outset but does give concern that companies may struggle to service the debt if interest rates rise and the company's performance dips. Vendor finance (in the form of deferred consideration/equity issued in the buyer company) is a common means of funding any 'gap' between the consideration to be paid by the buyer and the amount of external funding it can attract.

Mezzanine finance on larger transactions has also increased in popularity. This is debt that ranks behind the senior debt and is therefore slightly riskier from the lender's perspective. To compensate for this, interest rates are usually set higher, the debt is normally repaid as a 'bullet' after the senior debt has been repaid, and a warrant normally attaches to the loan, enabling the lender to subscribe for equity in the borrower on certain trigger events. Mezzanine funding is often provided by specialist lenders, but it is not unusual for some private equity funds to provide this tranche of debt. Again, it is important to ensure that the borrower has the ability to service the level of mezzanine finance provided.

Invoice discounting facilities are increasingly being introduced alongside senior and mezzanine facilities. Often there, is a coupling of a senior and mezzanine offer with an invoice discounting offer, so lenders look at their return in the round. These facilities can be attractive to borrowers and they do give the debt providers additional comfort in terms of security over book debts. The documentation for these facilities tends to be more standard (and often therefore more onerous on the borrower).

Current account banking issues

Companies tend to focus on looking at the best terms that they can obtain on senior and mezzanine debt finance to allow them to make the relevant acquisitions, and therefore current account banking tends to be a secondary consideration. However, often the bank that has been providing current account facilities is keen to continue the relationship, and it may therefore be one of the banks tendering for the acquisition facilities. Certain of the larger banks are seeking to differentiate their business accounts, and therefore corporates are becoming more discerning about where they go for current account services. The main clearing banks offer a large range of facilities which should accommodate most corporates, but where there are particular requirements for certain treasury products, for example for certain bespoke services or international coverage, some banks are able to differentiate themselves from their competitors. Often these facilities are documented between the bank and their customers directly, but where the overdraft and ancillary facilities are committed, these may be referred to within the negotiated acquisition debt documentation.

Parameters for investor-friendly business planning

In order to access funding for a transaction, it is important for the buyer (or the management team in the case of a private equity-backed transaction) to have in place what is commonly referred to as a business plan. This is perhaps the key documentation for a buyer in the fundraising process. It should be prepared to a high and verifiable standard, as a funder may seek warranties on the business plan as part of the funding documentation. Often the involvement of a financial adviser at this stage can be crucial, as they are familiar with how business plans should be prepared and what funders expect to see covered (such as a description of the business, its products/services and the marketplace in which it operates, some basic financial forecasts and historical financial information, details of the overall strategy and how the acquisition strategy is compatible, and details of the level of finance required). Making sure that a detailed and robust plan is prepared, containing the confirmation and level of detail a funder would expect, is time (and money!) well spent by a buyer if it is serious about its acquisition strategy, and about seeking the required level of funding for its implementation.

In addition to preparing the business plan, the buyer should also seek to do some initial due diligence on the acquisition target. This may be done before talks are formally entered into with the target or its advisers, or afterwards (in which case the buyer will be expected to sign a confidentiality agreement). If this is undertaken before formal talks commence, there is a great deal of information in the public domain that the buyer can get hold of: for example, audited accounts and annual returns are public documents which contain valuable (although slightly historical) information about the target. There may also be press articles about the target, or if the target is operating in the same market, it might already be well known to the buyer. Being able to spot any difficult issues at the outset could avoid a lot of time and money being wasted by the buyer during the funding process.

A management team looking to lead an MBO will already know a great deal about the target company, but will need to ensure they take appropriate legal advice at the outset to ensure they do not breach their terms of employment and (if they are directors) their fiduciary duties in spending time putting together a possible bid and lining up the funding for it, as opposed to concentrating on their duties to their employer. This point is considered in more detail later in this part of the book.

Negotiating the finance

So the acquisition strategy has been established, a target has been identified, and offers to fund the acquisition have been made. Alternatively, the management team has agreed terms to buy out the business. The next and final stage in the funding process is to negotiate the terms of the finance and ultimately reduce these to legal documentation. It is important that the buyer or the management team takes proper legal and financial advice on this aspect of the transaction to ensure that the best possible terms are negotiated. The advisers should have a thorough understanding of the funding markets to ensure non-market practice points are not taken, since these delay the process and can frustrate funders. A good adviser can help steer the buyer through the process and shoulder a great deal of the work. Typically, if it is a private equity transaction, the advice may include running with a couple of funders on the debt side for as long as possible to ensure that competitive tension remains in that aspect of the process, and to try to minimize the risk of terms being altered to the detriment of the buyer.

The key areas to be negotiated on the funding aspects of the acquisition process are considered in more detail later in this part of the book.

Private equity and VC investment perspectives

Paul Rivers-Latham, Cobalt Corporate Finance

Corporate finance for technology and media companies

Private equity and venture capital – one size does not fit all!

The terms 'private equity' and 'venture capital' are sometimes used interchangeably but it is worth clarifying what is meant. Venture capital (VC) in its stricter sense usually refers to an unquoted investment in a start-up or an early-stage company with strong growth prospects. (For example, technology companies are a high-profile group that has historically attracted significant amounts of venture capital.) By their nature these companies are relatively unproven, often loss-making, and hence the amounts invested today are usually relatively modest (typically a few million pounds). VC usually comes from either angel investors or from VC firms that specifically target or allocate part of their funds to early-stage investing.

Private equity (PE) by contrast usually refers to later-stage investing where the technology and/or business model is more proven and some of the business risks have been partially or fully mitigated. While simplistically this is true, PE covers an enormous breadth and diversity of companies and types of investment. For example,

Esprit Capital Partners (formerly Cazenove Private Equity) made a PE investment of £6 million, of new money, in May 2006 into Lagan Technologies, a provider of relationship management applications, which increased revenues to £17.5 million in the year ended March 2006 (up 60 per cent on the previous year). By contrast, in August 2005, an investor group led by Silver Lake Partners acquired SunGard – a global leader in software and processing solutions for financial services, higher education and the public sector, with annual revenues of US \$4 billion – in the largest ever technology privatization, valued at approximately US \$11.3 billion.

Clearly the size, nature, financial structure of the transaction and the investor(s) funding these two transactions are very different. It is therefore difficult to make generalizations; however, I will endeavour to highlight common ground. The reader should note that Cobalt specializes in high-growth technology and media companies (with turnover below £100 million) and hence our views and experiences are naturally biased towards the VC market and the smaller end of the PE spectrum.

What does the VC or PE investor want?

A glib answer might be 'maximum return for minimum risk'. However, before we get to the financial considerations it is worth touching on what are perhaps the top three key criteria that financial investors assess when considering an investment opportunity.

Operational considerations

Management

The most important constituent part of almost every deal is the management team that is being backed. The majority of VC/PE investors do not want to run the business themselves, although turnaround investors often do. Key areas that will be closely examined are:

- Does the management team have a proven track record in its industry?
- Does the team fully understand the market the company operates in (and does it have a clear vision of how the industry is likely to develop): market dynamics, competition, regulatory environment and so on?
- Is there breadth and depth of talent in the team. Gaps can always be filled, but is the backbone of the team of high calibre?
- Is the management team well incentivized to deliver the plan *and* is there financial downside risk (as well as reputation risk) for the management team if things don't go to plan? That is, have management invested and will they invest their own money in the venture?

As Accel Partners express it, 'Accel-backed companies are driven by extraordinary technology entrepreneurs and seasoned management teams who have sparked many of the most significant innovations in business and technology.'

Market opportunity

Is the opportunity that the team wants to address sufficiently large? The investor is assessing whether or not the company has the potential to grow to be a sizeable company in its own right and become one of the top two or three companies in its particular market niche. It is increasingly a global marketplace, and the larger investors in particular will typically only invest in companies that can address the worldwide market. For example, Benchmark Capital's stated strategy is 'to be the first investor in technology-driven companies that seek to create new markets with significant growth potential'. Similarly, Atlas Venture's mission is to 'apply our operational and venture capital experience to help early-stage companies become successful, high-growth global businesses'.

Defensible market position/competitive advantage

So assuming that the management team and the market pass muster, the next key question for any potential investor is, how is your approach to solving a business problem different from that of your competitors, and do these differences bring a sustainable competitive advantage? It could be that the differentiator is a new and patentable technology; the strategic partnerships the company has, or the route to market. But whatever it is that sets a company apart, there needs to be a clear sustainable differentiator.

Financial considerations

Financial return

It's all about the money. The VC/PE world is highly competitive, with firms constantly trying to outdo each other, striving to generate the most impressive returns. For example, Apax Partners put out a press release earlier this year to high-light that it had made a 27 times multiple on the IPO of Q-Cells, a solar cell manu-facturer, after holding the investment for a mere 22 months. Apax's return of £190 million, after costs and net of its original investment, is the single largest capital gain made by a European venture capital firm since the dot.com boom. This phenomenal return also beats the £170 million return that Index Ventures made on the US $4.1 billion sale of Skype to eBay (*Independent*, 31 January 2006).

The return that the VC/PE generates is often expressed as either a multiple of the money invested or as an internal rate of return (IRR) and it is insightful to under-stand how the two relate and how they help to frame the investment decision. 3i's press release of June 2006 on its exit from Azzurri is a good example:

> 3i announce today it has sold its 75 percent stake in Azzurri Communications, the leading UK converged voice and data communications company, to a secondary buyout vehicle backed by Prudential Ventures (PPM) in a deal valuing

the company at £182.5m. 3i's proceeds from the sale of £115m represent an IRR of 38% and a money multiple of 4.9 times initial investment.

Ideally, an investor would like to generate, and therefore deliberately structures the investment to target, both a high multiple (a minimum of at least doubling its money) and a high IRR (40 per cent plus). For example, an investor that invests £5 million and receives £15 million precisely one year later has made a three times money multiple on the original investment and has achieved an IRR of 200 per cent. By contrast, the same return (money multiple) but received after five years would result in an IRR of 'only' 24.6 per cent. So the IRR is a function of the time taken to generate the return: the higher the IRR, and assuming the same absolute return, the more quickly the return has been generated.

As a priority the VC/PE technology investor is more interested in the absolute return rather than a high IRR. A 'quick flip' for example of making £1 million profit on a £5 million investment in three months generates a very good IRR (75 per cent plus) but only a 1.2 times return on the money invested. The VC/PE investor will typically have spent six months or more analysing and carrying out due diligence on the opportunity prior to making the investment, and hence most investors (as distinct from hedge funds and shorter-term players) want a larger absolute return on their money over a longer period. As Benchmark Capital declares, 'We invest for the long haul, not quick flips, and look for entrepreneurs with a similar perspective.'

Time horizon

The expected investment horizon (from initial investment to exit) for PE/VC investors is often given as three to five years. Within this range their preference is usually for shorter rather than longer (the impact on the IRR is significant over the additional two years and hence the absolute return required is materially increased). This timeframe conveniently tallies with the fact that three years is usually accepted (for high-growth companies especially) as being the maximum period for which a forecast can reasonably be produced. More stable, established industries – for example in the mining, utilities and oil sectors – can (theoretically) be forecast accurately over a much longer time period. Equally, we have met many reasonably well-established technology companies that struggle (through no fault of their own) with forecasting the next 12 months' performance. We should always remember the Moltke maxim, 'No plan survives contact with the enemy'!

A three-year business plan is one of the core pillars of the investment decision. Over this time period the investor typically expects top-line growth and improving profit margins, but there will also be key operational developments that are targeted because they are expected to improve the company's valuation significantly, such as expansion into new geographies/industry verticals, launch of a new product/service line, or securing new key customers or supplier relationships. The three-year investment target also gives the VC/PE investor flexibility to make changes and recover performance if the plan slips or if there are more serious issues with the business.

At this point, it is worth touching fleetingly on the typical structure of VC/PE funds. These are usually independent pools of funds made available by international investors, principally financial investors such as pension funds and insurance funds (these investors are the 'limited partners'). These funds are usually closed ended, limited life (10 years is common), self-liquidating funds, in that they receive commitments from investors at the outset, draw down cash as needed to make the investment, then as each investment is sold the 'general partner' (that makes and manages the investments) distributes the proceeds to the limited partners without reinvesting.

Therefore, given that a typical fund has a life of 10 years, the VC/PE investor will usually spend the first three to five years of the fund's life making investments and spend the rest of the fund's life trying to exit the investment while seeking to maximize the absolute return. In this context the quick-flip investment has only limited appeal.

Mitigating risk/deal structures

VC/PE money is often referred to as risk capital. Many management teams/founder shareholders that have received term sheets may wish to take issue with this description. However, whatever the view, the VC/PE provider is offering to provide the funds when other potentially cheaper sources of funds are not available.

There are clearly many different ways that the financing for a particular transaction can be arranged but a typical PE deal involves a number of different layers of financing. Broadly these can be summarized as follows:

- *Senior debt:* At the top of the funding tree and the most secure, and hence usually one of the cheaper sources of finance. It has repayment priority in a liquidation. Secured with a mortgage over the company's assets (and anything else available). The amount that banks may be prepared to lend varies from relatively little (if anything) for early-stage technology companies to up to nine times EBITDA (earnings before interest, tax, deprecation and amortization), in today's market for a well-established business with long-term contracts, a dominant market position and strong cashflows.
- *Mezzanine debt:* Debt that incorporates equity-based options, such as warrants. Ranks behind the senior debt. 'Mezz' is often used to bridge the gap between the senior bank debt and the VC/PE investment. It is less secure than the bank debt and hence is more costly.
- *Preferred equity:* This is the form of equity usually held by the PE/VC investor. It could take the form of preference shares or 'A' ordinary shares with different rights from 'ordinary ordinaries'. Whatever the term used and however disguised it may be, the PE/VC investor is looking to build in protections. The different rights attaching to the shares come in many different forms but preferred equity is a very common mechanism for achieving this.
- *Ordinary equity:* Usually the class of equity that management receives. It is fairly common for there to be a ratchet mechanism attached to management

equity such that if the company performs well management's equity stake increases, and if the company performs badly its stake may reduce.

Investor protections

As mentioned above the VC/PE investor has a number of ways through which it can look to protect its investment. The most common include:

- *Differential dividend policies*: For example preferred equity holders might receive one whereas the ordinary shareholders may not, the dividend may be at different rates, or the management dividend may be performance or time-dependent.
- *Drag-along rights*: In an ideal world a financial investor would like to have an unfettered ability to sell its stake as and when it likes. In reality, it is usually the case that unless management and shareholders are aligned it is difficult to sell a business at all. Certainly, it is likely to be impossible to get full value without management's agreement. However, at the point of making the investment the investor will be looking to retain as much flexibility as possible, while tying management closely to the investors' wishes.
- *Under-performance rights*: These kick in when a business is not performing to plan, and can trigger a wide range of recovery or compensatory measures. The first breach may require certain changes to be made, issues to be addressed, or may give the company a period of time to rectify the situation. Over time, if the under-performance persists the measures will quickly become more penal, and they could ultimately give the investor the right to change the board or sell the company. From the investors' perspective these rights are crucial in allowing them to safeguard their investment, and their concern is that they (the investor) must have the time and the ability to rectify the situation before other covenants are breached, such as banking covenants. If banking covenants are breached the powers to control the business pass to the bank, and in the extreme the bank could sell the company to repay its debt. Clearly from the VC/PE investors' perspective this is to be avoided at all costs. How under-performance is defined is always an emotive question, but it is typically measured against profit or cashflow, or most likely both.
- *Enhanced board rights*: This is frequently tied to under-performance. Again if the business is not performing the investor may have the right to appoint new directors to the board ('swamp' the board) or the voting rights may change such that the investor's voice carries more votes.
- *Negative controls:* These can cover a broad range of areas, including a ban on management selling the business without the investors' agreement, no material change in the nature of the trade/no significant acquisitions, no significant capital expenditure above a pre-agreed level, and no senior-level hires.
- *Liquidation preference:* A perhaps much maligned term, but this gives the VC/PE investor priority on receipt of proceeds such that it gets back its money or even a multiple of its money ahead of other stakeholders if things do not go

well. From the VCs' perspective it is a reasonable right given the asymmetry of information about the business and its prospects. From the entrepreneur's perspective the mere mention is enough to get the blood boiling. In reality it is rarely easy to sell a business without the willing collaboration of the founder management. In essence, the liquidation preference merely establishes a starting point for negotiation.

Summary

This has been a somewhat brief discussion of quite a complex topic covering both financial and operational considerations. Most entrepreneurs have little opportunity to gather extensive experience of the topic precisely because they are so focused on their day-to-day business challenges, and yet it is of vital concern to them. Seeking out good-quality advice in order to address this concern is something that any entrepreneur should prioritize.

Consideration

Edward Hoare and Nick Jennings, Faegre & Benson LLP

In this chapter we focus on the main types of consideration used to finance acquisitions, and look at some common consideration structures.

Types of consideration

While a wide range of different forms of consideration may be used, the most common types are cash, shares and loan capital. For a buyer, the choice usually depends on its own financial circumstances and whether it wants the seller to remain involved going forward. For a seller, the choice usually depends on whether it wants cash or a continuing interest in the company or business being sold. Tax considerations also apply: for instance, the seller may wish to receive shares or loan notes to defer or reduce any capital gain on the sale.

Cash

Cash is likely to come from reserves or borrowings, or by way of an equity or debt offering. Both the size of the transaction contemplated and the financial position of the purchaser will determine whether sufficient cash reserves are available.

Where cash is raised from bank borrowings, it is usually a requirement of the lender that the purchaser provides security over the amounts borrowed. If it is intended that the target company or its assets are to form part of the security for the borrowings required for the transaction, then the financial assistance provisions of the Companies Act 1985 (the Act) must be complied with. In short, and subject to complying with the provisions of the Act (see below), a private company may engage in financial assistance.

Financial assistance is defined by the Act as the giving by the target company or its subsidiaries of financial assistance directly or indirectly for the purpose of the acquisition (either before or at the same time as the acquisition takes place).The relevant section of the Act is extremely wide-ranging and includes assistance by way of gift, loan, guarantee, security or indemnity, or any other financial assistance given by a company whose net assets are thereby reduced to a material extent. If a private company does provide financial assistance, the following requirements must be complied with (commonly known as a 'whitewash'):

■ The financial assistance must be approved by a special resolution of the members (unless it is a wholly owned subsidiary).

■ The directors must make a statutory declaration in the prescribed form attesting that the company will be able to pay its debts as they fall due during the year immediately following the date on which the financial assistance is proposed to be given.

■ The auditors must produce a report supporting the directors' declaration as to the company's solvency.

■ The financial assistance can only be given within the time limits set out in the Act.

■ The assistance can only be given if the company's net assets are not reduced by the financial assistance, or if any reduction in those assets resulting from the assistance does not exceed the company's distributable profits.

Financial assistance given in breach of the Act may result in the directors facing criminal penalties and/or a civil action by the company against them and/or the party that receives the financial assistance.[1]

Share capital

A corporate purchaser may wish to use its own shares to satisfy part or all of the purchase price. The issue of shares as consideration is most common where the purchaser is a listed company, as there will be an established market for its shares and it will be easier to assess their value. If a significant amount of consideration shares is to be issued to the sellers, the purchaser will be likely to impose restrictions on dealings in the shares received by the sellers for a limited period following completion, so as to maintain an orderly market for the shares.

Where consideration shares are being issued, the parties will need to ensure that the issue complies with applicable requirements of any exchange on which the company's shares are traded. Care must also be taken over compliance with the Act. This includes ensuring that the issuing company has sufficient authorized share capital, that its directors have sufficient authority to allot the shares, that any pre-emption rights under Section 89 of the Act or the issuing company's articles of association are taken into account and/or disapplied as applicable, and that a valuation report be produced if required under Section 103 of the Act.[2]

Loan capital

For tax planning purposes the sellers may wish to receive consideration in the form of loan notes from the purchaser. A loan note (usually issued as a series of loan notes) is a record of the purchasing company's indebtedness to the sellers to whom the loan notes are to be issued. The holder of the loan notes will be issued with a certificate which sets out the amount of the indebtedness, the amount of interest payable on the principal sum and the terms and conditions of repayment.

Depending on the creditworthiness of the loan note issuer, the sellers may require that the loan notes be secured, or alternatively this risk might be offset by the purchaser offering a higher level of interest repayable under the loan notes.

Consideration structures

A distinction is often made between initial consideration and deferred consideration. Initial consideration is simply the term for consideration that is paid to the seller on completion of the transaction. Deferred consideration is the term for consideration that is to be paid to the seller at a later date. Often the sale agreement will provide for a combination of these.

Deferred consideration is a popular mechanism to deal with situations where the final price is not known on completion. The most common situations where it arises are in the context of post-completion adjustments, retentions as security for future claims, and earn-outs.

Adjustments

In many cases the total consideration will be subject to an adjustment depending on whether an agreed net asset valuation has been achieved. This adjustment will usually be calculated by reference to a set of accounts which are prepared following completion. In the event that the seller has delivered more net assets than the agreed amount, usually any surplus in value will be paid to the seller in the form of additional consideration. Conversely, if there is a shortfall, the seller will be obliged to pay the shortfall amount to the purchaser (in which case the initial consideration originally paid will be treated as having being reduced by the amount repaid).

Retentions

Sometimes the purchaser's due diligence will discover a potential liability which is of such magnitude that the purchaser requires a proportion of the consideration to be held back for an agreed period as security, should a claim arise. In those circumstances it may be agreed that payment of part of the consideration is deferred, perhaps until any agreed warranty period has expired, on the basis that if a claim does occur in that period the purchaser may set off the amount of the claim against the deferred amount. The amount of the retention is often subject to much negotiation between the parties. The sellers may also request that interest be paid to them on any amount deferred but paid.

Earn-outs

Essentially, an earn-out is an arrangement whereby at least part of the purchase price is calculated by reference to the future performance of the target company. Earn-outs are commonly used as an incentive where owner-managed companies are sold and the managers are to continue to work within the business following the sale. They are also a useful device to link the overall purchase price to the future profitability of the target company where a greater degree of value is expected to be realized post-completion. Often target companies are acquired on the basis of their future income stream, with the purchaser willing to pay an additional amount of consideration in respect of contracts to be performed and in the pipeline, and receivables to be paid to the target company. This is most relevant in service industries where the company in question does not have a large number of valuable assets but the majority of its income is earned through the provision of services to its customers.

From a purchaser's perspective, the main advantages of paying earn-out consideration are the ability to ensure a link between the purchase price and actual performance of the target company, so as to avoid overpayment; the cashflow benefits of deferral; and the creation of a mechanism to incentivize key employees who are central to the target business going forward. From a seller's perspective, the main advantage is the potential to achieve a higher overall price.

There are also negative factors associated with earn-outs. For example, it is not possible for the sellers to have a clean break from the business following completion. The period covering the earn-out is usually a transitional period, during which time the sellers will have a retained and significant interest in the management of the target business. Also, extraneous factors, not necessarily related to the management or perceived profitability of the target, may impact on the profits actually realized by the target business during the earn-out period.

The negotiation of earn-outs can be difficult, and often requires considerable skill in terms of drafting the sale agreement. Each of the parties will be interested in ensuring that the calculation of the earn-out does not involve either an artificial inflation of the profits (resulting in the purchaser paying more than anticipated) or producing a figure that is artificially low (resulting in the sellers not achieving the maximal earn-out potential).

Most earn-out targets are profit-related, so it is essential to be clear about what is to be counted as profit and what shall be counted towards the *calculation* of profit. The normal starting point is by reference to the target company's audited accounts and the accounting practices and principles used in their preparation. However, adjustments may be required to deal with specific items that inevitably come about as a result of the target's ownership by the purchaser. Where the target company joins part of a larger group of companies, this might include having access to preferential borrowing terms, decreases in staff headcount, lower property costs (if there is relocation), and the general benefit in terms of purchasing power associated with the purchaser and its larger group. However, in practice these benefits are difficult to quantify and may be problematic if the means of their calculation and adjustment to the future accounting practices are not agreed in advance. Certain extraordinary items are also commonly excluded, such as one-off costs associated with relocating or making redundancies, and any other similar expenses associated with the transaction that do not form part of the usual spending of the target business.

The mechanics of preparing the accounts to calculate the profits are also important. The default mechanism is to provide that the purchaser's professional advisers prepare a statement of calculation stating what earn-out amount is due to the sellers. This should take place within an agreed time after the end of the particular accounting period. The sellers and their professional advisers are then afforded an opportunity to raise any comments or disagree with the calculations involved. If no comment or disagreement is raised within an agreed period, those calculations are deemed to be final. If the sellers disagree with the calculation and the parties cannot reach an agreed calculation among themselves, the disagreement may be referred to an independent expert for final determination.

While the purchaser will want to enjoy freedom in the operation of the target business after completion, the sellers are likely to want to retain some control after the sale so as to maximize their chances of achieving the earn-out target. This is done through earn-out protection (sometimes called 'ring-fencing') provisions in the sale agreement, and these are often the subject of tough negotiations. The impact of a breach of one of these provisions can be drafted so as to constitute a simple breach of contract which is actionable, or by giving rise to an accelerated earn-out payment triggered by the occurrence of specific events, or alternatively by impacting on the calculation of the earn-out itself.

The sellers might also insist on being granted some security for payment of the earn-out consideration. This might take the form of a bank or parent company guarantee or a charge over assets, or by putting the potential earn-out amount on deposit in an escrow account.

Notes

1   The Companies Act 2006 will, when it comes into force, abolish both the prohibition on the giving of financial assistance by a private company for the purchase of shares in itself and the private company whitewash procedure. However, the prohibition on the giving of financial assistance will be retained for public companies.
2   The Companies Act 2006 will, when it comes into force, abolish the concept of authorized share capital and remove the need for shareholders' authority to allot shares for private companies.

Crystallizing value

Adrian Alexander, Mazars LLP

Strategy for exit

In order to understand how to unlock and crystallize the maximum value in an unquoted company, it is imperative that the shareholders have a full understanding of their position as early as possible before selling their shares. They will then be able to formulate an effective strategy in the period leading up to exit.

They must ask themselves a number of questions, considering key issues such as:

- Where are we now?
- Where do we want to be?
- How do we get there?
- Who do we need to be talking to?

The analysis required is summarized in Figure 2.4.1.

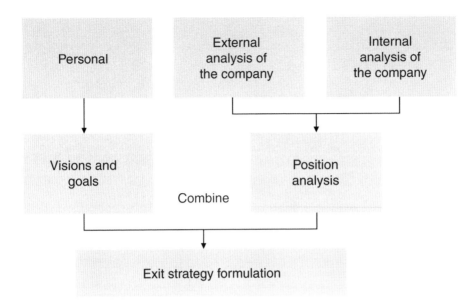

Figure 2.4.1 Exit analysis

What are the exit routes?

The main exit routes are summarized in Figure 2.4.2.

Identifying the best exit route for the shareholders and comparing the benefits of each option is a very individual process. Ideally a decision on the preferred method should be made several years in advance so that it can be planned for, although in many cases the decision is prompted by external factors: for example, receiving an unsolicited offer from a potential trade buyer or a management buy-out (MBO) team. A dramatic change in the personal circumstances of the shareholders or significant changes in other group companies can also determine the timing of a sale. However, while these events cannot always be planned for, all companies, from the largest listed plcs to the smallest owner-managed businesses, should attempt to plan a timely exit strategy.

Figure 2.4.2 Exit routes

Grooming the company for exit

Whichever exit route is chosen, it is essential that the exit strategy includes a rigorous 'grooming' process. Many businesses undertake little planning, which can result in the exit process becoming far more arduous and complicated than necessary, can have a negative effect on value, and in some cases may mean that an exit is not achievable.

The grooming objectives are to:

■ achieve the best value;
■ retain the maximum amount after completion through taxation mitigation planning;
■ have as little disruption through the exit process as possible;
■ avoid nasty surprises in the completion phase.

Commercial planning points

There are a number of commercial, accounting and legal aspects that can be planned for which will help maximize value at the point of exit. Areas that should be considered in the planning process include:

■ Maintainable earnings should be as high as possible. The quality of the underlying maintainable earnings and future growth prospects are key for all prospective purchasers. To achieve this:
  – Cease any loss-making activities, divisions or speculative development work which has a long-term payback period.
  – Review any major supply or sale contracts which underpin the business going forward. Any contracts about to end should be renewed or extended.
  – Ensure that any acquisition programme is completed at least a year before the planned exit.
  – Review overheads, but be careful not to cut out anything that will damage the long-term health of the business, as this will be identified by purchasers when they carry out their due diligence.
■ Growth should be demonstrated in the period preceding the sale and in a justifiable forecast with increasing profits, ideally from improving market share.
■ Reduce the gearing as much as possible and increase the net asset value. The potential increase in value will have to be assessed against remuneration and dividend policy, although most purchasers will discount 'proprietorial' remuneration in their valuations.
■ Review items such as freehold properties. Are they to be sold as part of the company or excluded from the deal? The position relating to property needs careful consideration before the deal; property can be a major issue to prospective purchasers. Many purchasers will be attracted (or not put off!) if there is flexibility in the property portfolio.
■ Unless the business being sold is property-based, the purchaser may find that a short lease is preferable so that parts of the business can be closed and savings made. Alternatively, the purchaser may have unutilized space which it wants to fill, or have ambitious expansion plans which will require a move of premises. If the vendor has a particular requirement, the necessary action needs to be made in advance of the sale.

- Sell off any surplus assets or subsidiaries not required for the core trading activities. These will be discounted anyway in future valuations.
- Identify surplus cash and a mechanism to realize this additional shareholder value.
- Avoid any unnecessary capital expenditure as this may not be fully reflected in the purchaser's valuation.
- Consider legal, VAT and PAYE/NIC audits to make sure there are no hidden problems.
- Does the business have reliable management information? The reliability of management information is more likely to be an issue for smaller businesses. However, being small is not a valid excuse when the time for the sale approaches. Potential purchasers will quite rightly ask for fairly detailed management information including forecasts. Just because the vendor has successfully run the business for 25 years without producing a single set of management accounts or forecasts, it is unreasonable to expect other businesses to act in the same way. Many owner-managed businesses are sold to listed plcs that have stringent reporting methods. They are likely to be more impressed if the quality of management information is good. This issue must therefore be addressed as soon as possible in the planning process.
- Ensure that there is a suitable management structure with the right individuals in the key roles. This is particularly important when it is not a trade sale or the vendor is seen to be key to the running of the business. However, beware of increased costs in the short term without increased revenue, as this will reduce the maintainable earnings.
- If the vendor is an owner-manager and closely involved in the day-to-day running of the business, certain key questions need to be addressed:
  - Does the owner wish to remain involved on a medium to long-term basis after the sale?
  - Is the owner fulfilling a vital management function not performed by anybody else?
  - After the sale will he/she retain the motivation to carry on working?
  - Can the business function without the owner-manager?
- If part of a business, for example a division or a subsidiary of a larger group, is being sold you should identify whether it can be sold as a stand-alone entity:
  - Can group functions be easily replaced?
  - Are the buildings, assets and employees separate from the rest of the group?
  - Is the accounting information on which valuations are to be performed accurate? Does it reflect all the costs and identify inter-group items?
  - Will inter-group pricing policies be maintained after the sale?
- Address matters with dissenting shareholders and ensure they all want to sell. If not, action needs to be taken to ensure they will not hold up any deal.
- Finally, give the factory a coat of paint to improve the image. Every little helps!

Companies that are most likely to sell at the best price are those that have planned properly, on a timely basis and where the owners have become 'investors' in their own companies and are not involved in day-to-day management. Prospective purchasers will be looking for well-run, profitable companies with future growth prospects and good-quality management and employees. To ensure the company is well placed to achieve maximum value for the vendor, the importance of forward planning and meticulous grooming should not be overlooked. In addition, taxation planning is normally an important consideration in any sale.

Marketing the business for sale

Careful and skilled marketing is vital to the successful sale of a business. The marketing process is one of the most critical phases of the process, and unless handled by experienced advisers, the most difficult to control. Once the process starts, it is the first time that the 'for sale' sign is put up, the information becomes public knowledge and confidentiality procedures are put to the test.

For the vendor it is the most uncertain time, with the following questions always in mind:

- Will a buyer be found?
- How much will I receive?
- Will the employees or customers find out?
- Will the business be damaged in the meantime?
- How long will it take to complete a deal?

Information memorandum

The information memorandum is the most important document in the sale process, with the exception of the final sale and purchase contract. It is, effectively, the company's 'shop window', and its quality and content can determine whether or not a prospective purchaser decides to take an acquisition further, especially if the purchaser has no first-hand knowledge of the company or the sector in which it operates.

One of the primary functions of the information memorandum, especially for owner-managed businesses, is to highlight the maintainable earnings of the business, which are usually higher than the reported profits. This will lead to a higher price for the business if the prospective purchaser understands the position fully from the outset.

The information memorandum should have a very positive tone, and highlight all the key areas of the business. It is likely that the information memorandum will be the key document upon which the prospective purchasers will base their bid, and negotiations could be concluded based on the information in this document alone. No information should be included or claims made that will not stand up to detailed investigation later on in the process. Otherwise, both sides could end up wasting significant management time and incurring unnecessary costs. The purchaser could validly claim during due diligence that false claims were made in the information memorandum and that this was misleading. This could lead to a renegotiation of the price, or at worst the purchaser could end up withdrawing from the deal.

Finding a purchaser

Once the information memorandum has been prepared, a method of identifying potential purchasers has to be agreed. Assuming that an adviser has been retained, the business can be marketed, on a no-names basis, in one or more of the following ways:

- to a single company only, possibly because it has already made an unsolicited approach;
- to a highly select list of likely purchasers, most of whom would be well known to the vendor;
- to a researched, targeted list of companies in the industry, or in related industries, some of whom may have registered their interest in making acquisitions or may be considered suitable as potential purchasers;
- to the agents or specialist accountants who carry out corporate finance work, or 'boutiques' and other intermediaries, such as financiers and solicitors who engage in mergers and acquisitions work;
- by advertising in the *Financial Times*, trade press or other suitable publications (including mergers and acquisition websites if they are properly controlled and regulated).

Choosing the marketing method

It is likely that a combination of methods will be used and all have their merits and their drawbacks. If the sale has arisen as a result of the business being approached by a company, and it is intended to try to conclude a deal without marketing the company for sale, breaches of confidentiality are less likely. However, in practical terms many vendors who only deal with one prospective purchaser can, at some point in the transaction, have serious doubts over the price being achieved for the business, as they have no idea whether other prospective purchasers would have bid a higher price. This also applies to a lesser extent to marketing to a highly select list of purchasers.

Using a researched and targeted list of companies in the same industry widens the net for prospective purchasers, although this does still limit the exposure to one industry only. Companies in that industry may not be in the best place or in a position to carry out an acquisition, or may feel they can obtain access to the customers or clients without making an acquisition. The use of agents, accountants or other advisers ensures that companies outside the industry who may be looking to break into a particular sector or have reasons for making an acquisition are included in the process. It also ensures that any management buy-in (MBI) candidates or financial purchasers are made aware of the opportunity.

If the business being sold is very large or highly specialized, there are likely to be only a limited number of potential purchasers. If this is the case, direct approaches will be made to the companies in question.

Handling offers

At the outset it is important to have agreed the procedures for handling offers. Some businesses prefer to keep the process informal. Interested parties are allowed to visit the business, meet with the owners and ask questions on the information memorandum before making a bid. This allows the management to explain the operations and impress would-be purchasers. Alternatively, first meetings can take place off-site to avoid arousing suspicion with employees. A timetable with a deadline for the first round of bids is set and a shortlist drawn up. Prospective purchasers are then allowed to visit the business before finalizing their bids. This process is desirable if there are likely to be multiple bids for the business.

If the business being sold is likely to attract only a few interested parties, the bidding process should be less formal. The vendor should always ask the question, 'Would I bid for a company without having seen it?' The information memorandum can only go so far in attracting interested parties to the business. When they have seen it and met with key managers, they may well have a much better understanding of how the business operates, and be encouraged to bid more than they may otherwise have done.

Ultimately, the method chosen will depend on the size of the business for sale and the likely number of potential bidders. Whichever method is chosen, all bids should be in writing and supported by at least an outline of the financing arrangements that are in place to support the bid including indicative offers from financiers where appropriate. The ability of the purchaser to pay for the acquisition will be key in deciding which offer to accept.

Negotiating the deal

Before negotiations commence the requirements of the purchaser must be understood, as the same deal structure will not be acceptable to all. For example, a listed plc with plenty of spare cash will be more worried about enhancing its earnings stream and its potential of future dividends to its shareholders than the balance sheet gearing. However, an MBI team could be faced with considerable personal risk in making the purchase, and could have a particular worry about the composition of the balance sheet after the deal. These factors will influence the way the negotiations are handled.

The first decision that needs to be made in the negotiation process is who will carry out the negotiations. Even the most experienced businesspeople should seriously consider whether they should negotiate on their own behalf. Very few people are good at sitting across the table with the prospective purchaser and extracting the best deal for themselves when their own money is at stake.

If an experienced adviser is involved, he or she will provide the opportunity to give input and advice on a 'real-time' basis as the negotiations progress. He or she may also be able to influence key areas before they are conceded, and ensure that taxation or other issues are addressed as early as possible in the process. Alternative deal structures and methods of consideration can be suggested at the appropriate time. However, the main benefit of a skilled negotiator will be to improve the deal. Certainly with small owner-managed businesses, it is less likely that a purchaser will try to take advantage of the situation.

If it is agreed that a third party is to carry out the negotiations, clear parameters should be agreed before the negotiation process commences. All relevant parties must understand who is going to carry out the negotiations, and only one person should be involved in the direct communications with the purchaser or their advisers; otherwise it can result in confusion and ultimately the purchaser could take advantage and undermine the position of the vendor.

If the purchaser is a large company or listed plc, remember that it will have management experienced in buying and selling companies. It will generally have the resources to spend time on the deal, and the managers will be 'streetwise' in what they can achieve. The vendor's corporate finance adviser will be able to ensure that the communication process is managed effectively between the parties, as the expectations can be very different on the two sides.

It is important to remember that even if formal negotiations have not yet commenced, the negotiation process begins on the provision of the information memorandum. As a result any meetings, even at an operational level, with a prospective purchaser are all part of this process. More than one person should go to all meetings with the prospective purchasers in the period leading up to the formal negotiation process, and it is recommended that advisers are present at most key meetings even if the terms of the deal are unlikely to be discussed.

Each meeting should be carefully planned, and all parties involved from the company should be adequately prepared. At some point it may be necessary for the vendors and their advisers to decide on the mechanism for the negotiation process. A controlled auction could be carried out including all of the prospective purchasers. Alternatively, indicative offers could be requested and a shortlist created based on those offers. Thereafter the preferred bidder will be asked to formalize the offer, and further negotiations will take place.

The position of the vendor can be enhanced during the negotiating process if 'good news' can be fed to the purchasers, for example gaining new orders. Finally, the negotiations should remain at arm's length and not become personal. Otherwise this can have an adverse effect on the relationships going forward and reduce the chances of successfully completing a deal.

Conclusion

In summary, in order to crystallize value and maximize the return for shareholders there are a number of key stages to go through:

- Carefully plan the exit strategy.
- Choose an exit route early if possible.
- Effectively groom the company for sale, in both commercial and taxation terms.
- Implement an organized marketing process with a high-quality information memorandum and proper procedure for identifying strategic purchasers.

- Use professionals to negotiate the deal with the purchasers.
- Ensure the completion process is properly project-managed.

If these key steps are implemented, all concerned will be sharing champagne at the completion meeting knowing they have achieved maximum value for their company!

Pensions issues

Richard Jones, Punter Southall & Co

Background to pension arrangements

In the UK, employer-sponsored pension schemes tend to operate on a pre-funded basis rather than the pay-as-you-go approach adopted in many other territories and by the UK government. Pre-funded occupational pension arrangements can be divided into two main categories, those that operate on a defined contribution (DC) basis and those that operate on a defined benefit (DB) basis. Similar arrangements are seen in most developed countries, although pre-funding is less common in some jurisdictions such as Germany.

In a DC arrangement, the sponsoring employer pays a set level of contributions each year, usually expressed as a fixed percentage of salary, into the each member's individual fund. The pension a member receives depends on the amount of contributions paid in respect of that member by both the employer and the member, the level of investment returns generated on those contributions and annuity rates at the time the member retires.

From an employer perspective, a DC arrangement has stable and predictable costs and hence presents little in the way of financial risk to the sponsoring employer. The financial liability in respect of a DC arrangement is limited to the set contributions payable each year that a member remains employed, and thus DC arrangements do not present any significant issues in mergers and acquisitions.

A DB arrangement presents much greater risks to the sponsoring employer, as the benefits are defined by reference to a set formula, typically based on salary and service. The employer remains responsible for ensuring that sufficient funds are available to meet the benefits. The sponsoring employer is exposed to fluctuations in costs as a result of investment returns, mortality experience and other experience such as salary increases, inflation and the exercise of member options. In a DB arrangement, the assets are compared with the value of liabilities at regular intervals (every three years in the UK for cash funding purposes, every year for accounting purposes) in what is known as a 'valuation'.

The presence of these regular valuations creates a significant risk for sponsoring employers if the measure used to place a value on the liabilities is different from the asset classes in which the DB arrangement's assets are invested (known as a 'mismatch' risk). Most measures of the DB liabilities are based on bond yields, while most DB schemes invest in other assets – typically equities – creating a significant mismatch risk. The accounting and cash funding requirements can be extremely volatile in such a situation. Furthermore, the assets held can be greater or lower than the valuation of the liability, and thus there will be a 'surplus' or a 'deficit' in the arrangement.

A deficit requires that the sponsoring employer makes contributions to make good the deficit in the arrangement. A reasonably long period of time of at least five years, and often more than 10 years, is granted to make good any such deficiency. A surplus can often be used by the sponsoring employer to provide for new benefits for its employees at no cash cost. However getting full value from a surplus is nearly always impossible, as the members usually have some form of claim on the surplus or part of the surplus.

A significant issue with DB arrangements in the UK is that they are nearly always established under trust, and thus the sponsoring employer has only a limited degree of control over how the arrangement is run. Typically, the trustees retain powers over the investment of the assets and the contributions that are payable. The trustees must act independently of the sponsoring employer and in the best interests of the members of the arrangement.

Under UK GAAP and IFRS, DB arrangements must be fully accounted for, with any deficit reflected on the balance sheet. The cost of the extra benefits granted to members in any accounting year is taken as a charge to operating profit. Outside of the EBITDA calculation is a notional financing charge, consisting of the difference between the interest on the total liabilities and the expected return on the assets, which serves to reflect the impact of the funding position of the arrangement on the profit and loss account.

Due diligence issues

The nature of a DB arrangement is such that due diligence is nearly always required. The future benefits payable from a DB arrangement can only be estimated by making assumptions about such factors as mortality rates, inflation, salary growth and the exercise of member options. Different assumptions about these factors can change the cost of the expected future benefits significantly, and thus a purchaser will need to take its own independent advice on these estimates to assess whether the benefit outgoings are being understated.

A further significant issue is that members often have options in regards to their benefits – such as the ability to take early retirement – that are not fully reserved for in the valuation(s) and could lead to an increase in the benefit outgoings. The benefits need to be studied closely to investigate the risks within the DB arrangement.

The construction of the trust deed and rules that govern the DB arrangement sets out the balance of powers between the sponsoring employer and the trustees. There are a wide range of different powers specified in such trust deeds, and these can present significant risks to a potential purchaser. They cover such matters as the setting of contributions payable, the timing of valuations and the termination of the arrangement.

Termination (or 'winding up') is the most significant risk in UK DB arrangements, as the sponsoring employer is then responsible for ensuring that sufficient funds are available to secure annuities with an insurance company for all members. Because of the different regulatory regimes and the profit requirements of insurers, annuities are significantly more expensive than accounting charges and the ongoing cash requirements.

Pricing a surplus or deficit

Where a surplus or a deficit exists in a DB arrangement at the point of a transaction, the potential benefit or the expected future cost needs to be reflected in the pricing of the transaction. Once the appropriate assumptions about such factors as mortality rates, inflation, salary growth and the exercise of member options have been chosen, the only decision to be made is about the discount rate that should be applied to the projected benefit payments in order to calculate a liability value. This liability value is then deducted from the market value of the DB arrangement's assets in order to assess whether there is a surplus or a deficit.

While there are a number of ways in which a discount rate can be chosen, a bond yield is typically used. Accounting standards require that the yield on AA-rated corporate bonds of a suitable duration and currency is used to discount the benefit cashflows payable. An industry standard is emerging for pricing pension obligations in transactions, and that standard is centred on the UK GAAP accounting standard Financial Reporting Standard 17 – Retirement Benefits (FRS 17), now in force for all UK entities. There are a number of reasons for this emerging trend, including:

- FRS 17 is used for accounting for pension obligations under UK GAAP and is very similar to the requirements under the international pension accounting standard, IAS 19.
- Most private equity buyers price their transactions on an FRS 17 basis. A recent survey carried out by Punter Southall Transaction Services showed that more than 90 per cent of private equity firms use this approach.
- Lenders tend to treat an FRS 17 deficit as a debt in assessing provision of financing.
- FRS 17 is the level at which an application for 'clearance' from the Pensions Regulator for a transaction is not required, and is often the target level of funding to achieve clearance.

- The Pensions Regulator is using FRS 17 as one of the triggers for investigating schemes which it considers may have an insufficient funding target.
- FRS 17 is a well-understood methodology and a measure that is readily available in companies' accounts.
- At 100 per cent FRS 17 funded, a scheme can hedge its liabilities with relatively low volatility.
- At 100 per cent FRS 17 funded, a company would have to be 'unlucky' to not be able to run off the accrued benefits with no further contributions.

For this confluence of reasons, FRS 17 is usually adopted in transaction situations in order to price deficits. Typically, the treatment of an FRS 17 surplus is to include only partial allowance for this surplus to reflect benefits agreed, or expected to be agreed, with the trustees at the point of transaction.

As contributions made towards a deficit in a pension scheme are an allowable expense for corporation tax purposes, the FRS 17 deficit in the pension arrangements is adjusted for deferred tax where corporation tax is expected to be payable. This net amount is then deducted from the enterprise value of the business such that the FRS 17 deficit is effectively treated as a debt.

To allow for new benefits being granted each year, the FRS 17 service cost is then included in EBITDA or in a discounted cashflow model, as it is an operational cost which should be accounted for as and when it arises. Future service liabilities can therefore be discounted at the cost of equity until they arise, and thereafter treated as an additional debt accrual.

Reliance on accounting figures

When sizing up a new investment opportunity the FRS17 or IAS19 pension accounting figures disclosed in a company's published accounts are generally taken as a reasonable first estimate of the pension liability exposure. This may be a reasonable first pass, but because of the gearing effect of the assets, a small change in the calculation of the total liability will lead to a very large change in the surplus or deficit revealed.

Caution must be taken when looking at the figures shown in a company's accounts because of the following issues:

- Accounts might be a year or more out of date. For many schemes the long-term investment strategy creates huge funding volatility.
- Directors setting company accounts are not trying to ascertain fair value for a future transaction and might have bowed to other interests and pressures when setting the assumptions for pensions accounting.
- The mortality assumption is not disclosed, and the difference between mortality tables can have a very significant impact on the pension liabilities calculated.
- Other key assumptions are not shown in the accounts. For example, cash commutation allowance at retirement, expenses, early retirements and early leaver assumptions are not usually disclosed and might hide additional costs.

For these reasons the numbers shown in the accounts cannot always be relied upon to reflect the true funding position.

The Pensions Regulator

UK DB arrangements are supervised by the Pensions Regulator, who has powers to rectify situations where the pension scheme has been abused by its sponsoring employer. These 'moral hazard' powers could potentially come into play whenever there is a merger or acquisition contemplated that involves a DB arrangement. Generally however these powers can only be triggered when there is a material weakening of the covenant provided by the sponsoring employer, and this will not occur in many transactional situations.

The 'moral hazard' powers are wide-ranging, and thus the Pensions Regulator introduced a process whereby companies could voluntarily ask for 'clearance' with respect to a transaction. Clearance provides comfort that the Pensions Regulator will not impose any penalty on the parties involved with the DB arrangement as a result of the transaction.

Applying for clearance is however not always necessary or desirable, as it can prove to be relatively costly in accelerating funding requirements as the quid pro quo for the Pensions Regulator's seal of approval. An application for clearance should always be considered in some detail before proceeding.

Unfunded arrangements

Similar considerations apply where DB arrangements are unfunded: that is to say, arranged on a pay-as-you-go approach. Generally the cash requirements are clearer, as the benefits due can be predicted, and the valuation process is only used for reserving in the sponsoring employer's accounts for the future liabilities.

The FRS 17 reserve, adjusted for tax as appropriate, is generally utilized as a price adjusted for pay-as-you-go arrangements.

Overseas arrangements

In many other countries there exist DB arrangements of a very similar type to those in the UK. For example, in the United States and Canada funded arrangements similar to those in the UK are common, while in Germany unfunded arrangements are relatively common.

Although the regulatory regime is different, the approach taken will remain unchanged, with any benefit that is required to be reserved for under IFRS taken into account for pricing. As IAS 19 is broadly identical to FRS 17, a similar price adjustment is made taking account of local tax deductibility rules.

Summary

DC arrangements do not present many issues in mergers and acquisitions, but DB arrangements can present both pricing issues and risk issues which should be taken into account.

General practice in pricing a pension arrangement is to use the accounting figures under FRS 17 (or IAS 19), adjusted as appropriate for changes in assumptions and updated financial conditions, to take account of any liabilities to pension arrangements. However, the liability figures can be distorted and significant other risks can be hidden within a DB arrangement, and thus independent pensions due diligence advice is strongly recommended.

Part Three

The mechanics of M&A

a word in your ear

M&A

Buying or selling a business is probably the most serious decision you'll make. You need to ask the right questions and listen to the right people. Horsey Lightly Fynn Solicitors provide:

☐ **Experience and commercial awareness**
☐ **A personal, partner-led service**
☐ **Objectivity and integrity**
☐ **Competitive pricing**

For a no-obligation discussion about our M&A services, speak to **Simon Arthur** on **01635 517136** or email: **sarthur@hlf.uk.com**.

We promise to listen - then act.

Horsey Lightly Fynn
solicitor

www.hlf.uk.co

LONDON • NEWBURY • BOURNEMOUT

Overview

Simon Arthur, Horsey Lightly Fynn

Companies are driven by their shareholders to generate and increase shareholder value. That is to say, it is hoped that the significant capital risk taken by an investor in making equity capital available to a company will be made worthwhile by the rewards in income and capital. In order to maximize rewards, a company must grow, and it can achieve this either organically or by merger/acquisition. To combine the efforts of two companies will almost always have an immediate impact on the top line of a business: its revenues will almost inevitably increase immediately. Depending on the comparative synergy of the businesses, an increase in the bottom line, the profits available for distribution, may take longer to become apparent.

Commonly, an acquisition is sought either to increase market share or to diversify into alternative markets by way of a complementary bolt-on to the existing business of the company. Both of these strategies have a strong revenue focus at their core. Other acquisition strategies may look at increasing a portfolio balance, capturing a particular customer, moving a company's position in the supply chain, or expanding existing, or developing new areas of, expertise by building on or acquiring technology and/or know-how.

In the context of a small to medium-sized enterprise (SME), embarking on a corporate acquisition is likely to be a significant undertaking, in terms of time and effort and also of costs. The amount of management time and effort required should not be underestimated if a seamless post-completion integration is to be achieved. It is vitally important that having identified a suitable target, management go into the transaction with their eyes open and with reasonable expectations about the process and short-term goals for the enlarged business. Part of this process is to engage key advisers with particular areas of expertise (such as lawyers) to assist management with core tasks. In particular advisers are needed to:

- ensure legal compliance;
- ensure that the transaction documents accurately reflect the commercial agreement reached between the parties;
- bring potential trading and commercial concerns to the attention of management;
- help mitigate potential risks;
- help ensure smooth post-deal integration.

The due diligence process and negotiation of the sale documentation are the two key areas for the corporate legal team, and are important for ensuring that an acquisition both progresses smoothly to completion and delivers management's goals on integration. However, it is vital that the buyer's management team and deal advisers approach the transaction holistically, working together as a deal team, rather than as if it were a fragmented exercise between disciplines. In reaching a decision on the appointment of deal advisers, the importance of this team approach cannot be overemphasized. Almost all good law firms will provide excellent technical advice and be responsive to a client's needs. However, a good and relatively simple deal on paper can soon run into logistical and practical difficulties if the buyer's management team and its various advisers do not successfully integrate and coordinate their efforts.

Structure

One of the most important considerations when buying (or selling) a business is whether the target's assets and/or business should be transferred by way of an asset purchase, business purchase, share purchase or a mixture of these. The decision has important implications for both buyer and seller, and while the buyer and seller are likely to have a clear idea of their views on the structure of the transaction at the outset, the most appropriate structure may well become apparent only after detailed investigation into the target.

The alternative core structures for an acquisition are:

- *Asset purchase*: the buyer acquires certain specified assets (for example, machinery or premises), but importantly, the business remains with the seller.
- *Business purchase:* the buyer obtains a business through the acquisition of its assets and goodwill, usually as a going concern.
- *Share purchase*: the issued shares in the capital of the target, which owns the business, are transferred to the buyer.
- A *mixture:* for example, the business and assets (or certain of them) are transferred (or 'hived down') into a newly formed subsidiary company, the shares of which are then transferred to the buyer.

Of key concern to the buyer will be the ability to integrate seamlessly the target business into its own operation post-completion. In other words, the buyer will want to secure trade continuity so as to mitigate (as far as possible) client losses which would not otherwise have arisen, but for the sale. Commonly of course, the seller will have built up strong ties with its client base, and accordingly it is usually prudent to secure the services of an owner-manager for a period post-completion to successfully manage the handover.

Management continuity will depend on the aspirations of the owner-manager to a certain degree, but it will be particularly important in the event of an asset, or business and asset, purchase. This is because contracts entered into between the seller and customers and suppliers will need to be transferred to the buyer. The buyer's legal team has an important role to play here, in order to mitigate the disruption caused to the business by reason of such transfers.

In the event of a share purchase, there is no such legal interruption to the business of the target from a customer's, supplier's or employee's perspective. However, it can nonetheless be considered desirable to retain the services of a selling owner-manager for a period post-completion to ensure a smooth handover from a commercial perspective.

Effectively managing the handover process is the key driver here, and one would generally expect the seller(s) to be keen to assist with this process, particularly where there is a deferred element to the consideration, and, perhaps an earn-out mechanism.

Due diligence

Without question, the key principle for the buyer in an acquisition is that it should have a full and explicit understanding of the business it is acquiring. The due diligence process (usually legal, financial and, less commonly in the context of SMEs, commercial) ought to be key to establishing the viability of the synergy between the buyer's business and that of the target. Once that has been established, and equally important, comes the post-completion integration of the target's business with that of the buyer's.

However, the due diligence exercise undertaken by management, and more particularly the buyer's external advisers, will generally be brief-led. That is to say, the buyer will have a pre-conceived idea of what is required here, which will vary from transaction to transaction, depending on the sophistication and experience of the buyer. What is important is that the buyer clearly identifies the key areas of interest and key areas of risk that should be brought to its attention. The external advisers will be able to assist in outlining the common areas to be looked at, but any particular issues affecting the target business (for example, business-specific licences, authorizations or consents required for effectively carrying on the business) should be clearly identified early on. It is also vital that all involved have a clear understanding of the buyer's business, the rationale behind the acquisition and the buyer's goals post-completion for the enlarged business.

An initial briefing meeting, if properly conducted, will go a long way to ensuring the smooth running of the transaction and, in particular, post-completion integration.

Without clear parameters, there is a real danger that the target's business will not be fully understood at an operational level. Accordingly, the overall deal synergy may not be fully appreciated and a successful post-deal integration plan may not be as easily implemented.

The key to a successful due diligence process is to ensure that the buyer's management and the external deal team fully understand and appreciate it, and the initial briefing meeting should cover, among other more specific issues:

- the operational scope, capability and state of development of the target;
- the level of true synergy/compatibility with the buyer;
- the scope of the business plan post-deal and the true likelihood of its successful implementation;
- the underlying business reasons for the acquisition and its reality;
- the likelihood of meeting rationalization improvements/potential;
- logistical and technical legal issues, such as geographical location of employees, premises and technical requirements.

The due diligence process should therefore be specifically tailored to meet the needs of the particular transaction and the realistic aspirations of the buyer post-completion.

Apportionment of risk

Whether an acquisition is achieved by way of an asset or share purchase, a key issue for the parties will be the apportionment of risk between buyer and seller. Notwithstanding that the buyer will have carried out its due diligence investigations, it will want to ensure that there are no hidden matters that were not immediately apparent from this process. Accordingly, the sale documentation will contain 'warranties', which in this context are contractual statements made by the seller to the buyer that a certain state of affairs exists at the point of completion of the transaction. Warranties often account for the principal area of negotiation in the documentation, and are used by the buyer for two main purposes.

First, they are used to apportion the risk more evenly between the buyer and seller, by providing the buyer with a remedy if the statement proves to be inaccurate, false or misleading and the value of the asset(s) acquired is thereby diminished. Second, warranties act as a tool to encourage the seller to disclose any final issues that may not have been made apparent to the buyer from the information supplied to it under the due diligence process.

However, it is vital that the buyer does not endeavour to substitute the use of warranties for due diligence. Warranties, by their nature, provide a remedy 'after the event' and will invariably be limited in scope and value under the sale documentation. It is far better to know and understand fully any potential issues prior to completion of the acquisition.

The warranties will generally take up half (or more) of the sale and purchase agreement, and are particularly important on an acquisition of shares, because the buyer will acquire a distinct entity as a package with all of its liabilities, past and present. However, warranties are also important in relation to a purchase of assets, as it will be rare for there to be no liabilities attached to a business asset. For example, the buyer will likely take on employment obligations, and on a novation of business contracts the buyer will take over the contractual liabilities of the seller (although, the buyer will look for the comfort of an indemnity from the seller here).

In addition to general warranties, the buyer's adviser should seek specific indemnities from the seller in respect of any issues arising out of the due diligence process. An indemnity differs from a warranty in that an indemnity is a promise to reimburse the buyer in respect of a particular liability, should it arise. The due diligence process should therefore be a key driver in the preparation of the principal sale documentation, and again it is vital that the scope of this process is clearly set out and understood from the outset by the deal team as a whole.

Key considerations for management

The deal team must identify at the earliest opportunity the fundamentals of the proposed transaction: who, what, where, when, how and, perhaps most importantly of all, why. Once the buyer has established its deal objectives, pre- and post-completion, the deal team (including the external advisers) should set clearly defined transaction parameters, and any overlapping areas must be carefully considered. In particular, the external advisers must show a clear understanding of the buyer's business, the seller(s)'s business and the buyer's aspirations for the enlarged business post-completion.

Therefore, in considering the appointment of external advisers, the management team should ensure that those advisers have a clear understanding of the buyer's reasons behind the acquisition. The greater the understanding a lead corporate legal adviser has of the transaction, the more value he or she can add to the process.

Global M&A
information
when you need it

To find out how ZEPHYR can help your
business call us on 020 7549 5000 or
email uk@bvdep.com

bvdep.com

BUREAU VAN DIJK
ELECTRONIC PUBLISHING

Identifying partners and targets

Lisa Wright, Bureau van Dijk Electronic Publishing

Objectives decided

So the directors have reviewed the company's strategy. They have determined on horizontal or vertical growth, market penetration, expansion, creation or diversification. They have decided whether to pursue opportunities via strategic acquisition, merger or partnering (a joint venture). Their strategy may be formally documented or be an informal understanding between them and their senior management team. Strategic objectives will have been set for the proposed investment in time and cost that expansion will incur. It is essential that these actions precede the location of appropriate targets for acquisition or merger.

Acquisition approach

An acquiring company can adopt a variety of different approaches to locating a target. These range from completely 'hands off', to undertaking significant work in locating and negotiating a deal with the target. A decision over when to involve professional advisers will be influenced by time, skill and cost factors. For example:

- *Commitment*: Do the directors/management have the necessary time to commit to the research and search process from start to finish?
- *Size of the target group*: Is the target company one among many or few?

- *Time constraint*: How much time will be needed to gather the information on all appropriate targets and produce profiles that support the decision-making process?
- *Resources*: Does the acquiring company have the necessary financial, legal and technical skills to evaluate the value that the target company could add – and then negotiate an acceptable price or agreement with the future partner(s)?

Only the directors can decide at which point to involve external agencies, and on the appropriate balance between internal and external resources. Searching and selecting targets involves significant time. However, the process remains the same irrespective of who undertakes it.

Acquisition process

The acquisition process involves a continuous, and increasingly detailed, review of a declining number of prospect organizations until the target(s) is identified. The process starts with drawing up a 'long list' of potential targets. Each company is reviewed against key criteria to arrive at a short list. Short-listed companies are subjected to further analysis and review. Increasingly detailed profiles of each company are produced. The short list can be further refined by re-comparison with the key criteria. As more is learnt about a company, it may become apparent that it does not meet the selection requirements. A number of iterations of this part of the process should be undertaken until the short list is of a manageable size. Once all required information has been gathered on potential targets, they should be compared using an objective scoring method.

Creating the target list

The directors will have their knowledge of companies that are considered 'interesting' candidates. However, the long list must be populated with as many relevant potential targets as possible. This will give the searching company the opportunity to locate objectively a target that best meets its strategic objectives.

Sources of target companies can be drawn from:

- exhibitor lists from trade shows;
- known competitors (from sales visits etc);
- known organizations gained through informal networking of directors;
- names gleaned from an internet search;
- the financial and business press;
- government agencies (for example Business Link);
- *Yellow Pages;*
- trade associations;
- the Patent Office;
- commercial databases.

Some of the above are obvious sources, but many others exist. The importance of any single source will depend on the nature of the business undertaking the search. For example, a business involved in high-technology manufacturing might find that a review of filed patent applications yields some potential targets. Patent applications are not just made by large companies. Many small organizations and individuals file patents too. They may require help to exploit opportunities that the patent provides. However, it is best to avoid trawling sources that may only yield a small number of potential targets too early in the search process. Sources such as the Patent Office are best used in the iterative review process to eliminate or confirm the suitability of companies for inclusion in the short list. If the initial search is confined to evaluating just a small section of the available set, profitable opportunities may never be discovered.

The key to finding a 'good' target is to first generate as large a set of potential targets as possible. A commercially produced database is arguably the best source.

Benefits of database searching

Commercial databases offer a fast and cost-effective way of identifying targets. By their very nature they allow complex searches to be undertaken at great speed. They enable users to search for companies that comply with their own criteria. Users can combine as many conditions as they like, to help pinpoint companies that satisfy these conditions and then allow for further analysis of the set of companies returned. For example, a list of all companies having a particular SIC (Standard Industry Classification) code with a turnover between £1 million and £6 million and located in the north-west of the UK can be produced. In this way a suitable list of targets can be drawn up and work started on the review process. Many electronic databases also assist with the review process by providing financial and other important information about the company, for example:

- financial accounts and key financial ratios (for a number of years);
- holding company/companies and shareholders;
- the latest news about a company;
- other company directorships held by directors;
- a company's competitors;
- other companies within your chosen company's peer group (thus enabling you to broaden your list of target companies if need be).

One of the advantages of using a database search approach is that it supports direct comparison of the same data item between potential targets. The database supplier should ensure that data capture and data definition are consistent. For example, the data item 'liquidity ratio' will always be provided for each company held in the database, and will always be calculated as 'current assets' divided by 'current liabilities'. Likewise 'current assets' and other items will always be calculated to a standard formula.

In the UK the accounting profession and the regulatory bodies ensure that financial information is generated in a manner that supports direct comparison. The measure of a 'good' database supplier is that it has in place processes and procedures that support comparisons for data drawn from EU/global sources. It should also provide additional non-financial information that helps create a fuller picture of the company under review.

Access to search tools

A number of companies generate databases of the type referred to above. A few generate a suite of integrated products. In the main, databases are sold to adviser organizations such as banks, law firms, accounting practices, consulting firms and some of the largest enterprises (which constantly scan their environment looking for opportunities or threats to their businesses). However, increasingly medium and smaller sized organizations are seeing the value of having one of these databases in-house.

Many companies still require the assistance of adviser firms in the process of identifying targets. Advisers generally gain access to the databases via a subscription arrangement. Access to these databases for non-adviser organizations is also available via an annual subscription or limited usage charge. This allows companies to generate their own long and short lists of targets. Advantage can be obtained by direct involvement in the iterative 'sifting' process. The directors and senior management will have a great deal of knowledge about a number of competitors. However, the use of database tools forces an objective and evaluative approach that may well change their perception of any one target. Additionally, direct access to the database provider gives a greater degree of control over the search process. The search company can decide when to involve specialist advisers, say for the drawing up of contracts or negotiating the details of the joint venture or acquisition, thereby reducing the overall cost of the search.

Given the value of the database in the search process, it is important to select the right database supplier for your search project.

Database supplier selection

Before purchasing access to a database, check that it will meet all of your needs. A number of suppliers offer single products that only cover a particular data set or limited level of data. While they are very useful in identifying, for example, UK company names, the database will not help with the review process. Some may concentrate on supplying related financial data to the exclusion of other relevant information. If a supplier of a number of databases is being considered, check that the databases 'work together' and cover all of the search process. For example, can the suppliers' databases give the list of potential targets, relevant information about the company, and help arrive at the amount that should be paid for the company if a merger or acquisition is being considered?

Most database suppliers draw their base data from a source subject to governmental control. In the case of the UK that source is Companies House. It is a legal requirement that all UK incorporated companies file an annual return and statutory accounts with Companies House within specified filing dates. The database supplier can add value to this data by supplementing it with information from a variety of other sources.

In selecting a supplier the factors to be considered include:

■ *Timeliness of data*: The database should be as up to date as possible and updated on a regular basis.

■ *Breadth of data*: does the database focus on a particular type of organization (for example, just listed public limited companies) or cover a wide variety (such as all plcs and all limited companies)?

■ *Quality of sources and data quality procedures*: does the database company apply consistent processes to its data collection techniques, and has it achieved ISO recognition?

■ *Is data presented and collected in a standard format?* This is particularly important if the potential targets to be compared are drawn from the UK and other countries.

■ *Value added*: as mentioned above, does the database(s) contain more information than that required by governmental agencies?

■ *Functionality*: does the database provide adequate user tools to search and analyse the required data? Does the database have extraction links to, for example, spreadsheet software to support review and reporting?

A SEARCH EXAMPLE

To illustrate the power and possibilities of a database-supported search, a worked example follows. The databases used have been supplied by Bureau van Dijk Electronic Publishing (BvDEP). All of the data is 'real'. However, care has been taken to avoid providing a level of detail that would infringe data protection rules.

In this scenario we shall look at a company operating a chain of butcher shops. The company has decided to look at acquiring a UK meat processing plant.

SEARCH CRITERIA

It is important to create relevant criteria for any search. For example, are the targets to be drawn from UK-based companies, US, Asian, European, or is a global search to be undertaken? If in doubt, start with only a few 'limiting' search criteria and then 'drill down' to greater levels of detail and more restrictive criteria.

For this example the search criteria are:

■ all non-listed companies (ie non-publicly traded companies);
■ companies with a UK SIC code of 151 (production, processing and preserving of meat and meat products);*

- turnover greater than £1 million;
- profits greater than £100,000;
- located in either the north-west, northern region or Humberside and Yorkshire;
- liquidity ratio greater than 3;
- profit margin – maximum of 5.

*SIC codes are Standard Industrial Classification codes that classify a business or facility according to its primary kind of activity, such as chemical manufacturing or electricity generation. Two-digit codes are the most general; four-digit codes are the most specific.

As only UK-based companies are being considered we will first use BvDEP's FAME database (see Figure 3.2.1).

		Search summary		
	Selected criteria	Specified values or options	Step result	Search result
1	All Active Companies		2,440,553	2,440,553
2	UK SIC (2003)	All Codes: 151 – Production, processing and preserving of meat and meat products	1,934	1,493
3	Publicly listed status	Publicly listed – Unlisted	3,408,122	1,493
4	Turnover (using estimates) (th.GBP)	Last available year, Max = 1,000,000	2,366,732	1,153
5	Profit (Loss) before Tax (th.GBP)	Last available year, Max = 1,000,000	653,539	376
6	Regions / Postcode Area / Post Town	Registered Office Address, Primary trading address: 06 – North West, 07 – Northern, 14 – Yorks & Humberside	583,618	75
7	Liquidity Ratio (X)	Last Available Year, Max = 3	1,489,149	66
8	Profit Margin	Last Available Year, Max = 5	195,604	35
		Total number of companies selected:		35

Figure 3.2.1 Extract from BvDEP's FAME database

The search criteria used returns 34 potential companies, some of which are shown in Figure 3.2.2. The turnover figure, the profit (loss) after tax, the long-term debt, the current ratio and the liquidity ratio have been chosen as the financial items to be used to compare the companies at this stage.

Company name	R/O Full Postcode	Registered Number	Primary UK SIC (2003) Code	Last Year	Turnover th GBP Latest Year	Number of Employees Latest Year
Convenience Foods Limited	LS15 8ZB	02226886	1581	31/03/06	392,945	6,206
F.W. Farnsworth Limited	LS15 8ZB	00255912	1513	31/03/06	267,682	4,141
Neerock Limited	BB8 8HL	02572702	1513	31/01/06	249,502	892
Edward Billington and Son Limited	L3 1EL	00059883	1513	31/08/05	131,502	571
Kepak U.K. Limited	PR5 6AL	02617732	1513	31/12/05	124,792	783
Key Country Foods Limited	DN15 9YH	02646525	1513	31/12/05	124,568	526
Grampian Country Park Suffolk Limited	YO17 9HG	00635964	1513	31/12/05	102,916	1,085
Sovereign Food Group Limited	YO17 9HG	00779259	1513	31/12/05	97,345	898
Hazlewood Convenience Food Group Limited	S80 2RS	00621496	1589	30/09/05	90,613	
Favor Parker Limited	YO17 9HG	00733060	1571	31/05/05	72,227	130
Dovecote Park Limited	WF8 3DD	03167280	1513	30/09/05	71,570	326
Thorne Poultry Limited	YO17 9HG	02575875	1513	31/12/05	56,652	351
Seamark plc	M43 6BB	02575875	5138	31/12/04	54,898	148
Oeff Limited	LS1 4JP	03286770	1533	30/06/01	50,826	467
Marr Foods Limited	DN31 3SW	00467148	1513	30/09/05	42,058	382
J&J Tranfield Limited	SL13 9NP	04617095	1511	31/03/05	39,015	466
Machin Yorkshire Lamb Ltd	YO7 4EQ	03546111	1511	31/05/05	31,208	72

Figure 3.2.2 A first return of potential companies from the FAME database

Company Report

Report Sections:
Header
Used Peer Group
+ Financials
+ Ratios
+ Trends & Changes
+ Stock Data
+ Credit Score & Rating
+ Actvities / Brand Names
+ Directors & Contacts
+ Ownership
+ Subsidiaries
Advisors
Audit Details
County Court Judgements (CCJ)
Mortgage Data
Filing Details
Trading Addresses
Mergers & Acquisitions
News Section

KEY COUNTRY FOODS LIMITED

R/O Address: Unit 10
Billet Lane
Scunthorpe
Lincolnshire

R/O Phone: 01724 – 274000
R/O Postcode: DN15 9YH

Website: www.kcs.co.uk

Registered No: 02646525
Legal Form: Private Limited

Date of Incorp: 18/09/1991
Accounting Ref.
Date: 31/12
Accounts Type: Full Accounts
Company Status: Live

Latest Turnover: 124,568thGBP
Latest No of Employees: 526

No of Holdings: 2
No of Susids: 5

Activities: Production of meat and poultry products
UK SIC (2003) Codes: **Primary Code:** 1513 – Production of meat and poultry meat products
All Codes: 1513
Standard peer Group: 1513 – Production of meat and poultry meat products (VL: Very Large Companies)

PROFILE	31/12/05 12 months th GBP Uncons.	31/12/04 12 months th GBP Uncons.	31/12/03 12 months th GBP Uncons.	31/12/02 12 months th GBP Uncons.	31/12/01 12 months th GBP Uncons.
Turnover	124,568	114,650	101,457	75,716	61,448
Profit (Loss) before Taxation	895	1,581	–199	217	–3,920
Net Tangible Assets (Liab)	12,030	7,930	9,139	2,780	2,292

Figure 3.2.3 A detailed company entry extract from the FAME database

As Figure 3.2.3 shows, there is the opportunity to look at very detailed sections of a full company report, including key financial indicators, ratios, trends and changes, credit scoring, ownership and subsidiaries, along with director details, etc.

REDUCTION OF NUMBER OF TARGETS

At this point the list needs to be narrowed down to some key contenders on which further investigation will be carried out. Recently acquired or merged companies can probably be excluded at this point.

Zephyr – List of Deals – Subject Companies Involved In							
Deal Value Mil GBP	Date Announced	Date Completed	Deal Type	Deal Status	Acquirer Name	Acquirer country code	Target Name
16.50	10/05/04	10/05/04	Acquisition 100%	Completed	Uniq Prepared Foods Ltd	GB	Convenience Foods Ltd's Minsterley fresh chilled dairy products business
11.84	01/04/04	01/04/04	Acquisition 100%	Completed	Sovereign Food Group Ltd	GB	Uniq plc's poultry Business
10.01	30/11/99	30/11/99	Minority Stake	Completed	3i Group plc Charterhouse Development Capital Ltd	GB GB	Sauce Company, The
8.00	01/01/01	01/01/01	Acquisition 100%	Completed	Sauceinvest	BE	Sauce Company, The
6.30	10/09/04	10/09/04	Acquisition 100%	Completed	J&J Tranfield Ltd	GB	Kinscourt Foods Ltd
4.50	06/12/05	23/12/05	Acquisition 100%	Completed	J&J Tranfield Ltd	GB	Canterbury Food Group plc's meat Products business
4.00	03/05/03	03/05/03	Management Buy-out 100%	Completed	MBO Team – UK	GB	J&J Tranfield Ltd

Figure 3.2.4 A sample search using BvDEP's global M&A database, Zephyr

Figure 3.2.4 essentially shows how easy it is to take the set of 34 companies initially identified in FAME into BvDEP's global M&A database – Zephyr – and then to run a search to see whether any of the companies have been involved in any historical deals. There have been 14 deals involving companies from the initial list of 34. Depending upon when these deals took place, the companies involved might be excluded from further investigation.

At this stage the easiest way to do this is to create a scoring matrix where the criteria determined by the directors are compared. We should also be looking to ascertain the likely cost of acquiring the target. BvDEP's M&A database Zephyr can also help here.

Deals results financial overview

Search Criteria: **Target:** United Kingdom
Acquisition, Institutional buy-out, Joint-venture, Management buy-in,
Management buy-out...
After 01/01/00
Target: 151 – Production, processing and preserving of meat and meat products
All deals with a known value

Boolean Search: "1 And 2 And 3 And 4 And 5"

All values are Millions expressed in GBP

Number of Deals: 26

	Equity financial values Median	Equity value multiples Median	No of deals with available fin values	No deals with multiples
Deal Value	5.45	–	26	–
Equity Value	30.00	–	23	–
Bid Premium – Rumour date		–	1	–
Target Turnover (operating revenue)	138.77	0.57	19	16
Target EBITDA	13.18	7.45	18	11
Target EBIT	9.98	12.42	19	11
Target Profit before Tax	8.22	9.80	20	10
Target Profit after Tax	4.92	15.66	19	9
Target Total Assets	78.79	0.86	20	17
Target Shareholders' funds	34.03	2.31	20	15
Target Market capitalisation	149.66	1.03	8	7

Figure 3.2.5 The median range of completed deal values on Zephyr

Figure 3.2.5 shows the median range of completed deal values in terms of multiples and target company financials involved in UK companies in this sector since 2000. The data provides an indication of the range of values paid for the companies, and as with FAME it is possible to go to a level of more detailed information and see a complete deal record for each deal.

A scoring matrix should take in to account not only the financial performance of the contender companies but also factors like:

∎ who owns the company;
∎ what the current parent company does;
∎ whether all of the company or a part is to be acquired;
∎ size of market share;
∎ geographical location;
∎ customer and supplier perception of the company;
∎ whether the company is likely to be able to be acquired.

These are just a few of the factors to be considered. For each company they will be different. It is important to define as many factors as possible at the outset of the search. They will help define search criteria. Also, discussion of which factors should be included will help define the weight that should be placed on any single factor. This in turn improves the quality and objectivity of deciding which targets to pursue. For example, is it more important to locate a target within viable daily travelling distance of the acquiring company (to aid control and ensure smooth integration of operations) or perhaps customer perception of the product/service is more important?

Moving forward

In summary, decide how much of the search and selection process you want to be involved in. Set clear requirements for the database supplier – the search outcomes will only be as comprehensive as its database coverage and quality processes allow. Use the database to 'trawl' for interesting prospects. Then try to be as specific as possible on selection criteria to narrow down to a realistic number of targets for in-depth analysis. Utilize a scoring method that helps select the target(s) in an objective manner. Happy hunting!

Appointing advisers

Daniel O'Connell, Kerman & Co

Mergers and acquisitions are as well known for destroying value as creating it. The AOL and Time Warner merger is a classic illustration of this. It has been reported that more than half of all mergers and acquisitions fail to meet the objectives they were originally designed to achieve. Studies have illustrated that in many cases this failure can be attributed to poorly planned and executed integration of the transaction itself, rather than the strategic case for merger. It follows that organizations that invest sufficient time and effort in planning and executing their merger and acquisition strategies are much more likely to invest well and to increase the value of what they have bought.

Appointing advisers: what should you look for?

The right advisers can help you make better business decisions, protect you from liability, and increase your transaction success rate. The following are some practical pointers to bear in mind to help improve your chances of doing the best deal:

- *The right chemistry.* Chemistry between advisers and management is important not only in fostering a good working relationship but also in presenting your company to prospects. Find out exactly who will be working on your transaction. Even though it may be tempting to choose a firm based on name recognition, the people you work with will ultimately make the difference.
- *The right experience.* Find advisers with successful track records in your industry who understand all the complexities of the M&A process. Choose a firm that is partner-led, so you receive top-level support.

- *Size is not everything.* Size does not matter. Performance matters. Ability matters. Knowledge of specific industries and technologies matters. Connections and relationships matter. Dedication, devotion and passion matter. It is crucial that every part of the deal is handled swiftly and effectively at thought level. You need a firm with short lines of communication to enable it to be highly responsive.
- *Talk your language.* You need to have confidence that your advisers can provide objective and dispassionate advice. You need to have the assurance they know when to stand firm, when to negotiate and when to compromise. Finally, make sure you agree clear terms of reference and how the work of different advisers will be coordinated.

Every transaction has its own quirks and complexities. Kerman & Co works to solve them in a practical and efficient way. Each of them has added to the firm's knowledge and experience. Although clients may take knowledge of the law for granted, practical experience and commerciality is the key to assisting its clients to conclude their transactions.

Negotiating techniques

With any merger or acquisition, the following elements of negotiation all apply and are equally important:

- preparation;
- comprehending the interests of the parties;
- determining what information is needed;
- obtaining that information;
- acting on that information;
- dealing with relationship issues;
- conducting proper analysis of parties' best alternatives.

Due diligence

'The art of doing due diligence is being lost. Buyers aren't analysing the operations and books of prospective acquisitions with nearly enough vigour' (*Fortune*, 3 September 2001).

Due diligence is the process of uncovering all liabilities associated with the purchase. It is also the process of verifying that claims made by the vendors are correct. Directors of companies are answerable to their shareholders for ensuring that this process is properly carried out.

Conducting thorough due diligence is one of the most effective ways to reduce the risk involved in most major business transactions and to improve the chances of success. In recent years, the practice of due diligence has evolved substantially, and the level of detail and analysis now possible allows companies to take much better development decisions. Well-conducted and well-managed due diligence can help a business transaction to proceed smoothly, and can even enable companies to find ways of adding value to major business transactions. All major business transactions are highly risky: at least 50 per cent of acquisitions fail, and numerous other partnerships end in disappointment and acrimony. Due diligence is the essential step.

Make sure you carry out a proper due diligence exercise. If you do not ask, you will not find out. Do not just expect to be told about anything that is wrong with the target. Be prepared to act if you do not like what you find out, and do not hesitate to pull out of a transaction if you are not satisfied. When the pressure is on to conclude a transaction, deciding to withdraw because of something discovered from your due diligence investigation can sometimes be a difficult call. Do not be scared to make it, if the evidence indicates that you should.

For legal purposes, ensure that you:

- obtain proof that the target business owns key assets such as property, equipment, intellectual property, copyright and patents;
- obtain details of past, current or pending legal cases;
- look at the detail in the business's contractual obligations with its employees (including pension obligations), customers and suppliers – think about any likely or future obligations;
- consider the impact on existing contracts of a change in the business's ownership.

Always use a lawyer to conduct legal due diligence.

Approaching partners and targets

Dr Mike Sweeting, Acquisitions International

Once you know that you have a meaningful shopping list, one you know is worth persevering with, now is the time to begin approaches. Do *not* do a bit of research then a few approaches, then a bit more research, and so on. This method forfeits much of the benefit of being able to make true comparisons. It also can warp the context you are also trying to build up. Successful acquirers almost always work in parallel, rather than serially. They resist optimism-driven acquisition search.

What do I mean? I have seen so many supposed acquirers end up never buying. They wear themselves out and become discouraged through the serial approach. They chase a single target for three months, convince themselves it is ideal and then are cast down when negotiations fall through. 'Never mind, though, another target is now on the horizon.' Four months later there is more discouragement when someone else buys the target after a much higher offer. 'Never mind, here's another one!'

Method of approach

Make the initial approach by telephone. It is more time-consuming, and definitely more frustrating, but it is almost seven times more effective than mailed circulars. Written material can be used either to 'open the door' to the verbal proposal, or to back up such a proposal. There has been an exponential growth in what I call 'confetti' in the M&A world over the last few years. The use of information memoranda (IMs) has got out of hand. These documents are endlessly circulated not only to advertise companies for sale, but also as funding proposals, investment teasers and so on. Companies that are finding it hard to sell register with several different advisers, so that it is now possible to get several IMs on the same company – and not recognize them as such because of the different ways these documents may be constructed.

The whole nature of the above is reactive, not proactive. Merely trying to buy companies that are known to be for sale can be deeply frustrating. Do not make approaches because you are just responding to IMs. Make them because you are working your way through a 'wish list' of companies that meet meaningful criteria which you and your colleagues have already established on a good commercial basis.

The use of the telephone together with a short well-worded proposal letter will single you out from the crowd. But be warned: it will take you an average of six actual calls to have the right conversation with a key shareholder. Because the call and the proposal are so crucial, make sure they have been analysed, rehearsed and debugged well before you have a real conversation with any potential target.

Drawbacks of approaching companies that are for sale already

- They already have appointed advisers so you cannot deal direct.
- Everybody else is being offered them too.
- You risk getting into a bidding war.
- They are habitually overpriced.
- They have usually been valued too, so buyer expectations are hard to modify.
- Why have they not been snapped up by someone else already?

One issue that many people mention is the shareholder structure, and how to penetrate it effectively. There are two ways of interpreting the points I am now about to make. You may see them as a basis for avoiding certain types of company, or you may see these points as providing a great opportunity, because you can be sure few others will be interested in firms that do not meet the criteria below!

What buyers usually want

Most buyers look for:

- simple shareholdings;
- few shareholders;
- no legal problems in the target;
- transitional management;
- underlying profit capability;
- *future potential*.

As you can see above, there is a marked distaste for dealing with companies that have a numerous or complex shareholding. The deal figures bear out the reasons behind this. Quite simply, it is so much more frustrating to negotiate with a many-headed decision-making unit. You cannot even presume that the only decision influencers are the actual shareholders. In most owner-managed or family businesses there is at least a spouse or partner behind the scenes.

I shall give you an example from my father's career. He was chief executive of Richardson Merrill, the US holding company for Vicks (as in Vick Vapor Rub, Sinex etc) in the 1960s and 1970s. At that time the group was heavily into generic pharmaceuticals and Vicks was its only real brand. My dad was tasked with making worldwide acquisitions of privately owned companies with successful branded products to develop that area of the business. He came across a South African business that met all criteria. The brand was called Oil of Olay. The owner had lost interest because he wanted to farm ostriches – as you do!

The owner was an idiosyncratic person who wrote every piece of advertising copy for the company. Vicks were worried that the brand would dip without his tender loving care. They had what I think was around a US $90 million offer on the table – conditional on his continued participation in advertising. This gentleman was not prepared to budge, and his wife added that in her view he was a workaholic and that he would never sell. After all, he had been promising her a trip on the *Queen Mary* to New York for years, and done nothing about it.

My father returned to his hotel room to have a little think. What was absolutely clear was that raising the offer would make no difference at all. Instead he inserted a single sentence to the purchase document they had been discussing and went back at breakfast time. He made sure that he presented the document to the wife first. The document now said US $90 million *plus* an all-expenses-paid trip to New York on the *Queen Mary*. She leant across the table and said 'You're signing that' to her husband. Deal done. The true decision-making unit had been identified!

Style of approach

In our own work at AI, we always go in 'soft'. The line is not 'Do you want to sell?' Nor is it 'Do you want to sell to Bloggs plc?' Nor is it 'Do you want to sell to client 2593?' People are far more willing to talk about things if the topic can be distanced from the here and now. Ask them about their succession planning. Ask them how they feel about the marketplace. Most private company owners get little chance to talk with someone at a peer level about such things. At the Chamber of Commerce dinner everyone is in boasting mode. At a trade association event competitors are always present. Succession planning is the 'hot potato' of the next decade, and is a topic that will usually give you a way in. Do make sure, however, that you have mugged up on the real issues, so that you sound in touch and are able to offer genuine insight.

Allow the target the fiction of being able to say that the whole conversation is, of course, purely notional and that it only applies to 20 years' time! Very soon you will be getting interesting signals. It's just a matter of interpreting them correctly.

The mergers and acquisitions industry is a lazy one. Many of you will have learnt this the hard way. The norm is to be reactive. The same tired old companies are touted around the same old round of accountants. Acquirers are steered towards firms that are on existing brokerage lists, compromises are made and goals are not reached. Compromise is not the only problem, because these brokerage lists are circulating around and around the M&A world, and suddenly it is the vendor who has the choice, the vendor who has the upper hand, and the chance of an acquisition being successful or even being done at all goes rapidly down.

Why keep fishing in a muddy puddle when a fresh lake is available? Our main focus is on firms that are not actually on the market. We search the entire sample of companies that match our clients brief. Only 7% of done deals involve buying a company that is already for sale (PWC Mergers & Acquisitions Report 2004). The unique methodology that we recommend can be measured, can be monitored, and delivers, whether done by you or by us. Our clients are provided with a choice of potential purchases that will fulfill their growth strategy. Of course there is usually a 'front runner', but a true position of choice is established, which means you are not at the mercy of that one vendor, this gives you a better handle on negotiating, in terms of both speed and price. Many of our clients have been through the mill. They come to us after they have been under an exclusive retainer with their auditor, or a merchant bank, paid tens of thousands of pounds and got nowhere.

If any of this sounds familiar or you would like more information, please call Matthew Wilkinson on **00 44 1642 675965**.

Why not read chapters 1.6 (Identifying partners and targets) and 3.2 (Approaching partners and targets) for our unique take on the mergers and acquisitions industry.

Acquisitions Intl
a division of bcms

'The unique and refreshing different approach to corporate acquisitions'

Free morning seminars –
'Buying better companies at better prices'.

This acclaimed seminar is Europe's most popular
and well attended M&A seminar.
Please see
www.acquisitionsinternational.com/seminars
for monthly venues.

If you would like more information, or would like
a free one to one consultation, please call
Matthew Wilkinson on **00 44 (1)642 675965**.

Please see chapters 1.6 (Identifying partners and
targets) and 3.2 (Approaching partners and
targets) for our Managing Directors down to
earth take on the world of M&A!

www.acquisitionsinternational.com

After all, very few people are going to say their company is available for sale, and almost certainly not at first contact. If they do, give them a black mark. Either they are utter idiots or the company is already in distress. The 'normal' response is to be extremely guarded and say that the business is doing very well, etcetera. In our own work we seek to break through this initial shell, by thinking ourselves into the other person's shoes. We do nothing at this stage that he or she can regard as uncomfortable. We go in on our own credibility and reputation. It is only later that we need to turn the focus off ourselves and onto our client instead.

If you are making an approach as a big plc, this phase can be quite brief. If you are a management buy-in (MBI) team much more time is needed. Let us briefly look at these two extremes, since this will tease out some of the main issues.

The danger for the plc is that, while you have bags of credibility, this also means that the seller may automatically mentally double its price once it realizes who you represent! This seems to fit in with the received wisdom that by making the approach instead of responding to a seller, you will end up paying more for a company. When we look at actual deals, however, the picture is quite different. The issue is not who made the approach. The issue is which of the buyer and seller had the most real world *choice*. If the seller already had four offers on the table, the end price stayed high. If the buyer had several alternative purchases and could tactfully communicate that to the seller, the price always went down. Statistically, if you as a buyer make an approach in an environment where you are the one with choice, you will pay at least 10 per cent less than the going rate.

It is not your whole story that will influence the target at this early stage. It is simply your *credibility*. This is where meaningful time spent on the briefing process will repay substantial dividends. If your goals sound unrealistic and your company sounds vague, the better companies will instinctively shy away from you. This is a particular problem for MBI teams. They have been used to give instant credibility through their previous employers or activities. They know how credible they are as individuals, and are initially not well disposed to having to 'talk themselves up' to every seller. Rarely do they communicate this credibility very well. Their stance merely sounds boastful to a seller, which normally would prefer to stay within its comfort zone with a trade buyer from its own industry.

Over the years I can safely say that the most 'unbelieved' people are MBI teams. All sellers prefer trade buyers over all others. Private investors come next (money talks!). Private equity comes next. Venture capital comes next – well behind, though, except in the high mid and higher-end markets. MBI teams are last at the trough.

Content of approach

The written proposal should be a reinforcement of what has already been said. It should say nothing about price at all. It should be clear about the benefits of looking at things more deeply. It needs to communicate, whether subtly or bluntly, that a lack of information from the target will probably end things. After the situation has already been reconnoitred by phone, and the personality of the shareholders taken into account, the written proposal can be tailored. No wonder there is a maximum 3 per cent response from mail-outs. How on earth can they be truly tailored to each target?

There is enough 'corporate confetti' being circulated. Don't add to it! Bigger and better companies will be getting regular circulars inviting them to sell. They may well have responded to them in the past and found that they were speculative sales approaches from brokers needing clients. Some of the more unscrupulous ones imply that they have an interested purchaser already lined up. (A bit like some estate agents, isn't it?) You need to distance yourself from this world rapidly.

If you are making an international approach, make sure the text of any approach letter is perfect. Don't entrust something so crucial to the local university languages department. Use a national of the target country, who is currently in that country *and* who is familiar with the jargon of that particular industry. Electrolux is a Swedish company. It used a Swedish ad agency many years ago to design its first sales campaign in the United States. Of course the creative team all spoke excellent English. The firm still went to market with the slogan, 'Nothing sucks like an Electrolux!'

There is a danger in the proliferation of non-disclosure agreements (NDAs). The goal should be a single one that all are signatories to. Initially, it is good tactics to sign the other person's (if he or she has one), or at least offer to do so. This act of willingness reaps good dividends. It creates a comfort zone. It means that the person now owes you a favour. Most importantly, it gives you leverage. Plenty of other target companies will not even think of asking for an NDA. It should become pretty clear pretty fast to the one who has insisted on it that it will soon be left behind as the competitive choice environment is created.

At this point, about 20 per cent of the target group could be talking to you. We ourselves persevere until we have a decision from all. Some companies say a resounding *no*, and still will eventually turn into a definite *yes*. Because of the way the approach has been made, trust is now growing. After all, you are quite popular with these people really, whatever they might say out loud. Being approached is inherently flattering, and of course the chance of making a financial killing is also appealing! Remember they have no idea of their company's real-world worth. A small amount to you may sound like a lot to them. Do *not* presume that just because it is you making the approach, the price tag will automatically be exorbitant. What you *can* be sure of is that any price the seller happens to mention will be the most he or she can think of at the time. It is no reliable indicator.

The goals

You should aim:

- to convey credibility;
- to emphasize that you have several options but that you are not purely speculative;
- to indicate that they will only get a meaningful offer if they themselves convey meaningful information to you;
- to create a dialogue with the right shareholders.

We have a large client who does not wish to be named. Our first project for it entailed approaching seven firms who had already told it to get lost. The client had tried again, using its auditor as an intermediary; same result. At first the job seemed a real 'poisoned chalice', until we realized that there were no clearly understood reasons for the rejection. First of all, we went in soft. Then we made proposals that were within the prospect's comfort zone. Then we established the four aims above. We were able to engage the interest of four of the companies.

The best one still refused to engage. My research manager contacted the owner one last time, and received an immortal reply by fax. 'Didn't I tell you I have no interest in selling? By the way, can we meet in Copenhagen next Thursday?' Our client now owns that Danish company. Is my final point that my staff member has a specially attuned ear for the real meaning behind the words of a target? That may possibly be the case.

However, my last point is this: the more systematic and more professional the approach, the more 'luck' will be on your side. My colleague was successful because he persevered with a target that fitted ideally with the client, and helped both of them see it.

3.5

Negotiating techniques for the seller

Dave Rebbettes, BCMS Corporate

Introduction

This chapter is the sequel to Chapter 1.3 (Selling a private company) and focuses on the practical steps in the negotiation process.

Once you have identified perhaps several hundred prospects, careful attention must now be given to the way that these companies are approached. As we have already said, traditional methods of selling involve writing a detailed (but inappropriate) prospectus, which is then passed to a gap-year student, who is asked to identify between 12 and 14 competitors to whom the prospectus will be mailed. This course of action is followed consistently, despite the fact that premiums may be more forthcoming from complementary companies.

It is inadequate to approach just 12 companies, and to mail them is a serious error. The mailing may be well written and packed with benefits, but if the best purchasers are not looking to buy (often the case), then they will not respond to a mailing. The only people that tend to respond to such an approach are bargain hunters and short-term investors. Perversely, such mailings can have the opposite effect from that which is desired. They can end up alienating you from the best purchasers and only generating inquiries from the worst.

So how should you best approach these prospective purchasers in a way that will generate maximum results? Unfortunately, there is no short cut. BCMS has found that the only successful option available is to pick up the telephone and speak to the chief executive of each prospective purchaser. BCMS considers this so important that it has recruited and trained a large specialist team called the Prospect Generation Team (PGT). The objective of the PGT is to verbally present the prospect with the germ of an idea. The call must:

■ focus on the benefits that apply to the buyer;
■ introduce competition;
■ retain the initiative.

The call will be relatively short and to the point. Benefits must be used to establish interest, and the acquirer should be made aware that you are talking to a large number of prospective buyers. Competition has been established and the initiative now remains with you.

Only now should pen be put to paper. A short two-page summary should be drafted. Of course, the name of the seller should not be disclosed at this stage, and the content of this brief letter must be well thought out. The objective should be to:

■ establish credibility;
■ clearly state some of the benefits on offer;
■ form the basis of a future discussion;
■ maintain confidentiality.

Some readers will be familiar with the term 'benefits' and others less so; either way it is worth focusing on them. The absence of benefits is a major reason that so many companies fail to sell, or never sell for a premium price.

Early negotiations and competitive bids

Once you have made the first contact by telephone with each prospective purchaser, it is very easy to hand over the initiative to them. Resist this to ensure that you stay in control. Maintain the contact with each prospective purchaser. Start to trade information with them. Ask them questions and slowly feed them more benefits that you have to offer. BCMS finds that 200–300 prospective purchasers will be filtered down relatively quickly to somewhere between 25 and 35.

Most vendors that BCMS represents tend to be entrepreneurial in their personalities, which is unsurprising, given that they are generally self-made people. What is surprising is that, more often than not, the top person in the acquiring company is usually entrepreneurial as well. This is an important factor because most entrepreneurs tend to be driven by the 'feel' of a deal. Could we work with these people? What good reason is there not to proceed? Is the buyer excited about the potential of the acquisition? It is critical that the buyer feels good about the deal.

The words used in a discussion need to be considered carefully, because the 'flavour' of a meeting has a profound impact on its outcome. The following is an example of what not to do. In a meeting once, the buyer asked the seller, 'What's your staff turnover?' The seller replied, 'Very low, just 5 per cent – which is just as well because recruitment's a nightmare!' Needless to say, this response affected the feel of the meeting and left a 'slight bad taste' on that particular topic. What the seller should have said is simply 'We enjoy a very low 5 per cent staff turnover, so it's not an issue.'

While also making the acquirer feel good about the deal, the vendor also needs to have a compelling commercial argument that 'one and one makes three' through issues such as:

■ the nature of the fit;
■ commonality of client base;
■ financial strength;
■ strategic intent;
■ applicable benefits;
■ motives for purchase;
■ sharing of resources.

The competitive bid

Assuming that you have a choice of potential purchasers (which is why you will have endured the previous five months of hard work or research and preparation), the following is the bidding approach that BCMS advocates:

1. Each prospect should be informed that it is one of several companies with which you are in discussions; so its bid will need to be competitive.
2. Be open-minded regarding the eventual deal structure. The deal structure is limited by one thing only – your imagination. Generally speaking, the more flexible a vendor is about the deal structure, the more the business will sell for, because it reduces the acquirer's perceived risk. For example, if a vendor is prepared to receive 80 per cent of the monies on completion and 20 per cent in one year, linked to some performance criteria, the act of doing this reduces the buyer's risk and could result in, say, a 50 per cent increase in overall consideration.
3. It is important to collate a step change business plan for each buyer, which will factor in all of the various 'economies of scale' and 'added value'.
4. Always retain choice. Only retaining a choice will ensure a subtle change in mindset from 'How little can I get away with paying for this company?' to 'Why am I really buying this company?' If that change in mindset does not take place, then diverse motives will almost never be expressed.

It is at this point that the 270 per cent differential between the highest and lowest bid will be revealed. Although the lowest bid will almost certainly be rejected, so may the highest bid if the terms are inappropriate. BCMS normally finds that only two or three of the six or seven bids are of interest. From this point, you are now ready to move into the closing stages of negotiation, due diligence and legals.

Some negotiation points

Don't discuss value too early

Traditional routes to market involve calculating a value using traditional valuation techniques, which means that the value is almost certainly wrong. The company is then offered to the market with a brief description of the business and the value is attached. It's a bit like advertising a car for sale for '£2,000 or nearest offer'. Guess what offer you won't receive?

Be professional and credible

Good preparation is vital. It makes your negotiating position look serious. Construct all documentation in a professional manner and spend time on your 'step change' business plan.

Know your buyer

Go out of your way to investigate the purchaser. In particular, ask the question, 'What is its motive for buying?' Think yourself into its shoes. How badly does it want it to buy? Its motive for purchase will determine the price that it is prepared to pay.

Think benefits

We have said this already, but benefits are the all-important payload. If the benefits of a deal are unsure, then do not expect a premium to be paid. Benefits are the only reason premium prices are ever paid for any product.

Be confident

Don't appear reticent or nervous. As a rule, human beings tend to undervalue what they have built with their own hands. Maybe this is because you know the flaws and weaknesses in your own business, but can't see them so easily in others. You may need to develop more confidence in your business. Avoid weak statements such as 'We were hoping that the company might be worth …'.

Use choice

Ensure that the buyer knows that you have credible options. Don't worry about sounding or looking shocked if it makes a derisory offer. Saying nothing may well be seen as resigned acceptance. Remember that choice will ensure you sell not only for the right price, but on the right terms.

Trade concessions

This is simple and obvious, but so often overlooked. Negotiating can mean that, on occasion, you will have to make a concession. But always bargain a concession – never give them away. If you move, so does they buyer. However, try to make this one-way traffic. If the buyer concedes something, do not assume that you have to concede in return. It may also be better to trade several small concessions than one major one. Look for concessions that will provide high value to the buyer and low loss to you.

Plan the negotiation

What are your expectations? What terms would be acceptable or unacceptable? How will you pre-handle objections? At what point would you consider using deadlock? How will the team work together?

Keep sight of the objective

Be sensitive, flexible and quick to adapt, but never take your mind off the objective.

Win–win

Remember that every successfully concluded negotiation must, at least, be perceived as a win–win by both parties.

Triple think

Don't just think about what the other party wants out of this negotiation, but also think about what it thinks you want out of it.

Develop trust

Negotiation is a sophisticated form of dialogue, and always succeeds best when the other party has developed a trust in you. Go out of your way to develop trust. Keeping small promises will always aid the negotiation.

Listen

Develop the ability to listen beyond what is being said. Hear why people are saying things. Listen to the way people speak and their inflections. Observe non-verbal communications.

Prepare your alternatives

You need to consider the best alternative to the best solution in advance.

Concluding the deal

Following the competitive bidding process, your adviser such as BCMS will be available to facilitate during the due diligence and legal process. You will now be down to the final two to four candidates. That is, there are two to four bids out of six to seven that may be acceptable. What happens next?

Final choice

You can't sell to all three candidates, so a choice has to be made. This may be an easy selection, as one candidate may be head and shoulders above the other two. It may not be so easy, as all candidates have made good offers. However, a choice has to be made. At this point, you need to be careful not to make your choice at the expense of competition. The final candidate needs to be aware that you have not rejected the other two prospects, but parked them temporarily. Although you will not be entering any due process with them (indeed you may be happy to offer a degree of temporary exclusivity to the buyer), you will, however, retain a relationship with them.

The reason for this is simple. Both parties may be convinced that a deal is likely, but what happens if the buyer's parent company suddenly calls off any group investment? This is beyond anyone's control, and is not infrequent. What you are saying to the buyer is that you absolutely intend to sell to it, but you would be unwise to lose relationships with the others at this early stage. In other words, you still have alternatives and the choice remains with you. Deadlock holds no fear for you. The one that retains choice will dictate terms. Choice retained during this element of the process will significantly influence:

■ the speed of the sale;
■ the price secured;
■ the terms that you sell for.

Concluding thoughts

The principles outlined in this chapter and in Chapter 1.3 have been proven time and time again. I shall leave you with a few thoughts:

■ It doesn't have to be difficult to sell a company, but most people don't bother to sell. They hope that enquiries will somehow come to them. However you go about it, be active in your marketing.

- Don't forget that the best buyer may well not be looking to purchase. It will not be scouring the brokers' lists looking for bargains. Instead, it is likely to be successful and profitable without you. An acquisition of a company like yours is quite likely not to be on the agenda.
- People buy for many motives, and ultimately it is the motive of the purchaser, not multiples of profit, that will determine price.
- The single most influential matter when it comes to saleability and price is that you create a market of strategically motivated, financially strong buyers. If you compromise anything, don't compromise this. Don't even consider entering a negotiation without choice. Choice is not a luxury and could be worth millions.

Time to grow?

Is it time to take your growing business to new horizons? A merger or acquisition is a way of making that leap – but it may be the single biggest leap you've ever taken.

Confidence and experience are the make-or-break factors – and PKF can provide you with both. Our specialist M&A team have an excellent track record in everything from identifying acquisition opportunities to negotiating the final deal. Moreover, our technical excellence is matched by a personal approach and full support from beginning to end.

We can help your dreams to take off – so call us today for a chat about what we can offer you.

For more information please contact James Turner

PKF (UK) LLP | Pannell House | 6 Queen Street | Leeds | LS1 2TW
Tel 0113 228 4118 | Fax 0113 228 4242
Email james.turner@uk.pkf.com

www.pkf.co.uk

PKF (UK) LLP is registered to carry on audit work by the Institute of Chartered Accountants in England and Wales.
PKF (UK) LLP is authorised and regulated by the Financial Services Authority for investment business activities.

PKF

Accountants &
business advisers

Taxation and accountancy considerations

James A Turner, PKF (UK) LLP

Introduction

In pulling an M&A transaction together, there is a risk that taxation and accounting issues may not be considered until the transaction is well under way. This can lead to significant problems. While these issues should not drive the deal, they may have a financial impact, and hence necessitate some renegotiation of the proposed terms of the deal.

The following guidance is not intended to be comprehensive given the space available, but it should provide some insight into the key points to be considered. The most important point to remember is to ensure your M&A team includes individuals experienced in these areas, and that they are involved throughout the process including the drafting of the sale and purchase agreement (SPA).

During this chapter the company to be sold/acquired will be referred to the as 'the target', the group/company/shareholder(s) selling as 'the vendor(s)' and the group/company/shareholder(s) buying as 'the buyer(s)'.

Taxation issues

This section focuses on what buyers and sellers usually want from a tax perspective, the differences between assets and shares, the due diligence process, and an overview of some of the trickier areas encountered in M&A transactions. Readers are referred to Part Two for funding considerations, in particular private equity and VC investment (Chapter 2.2) and deferred consideration (Chapter 2.3). Personal tax issues for directors and shareholders are dealt with in Chapter 5.4.

From a tax perspective, the M&A process contains at least two phases, but these are often iterative and run alongside each other. They relate to planning the structure of the transaction so that both the vendor and the buyer know what after-tax cash-flows to expect from the sale and the target respectively, and the making and veri-fying of statements about the tax history of the target to ensure that historic tax liabilities are properly recognized and likely future tax flows can be predicted. The latter process is often referred to as tax due diligence.

The reader should be aware that it is not possible in the space available to cover all significant aspects of these topics, and taking adequate professional advice is recommended.

The tension between acquisition/sale of shares or assets

On a share purchase, the buyers gain no relief for the cost of their investment against either income tax or profit for corporation tax purposes. The only relief they will get is in the base cost of their shares on a subsequent sale. Contrast this with the corporate buyer of assets, who will be able to amortize any goodwill purchased for tax purposes and will be able to allocate the purchase price across fixed assets, some of which may qualify for writing-down allowances.

Buyers of shares also acquire historic actual and potential liabilities of the company, and this will require them to undertake much more work to verify their nature before acquisition. Of course, buying shares may enable them to access tax losses to the extent they exist in the target, although there is stringent anti-avoidance legislation for loss buying so this needs careful planning and is by no means certain. A share purchase will attract stamp duty at 0.5 per cent, whereas buying assets with real property could lead to stamp duty land tax (SDLT) of up to 4 per cent.

The vendor is likely to pay less tax on a share sale and is also likely to get a double tax hit on an asset sale – first on the profit realized by the company on the sale of the assets, and then individually as a shareholder on extraction of the proceeds.

However, like all generalizations, the above analysis is not always correct. In reality, most buyers are aware of the likely tax consequences for the vendor, and may be prepared to negotiate differently. Often a buyer is willing to pay less for shares than assets. Similarly, corporate vendors with losses brought forward or with significant future capital expenditure plans may be happy to sell assets because they know they can relieve or roll over any gain arising, and may not need the proceeds outside the business. The bottom line is that a share transaction will involve more work for buyers than an asset transaction and professional advisers' fees are likely to be higher. It is also likely that vendors will have put much more effort into planning for a share sale and mitigating their tax consequences on that basis, and may simply not be willing to sell assets in these circumstances.

The sale of shares is currently treated as exempt from VAT, with no VAT recovery on associated costs. With transfers of business, there is no VAT recovery restriction but a lot of anti-avoidance legislation needs to be checked.

Due diligence

The due diligence process from a tax perspective focuses on understanding the balance sheet provision for taxation and whether or not the historical P&L tax charge was reasonably stated. This is achieved by speaking to the vendors or their tax agent and reviewing their correspondence with HMRC. Tax due diligence will check whether corporation tax returns have been filed on time, whether corporation tax has been paid on time, and the nature of any enquiries that have been made into the corporation tax affairs of the company. Where enquiries have been made, whether or not any adjustments have been necessary, and their nature, will provide a potential buyer with information relating to the adequacy of the corporation tax returns prepared and signed by the company.

The scope of tax due diligence is often extended to a review of payroll matters and VAT, to check whether these processes are undertaken adequately, whether there has been a recent review of PAYE or VAT by HMRC, and what adjustments arose. These aspects of due diligence can often discover potential issues that vendors may not have been aware of, such as contractors that the vendors believe not to be employees but which the due diligence reviewers consider may be success-fully challenged by HMRC on a PAYE visit. A number of VAT issues may arise: for example, where property is transferred there can be many pitfalls, and with international transactions, local VAT risks need to be considered.

There is often a linkage between the tax due diligence and other aspects of the M&A process. From the perspective of the buyers, anomalies in tax returns may suggest there may be other areas of concern, and hence they should consider more extensive due diligence and high retention of consideration/indemnity provisions in the SPA. Issues with tax returns are a serious issue for vendors as they may result in a loss of credibility and the buyer may walk away.

Due diligence becomes more complicated where there is an international element associated with the target. In such circumstances the buyer will need to determine the extent to which overseas operations are material, and which overseas territories should be the subject of separate tax due diligence.

The international structure itself may justify review and comment by the tax due diligence provider. Intra-group cross-border financing and intra-group transfer pricing can give rise to complex international tax issues, and should be considered in the scope of any due diligence exercise, particularly when cross-border intra-group cashflows are material.

Some trickier areas

Often deal structures in M&A involving a privately owned target become complicated because of a combination of factors : the vendor's planning to mitigate his/her gain; planning to defer and/or control the timing of payment of any tax arising on a known gain; the desire (often) for a buyer to offer some form of paper as part of the acquisition to minimize cash outflow; and the desire for the buyer to tie in the departing shareholders through some form of earn-out, either to encourage them to support the business in its early years post change in ownership (and therefore to preserve goodwill), or because there have been some differences in opinion regarding value, particularly when based on projected profits, so that the parties agree to a deferred element payable on the occurrence of certain future events. Such structures often lead to share and debt consideration given for the purchase of shares, a proportion of which may be deferred or contingent on future performance.

Any or all of these can give rise to complex tax issues because they come close to a variety of anti-avoidance rules in tax legislation, including those that prevent shareholders receiving monies in transactions related to shares which are not taxed to income tax (ss703- 707 ICTA 1988), that provide a rollover in paper-for-paper deals but only when the transactions are deemed to be for bona fide commercial reasons (ss135–138 TCGA 1992), or which seek to tax under employment income certain proceeds that the shareholder may expect to be taxed as a capital gain (in particular deferred income).

These areas are too complex to cover in detail here, but most usually require tax advisers to seek clearance in advance from HMRC that the proceeds will not be taxed in a way the vendors are not anticipating. Where clearance is not available in advance, vendors will often instruct their tax advisers to work with advisers to the buyer to minimize the risk of an unexpected tax outcome. For this reason, the structuring of M&A transactions usually requires the early participation of tax advisers from both sides to ensure the desired completion timetable is not unduly affected by the tax advice and potential clearances needed from HMRC.

Accounting issues

The target and buyer may have differing accounting policies and accounting functions and these differences need to be evaluated so that their impact may be considered during the planning, investigation and legal drafting phase of the transaction. From the buyer's perspective, accounting issues may have particular significance if a future float or sale is planned.

During an M&A transaction, some of the accounting issues that should be considered are:

- accounting policies of the target;
- accounting for goodwill;
- fair value accounting;
- earnings per share;
- accounting system integration;
- completion accounts;
- implications of International Financial Reporting Standards (IFRS).

Accounting policies of the target

The accounting policies of the target should be considered at an early stage of the negotiations, and ideally a full list of the main policies should be documented. Key policies and estimation techniques might include:

- revenue recognition;
- profit recognition;
- long-term contracts;
- stock provisioning;
- bad debt provisioning;
- depreciation;
- research and development;
- prepayment and accruals recognition;
- accounting for financial instruments.

The buyer should compare the target's accounting policies with its own and quantify the impact of any differences, so that the impact of the acquisition both historically and on a combined projected basis may be determined on a like for like basis. It is important to get this right, as once a price has been set out in an offer to vendors, they will be reluctant to shift from this.

Accounting for goodwill

Calculation of goodwill is an issue for the buyer. The likely quantum and amortization period should be determined. The buyer should consider the quantum taking into account those factors that would be considered in an impairment review. The amortization period should have regard to industry norms and how well the income streams related to the acquisition can be predicted. The buyer's auditors may be able to assist in this exercise, although they will have to ensure that this does not compromise their independence as auditors.

Fair value accounting

In order to calculate the value of goodwill, the assets and liabilities of the target need to be stated at fair value. From the vendor's perspective, it is useful to conduct a fair value exercise before a sale commences. It is possible that there may be surplus assets with sufficient value to justify their being transferred pre-sale, or existing assets that have an alternative value well in excess of their existing use value. For example, the land on which the factory stands may be developed for residential use. The use of professional valuers for assets such as property may be disclosed as part of the negotiations to ensure that the vendor gets full value for those assets.

The buyer needs to exercise care in reviewing the fair value calculations during due diligence, and it would be wise to be comfortable on the value of key assets such as property at an early stage, as funding may depend on these. Other key areas to watch are:

- adequacy of dilapidation provisions on leases;
- specific provisions for product liability claims or legal costs;
- specific provisions for rectification of environmental contamination as a result of industrial processes;
- provision for corporation tax to the point of sale.

Earnings per share

While only quoted companies are required to disclose earnings per share, the directors of a private company should also ensure that the price paid for the acquisition of the target is earnings-enhancing (that is, earnings per share increase), as this is a good logical check to ensure that they have not overpaid for the business. If they are looking to float the company in the near future, the fact that they can demonstrate that an acquisition was earnings-enhancing will increase their credibility, and consequently the chances of a successful float.

Accounting system integration issues

This is often an area to which too little attention is given, and yet it can result in very serious financial consequences. Financial reporting systems should facilitate proper control of the operations of a business in conjunction with its other internal controls.

From the vendor's perspective, the accounting systems should allow monitoring of the performance of the business during the negotiation to assist with the buyer's due diligence requirements. Any issues with the production of reliable financial information may delay the sale and may result in the buyer withdrawing altogether. If the structure of the deal involves an element of deferred consideration, vendors should be comfortable that the system integration is properly planned.

From the buyer's perspective, it should request updated financial information during the early negotiation, and sufficient details on the accounting systems to be comfortable that integration can be completed within an agreed timetable. Businesses with a high degree of reliance on financial systems for stock control, issue of products or production control should consider the use of a specialist consultant to ensure the integration goes smoothly.

Completion accounts

The accounting policies applied to determine the value of net assets at completion are generally set out in the SPA as part of a completion accounts procedure. It is important for both sides to agree and understand the policies to be applied to prepare the completion accounts and any specific adjustments to be made (such as no debtors more than three months old). These should be reflected in the sale and purchase agreement together with a means of dealing with any dispute between the parties.

Implications of International Financial Reporting Standards (IFRS)

The convergence of accounting standards globally is set to continue, and it is therefore worth considering the impact of IFRS on historic and future financial reporting of the target, especially if the buyer may be considering a flotation or already be quoted. It may even be worth restating the historic financial results under IFRS or including a reconciliation of adjustments in the information released to potential buyers in order that any outline offer made takes this into account, thereby reducing the possibility of the buyer having to restate the offer following due diligence.

Despite recent convergence, there remain some major differences between UK GAAP and IFRS. Key areas that may produce significantly different results in the buyer's group accounts include:

- Merger accounting is not allowed under IFRS.
- IFRS require far more intangible assets to be recognized separately from goodwill, thereby reducing goodwill recognized on acquisition.
- Goodwill cannot be amortized under IFRS.
- Deferred tax accounting is quite different, notably in respect of providing for deferred tax on fair value adjustments.
- Financial instruments may be accounted for quite differently.
- More options are available for accounting for the cost of defined benefit pension schemes.

Other matters

Again, given the limited space available, it is not possible to cover all accounting issues that may impact on M&A transactions but some other areas where problems commonly occur include:

- form of consideration (if not cash) and fair value thereof;
- merger relief;
- post-acquisition restructuring such as hive-ups.

Conclusions

As a potential vendor, it is vital that you investigate both the tax and accounting issues at an early stage to identify any serious issues that could affect the sale process and the price the buyer will pay. For tax issues, the timeframe necessary to resolve certain issues may be months or longer, so it is important to plan well in advance.

As a potential buyer, you need to be aware that there are a number of serious pitfalls associated with tax and accounting issues, and the planning element is vital to ensure the process goes smoothly and the acquisition is ultimately earnings-enhancing. It is important that you get a grip on the key issues at an early stage, so if something does arise, the vendor's expectations are properly managed and the acquisition timetable amended if required.

This information has been prepared as a general guide. It is not a substitute for professional advice. Neither PKF (UK) LLP nor its partners or employees accept any responsibility for loss or damage incurred as a result of acting or refraining from acting upon anything contained in or omitted from this chapter.

Legal considerations in making an acquisition for smaller companies

Steven Conybeare, Conybeare Solicitors

Introduction

In this chapter we aim to provide readers with an overview of the legal considerations facing the smaller company when undertaking an acquisition. We consider some of those issues commonly faced by directors of and shareholders in such companies. In particular, we look at any special considerations they face in light of the participation of business angels and/or private investors in their companies, either before the acquisition or as part of the funding for it. The chapter looks at:

- What is an acquisition? – meaning and types.
- Why make an acquisition? – rationale and objectives.
- How to make an acquisition – planning and process.

What is an acquisition?

In its simplest sense, an acquisition is the purchase of a business, an asset or a company. This particular chapter concentrates on the acquisition of a company by way of a share purchase. This means taking on all of the assets and liabilities of the company – a so-called 'warts and all' approach. Contrast this with a more targeted approach of an acquisition of specific assets only.

Why make an acquisition?

The question may seem unusual, but the practical reality is that there are a number of reasons. These include companies wishing to grow their business by expansion or diversification. They need to acquire critical mass, in the form of more customers, a greater product range, a new market or indeed a combination of one or more of these goals. However, whatever the reason, it is critical that the key benefits of any acquisition remain in focus.

Company directors should be the first to appreciate the benefits of merging with or taking over another company. They should be aware of their market, their products, their key customers and of course their key competitors. However, sometimes in smaller companies directors do not have the same wide range of contacts and access to market information as more experienced or knowledgeable directors of larger companies. This is particularly true of both family companies and new start-ups.

Sometimes a driver for an acquisition is a third party in the form of a business adviser, such as an accountant or lawyer, or more usually a business angel or private investor. This group of people are far more likely to be looking at the bottom line of the financial performance indicators of a company, compared with a director in a private company, who may be more focused on other measurable performance criteria, such as sales, number of customers, turnover or profit margin.

How to make an acquisition

It is widely accepted that the key to a successful business is planning, which by its very definition means looking to the future. What are the market trends for this company's products? Who will be the new customers of the future? Where will they come from? What will be the effect of a new product?

Business angels are financial investors. Yes, there are some who after a successful career look to utilize their knowledge, experience and contacts for the benefit of a company, but more often than not, they are principally interested in a return on their investment. They are the ones who are usually monitoring and measuring the key financial indicators of a company. They are the ones who will be raising the difficult questions, and who expect answers!

Using their experience they may well suggest to the working directors solutions to the problems they have identified. Sometimes these solutions include a merger with or acquisition of another company, which may either be a competitor or a producer of a complementary product or service which would expand their market share.

It is not uncommon for business angels to have more than one interest, both commercially and financially, and their interests may actually be complementary to each other, even if they didn't realize it was so at the outset! By combining their interests into one vehicle they may well achieve a greater financial return on their investment, and also actually improve the value of the two separate companies.

Business angel investors will usually have their own preferred professional advisers. They are the ones with whom they feel comfortable and/or with whom they have worked on a number of transactions previously. However, directors must themselves be comfortable. It is they who sign the agreements, and more importantly, it is usually they alone who give the warranties, and thus take on the element of direct financial risk.

Investors may be significant shareholders and directors. Their role however is normally as an investor, and they would look to the directors to protect and enhance their investment. Quite often shareholder or subscription agreements entered into with such investors require the consent of investors to the acquisition or disposal of assets, including shares.

Clearly, it is imperative that a director of a company with an investor on board is familiar with his/her own obligations under the terms of any such agreements. Where necessary, obtain appropriate consents and permissions at an early stage, even if in principle. It is never a foregone conclusion.

Where a purchaser has itself received investment from a business angel investor, there will be various agreements and arrangements entered into with the investor by both the company itself and majority or all shareholders. The terms of such agreements must be carefully considered at the outset.

If the consideration for the acquisition is to be paid, whether in total or in part, by the issue of new shares of the purchaser, then there are even more issues to be considered, including the value of the shares of the issuer or purchaser, the post-acquisition shareholdings and the consequential dilution of these shareholdings. One would expect to find an anti-dilution clause in the shareholders' agreement, as a means of protecting an investor's position, and there may need to be formal consent obtained and/or a waiver from other shareholders.

Planning is critical. The transaction is far more time-consuming and complicated than anyone ever imagines at the outset; and this is true whether the deal size is large or small. There are always many more documents generated, more meetings to attend, lawyers' questions to answer and financial documents to be prepared, reviewed and relied upon. All of this costs money, including legal fees. It is always advisable to obtain firm quotes from your lawyer, or even better a fixed fee. This will help towards ensuring that the costs do not escalate beyond what makes the deal a meaningful and worthwhile exercise.

It is true to say that the process and procedures adopted in making an acquisition makes little distinction between a £1 billion or £100,000 purchase value. The fact is that the same questions, enquiries and protections need to be obtained.

The legal documentation required for an acquisition is dealt with in some considerable detail elsewhere in this book, so here we aim to give more of an overview of the process of a merger or acquisition, with a particular emphasis on the role of a business angel investor. We concern ourselves with the private company, whether it be a family company or a start-up.

Key legal considerations

These include the price to pay, how that price is calculated, the potential liabilities, the real value (not just the paper value) of a business, how to obtain and then protect the goodwill, how to retain key staff and customers, and who is going to run the newly enlarged business.

Game plan

The purchaser must have a game plan. As seen above, there are one or more reasons for the proposed purchase. It is of course essential that the purchaser has a clear and unambiguous game plan of how the acquisition will be made, the benefits of it, any potential problems and exactly what the new group will look like and how it will work in practice. The legal considerations are there to help ensure the company achieves its commercial goals as best it can, but it cannot replace them. Matters for particular consideration include the structure of the group going forward, who will report to whom, and how the 'old' and the 'new' will be merged together to actually drive the business forward.

Heads of terms

Once preliminary discussions have been held at board level between the two companies, an outline agreement or agreement in principle will be reached, and it is usually documented. Such a document provides an easy reference guide to the principal terms of the transaction, and serves as a useful guide for the solicitors.

It is normally only when this has been done that the lawyers are engaged to document the agreement reached by clients (or what they think has been agreed!). However, if this document is properly drafted, the principal terms are more likely to be both understood and agreed. Usually, such heads of terms are non-binding, but certain legally binding obligations and restrictions can, and indeed probably should, arise.

For example, it is sensible to obtain a period of exclusivity, as a buyer normally expends a certain amount of cash on preliminary investigations. In some cases, there is an argument for adopting break fees, whereby a party who pulls out of a proposed transaction is obliged to make a payment to the other for certain fees, costs and expenses.

Confidentiality

As part of the negotiations, there should be restrictions on the use and dissemination of the information relating to the target company, as well as the purchaser. It is pointless trying to protect all information, but it certainly should not be ignored in the hope that 'it won't happen to me'.

Legal due diligence

Due diligence is the generic term given to the examination of the company to be acquired. It includes a thorough and systematic review of the financial books and records of the company and the contractual obligations and liabilities of it, covering commercial contracts with suppliers, customers, advisers and not least employees.

The financial matters are dealt with by accountants and the legal aspects by solicitors. However, depending on the size of the company other professional advisers will also be required to deal with pensions (actuaries) and property matters (surveyors). In addition, a proper investigation should be carried out into the company, its history and its liabilities. Whilst warranties are used as a means of protection, they of course only give rise to a cause of action against directors/share-holders, rather than preventing the liability arising in the first place.

Once solicitors have been instructed, the process of due diligence will commence. This normally starts with a series of questions and information requests made to the target's solicitors. The subject matter will include items relating to the operation of the business, its contractual obligations, the benefits of any contracts and its employees. Clearly, a first attempt will be to flush out all of the issues that may arise and that may need to be dealt with.

Normally the financial due diligence exercise will have been carried out earlier in the whole process by the accountants. This itself will serve as a useful starting point for the solicitors, although remember that the information to be extracted by the legal process is and will be different.

Funding

At the same time as the due diligence is being undertaken, if not before, the purchaser needs to consider how it is to fund the purchase. In some cases, it is a simple matter of having the cash available, but usually there needs to be some form of funding. Sources of funding are beyond the scope of this chapter, but in terms of the ramifications these are covered in brief.

One option is to take a bank or other loan to finance the purchase and the terms of the loan should be carefully considered, including repayments, interest rates, security and restrictions imposed on the business. The alternative is to raise funds from existing shareholders, new investors or a combination of both. Where this course is chosen, it is critical to ensure that a game plan is thought through at the outset.

There are plenty of time periods that need to be complied with, discussions held and documentation produced. Shareholders and investors alike will expect verified information to be made available to them in order for them to make an informed decision. This is usually not available until the purchase documentation is near complete, which of course delays matters. The extent of any such delay depends on a number of factors, not least the preparatory work undertaken by the directors and their advisers.

Share sale and purchase agreement

Once the heads have been agreed, the exchange of business information made confidential, and the results of the due diligence exercise obtained, it is time for the real negotiations to be concluded. Depending on what, if anything, unexpected has arisen, the principal terms of the deal now need to be documented. These terms will be set out in the share purchase agreement, and may also be covered in ancillary documents. Depending on the complexity, the agreement itself could range from several pages to hundreds of pages.

Warranties and disclosure letter

Where warranties are to be given, it is usual for investors to state that they will not give warranties or otherwise be liable in respect of any breach of such. As this chapter is not aimed at the selling company, the circumstances in which warranties are given would normally be restricted to the issue of shares as consideration of the purchase price.

More often than not, one of the most contentious areas for negotiations relates to the warranties given by the vendors. Many directors are reluctant to risk their own assets in the event of a claim. Endless discussions can and often do ensue between the lawyers seeking to cap or limit the financial extent of the warranties, the time limits within which a claim may be brought and how such a claim may be made.

Consideration: cash or shares? delayed or deferred?

Sometimes this is overlooked or not properly considered at the outset. It is of course essential for any company wishing to make an acquisition to be aware of how it is to be funded and more importantly how and when it is to be paid.

Ancillary agreements/documents

In some instances, there are particular requirements to be dealt with. In smaller companies, the importance of customer relationships and non-compete restrictions is key. This is not to say that they are unimportant to larger companies, but rather that smaller companies rely more on personal business arrangements. In a good number of cases, a company's real asset is an individual or a group of individuals, rather than the company itself. It is hugely important to identify whether this is the case in your acquisition. There is absolutely no point in paying any amount of money for a business if immediately following completion the two key individual directors or shareholders set up in business directly competing against their old company. In this way, smaller companies must ensure that key staff are retained, or otherwise prevented from competing against them, and where retained are suitably incentivized to increase the financial performance of the enlarged group. This may take the form of cash bonuses, various share saving plans and share options. Of particular benefit to smaller companies is the Enterprise Management Incentive (EMI) legislation which provides very useful tax breaks for option holders and companies alike.

Employees

In the above section we considered the importance of key employees, but that is not to say that any other employees are less important. While a share purchase might avoid the need to consider the Transfer of Undertakings and Protection of Employees Regulations 2006 (TUPE), there is still much to be done in ensuring that all staff are kept informed of what is happening and when. Nothing creates fear and loathing as much as a lack of information, and the vacuum is easily and quickly filled by speculation and guesswork.

Practical matters

Driving the new business

Investors have normally been, or are, a director in one or more companies. They have normally been involved, directly or indirectly, with the purchase of another company or business. Even where they have not, then they will have undertaken a very similar process when making their investment in a private company. Their experience, good or bad, tends to guide them through any subsequent transaction. As investors, they are normally objective enough to see, or at the very least to form a view on, the commercial benefits of any tie-up. They can and do provide an interesting and useful soundboard for the directors' views and aspirations for the newly enlarged group or company, and in particular offer candid advice on how to ensure that the assumed financial and other benefits are actually realized.

New shareholders

If the consideration for the purchase has an element of new shares to be issued, then the purchaser will automatically have new shareholders following completion.

Should they become bound by the existing shareholders' agreement? Do the existing shareholders remain bound while the new do not?

New directors

Will any of the target's directors remain? Will they also become members of the purchaser's board of directors? Clearly, the purchaser's directors will either replace or substantially assume the board positions of the target, but consideration must be given to these matters, and not just from a legal point of view. Very often with smaller companies, the personalities of the individuals concerned are far more important, in the sense that they become apparent much more easily and quickly.

Summary

While a large number of the considerations facing a purchaser of a company remain the same whatever the size, there are specific matters that undoubtedly affect a smaller company much more than a larger one. As we have tried to explore in this chapter, in smaller companies there is a much greater need to ensure that from a commercial perspective there is a good fit between the purchaser and the target.

From a legal standpoint, there are likely to be specific issues relating to structuring and funding an acquisition, understanding and appreciating the risks in making an acquisition, protecting the goodwill of the business by retaining and motivating key directors and staff, and holding early discussions with existing private investors as well as any potential new investors.

Above all, it is essential to properly consider, plan and execute the proposed acquisition, to fully appreciate the depth and range of information required, as well as the time and effort needed to make an acquisition a true success.

CASE STUDY

We acted for a manned guarding services company, which had found an acquisition target. The managing directors of the two companies had agreed a deal, which may be best summarized by 'I will sell you the company for £2.5 million.'

Our client went away, discussed it with his board and they agreed that the purchase made commercial sense. The only problem was that the company didn't have the money to pay for the deal. The company discussed it with its key shareholder investors (business angels), who were supportive of its aspirations. It was led to believe that these shareholders would provide some of the funding required by way of a rights issue. However, the company had to speak to certain financial brokers in the City who would help it find new investors as well.

After considering the terms of the acquisition, the brokers advised that they could raise the money, but the basic terms of the deal would need to change, as their investors would not be prepared to take the risk of paying across all of the cash on completion. There would have to be an element of deferred consideration payable only on the successful conclusion of various financially measurable targets. This was then the position adopted by the existing investors as well.

In the meantime, we had been busy drafting documentation and negotiating the same with the vendor's lawyers. When we thought we had covered the main points which had apparently agreed, we held an all party discussion.

In fact, the principal terms of the deal (from the vendor's perspective) had changed substantively because of the requirements of the purchaser's existing and potential investors. The vendors were not going to get all of their cash on completion. Instead there were numerous targets and payment mechanisms to be agreed and documented. The deal was eventually consummated, but by the end it bore little resemblance to the deal upon which we were originally instructed!

Common features in the acquisition of private companies

Alan Kelly, MacRoberts

Whether you own a Bentley or a Beetle (or more likely, something in between), you will be aware that there are many parts of your vehicle that need to work together in order to propel you along the road you wish to travel. You may or may not know, or indeed care, what those various parts do, but you know that if you were to look under the bonnet of each you would be presented with very different pictures. Stripping down each car, however, you would find an amazing number of common parts.

To a large extent, the same can be said of any merger or acquisition. There are undoubtedly different issues faced by the large stock exchange listed public company in a merger situation when compared with a small private company, but if you strip down all the issues, there will be a surprising number common to both. Equally, it matters not whether a company is located in Scotland or in England or Wales; the same general principles apply.

This chapter looks at the mechanics of an M&A transaction from the viewpoint of directors of a private company (or in other words, from the perspective of the driver of your standard saloon).

non-circumlocutory, oral communication dispensed by an orator who has no predilection for verbiage and is far from prolix or magniloquent in manner

straight-talking

maCROBERTS

straight-to-the-point business law

The professional team

Before you are able to embark on your acquisition, you will need to appoint a team of specialists to help you. You should not underestimate the importance of selecting the right team at the outset. (If you are looking to acquire a new BMW 3 series, your first port of call is unlikely to be your local mini-dealership.)

The importance of selecting a professional team that possesses the depth of specialisms required in the acquisition is crucial. With the ever-increasing complexity of the legal and accounting regime and the growing practice of greater specialism, you need to ensure your team is able to cope with the various pensions, environmental, property, employment, tax and a myriad of other issues that are likely to arise. Failure to get this right at the outset can have significant consequences, increasing the risks that are being inherited and prolonging the acquisition process itself. Make sure, therefore, that your team has sufficient experience in the size and scale of acquisition that you are considering.

Approaching the seller

Once you have identified your target, you need to consider the best way of approaching the seller. The circumstances can vary greatly. It may be the target is being marketed generally for sale, or it could be that the target is not actually for sale and you want to make an informal approach to the owner.

Whichever situation applies, if you are the potential acquirer, you should expect to be asked to sign a confidentiality agreement at some point, undertaking not to disclose any confidential information of the business. While this is standard practice, you should be careful that the undertaking you sign does not adversely affect any other business interest you may have. It is common practice now for these undertakings to include obligations not to offer employment to employees of the target for a period following conclusion of the negotiations, and to provide restrictions on dealing with the customers and suppliers of the target business and even restrictions on launching similar products. If your existing business has common customers, suppliers and/or products, or if employees regularly move between the businesses, you need to make sure you are not being unduly restricted under the confidentiality agreement.

Likewise, if you are the seller, you will want to make sure that business competitors are not simply using the process to obtain valuable confidential information about your business. From a buyer's perspective, you should also always be asking for an exclusivity period to ensure that during this period, the seller cannot enter into negotiations with any other party. Otherwise, you run the risk of incurring time and costs while the seller is negotiating a second deal with another party.

Notwithstanding that you now have a suitable confidentiality agreement in place, if you are a seller, you will still want to make sure that you are not putting your business at risk by disclosing business sensitive information to competitors.

In putting together your due diligence package, you can take steps to ensure that any commercially sensitive information is made anonymous wherever possible (for example, by not referring to the names of your employees but only their title, salary, benefits etc). Your advisers should be able to provide assistance here.

Kicking the tyres

Depending on the type and size of the acquisition, the due diligence process (essentially the exercise by which potential buyers will analyse and examine your vehicle from every angle in order to ascertain whether there are any hidden problems) can take many forms. If there are a number of interested buyers, it may be that a 'data room' is set up where all the diligence information is set out for the interested buyers to review before they make an offer for the business. It could be that there is only one interested buyer, and that the due diligence process takes the form of responding to the enquiries made by that buyer.

Whichever route is followed, it is critical from the seller's perspective to be as prepared as possible in advance of the process starting. The seller should (in conjunction with its advisers) be looking to rectify any problems within the business before they are seen by the buyer. If issues are not dealt with before they are put in front of the buyer, not only can it lead to the buyer looking to reduce the business's price (often quite considerably where this is based on a multiple of earnings), it can also lead to the buyer becoming suspicious that other problems could be lying undiscovered. Wherever possible, as a seller you need to be compiling all the information that a buyer is likely to want to see as early as possible, and identifying any defects before the information is handed to the buyer. This will not only save you time during what can often be a hectic negotiation and completion process (time which could have been spent during the process on looking after the business), but could also save you money. An organized and smooth-running due diligence process is going to give the buyer the impression that the business is well run and organized. (It also makes the adviser's job a lot easier and therefore less expensive.)

A shambolic process on the other hand, where information is incomplete (or incorrect) or late in being delivered, will give the impression to the buyer that there are deficiencies in the working practices of the business which could be hiding greater problems. (In other words, keep your service book up to date and the various working parts regularly oiled and maintained. If a potential buyer opens up a bonnet to see a sparkling engine, it gives a very good first impression.)

Paperwork

Many of those involved in an acquisition for the first time will be surprised at the amount of paperwork required to document the transfer. The principal document however, is always going to be the sale and purchase agreement itself. The issues that arise in this document will depend on whether the acquisition is proceeding by way of a sale of the business and assets, or whether it is the shares in the target that are being sold (clearly in the latter case more diligence will be undertaken). However, there are some common issues to be faced in both circumstances.

Who guarantees the obligations of the seller?

Particularly in an asset sale, it is always a concern that following the sale of the business and assets (and especially where the seller has no other business or assets), the seller will no longer have any assets with which to settle any claim under the agreement. If there is no suitable guarantor, consideration should be given by the buyer to a retention account into which a portion of the purchase price is paid for a period of time, to which the buyer can have access if a claim arises, or alternatively, to deferring some of the consideration to a later date and insisting on the right to withhold payment of the consideration in the event a valid claim arises.

The nature and extent of the warranties

The warranty exercise is to a large extent related to the due diligence process. In compiling the due diligence information for the buyer, the seller will also be compiling a bundle of 'disclosure documents' which have the effect of qualifying the warranties that the buyer will be looking for. (Warranties are essentially statements of fact made by the seller about the state of affairs of the business.) Unlike your standard three-month warranty on any used car purchase, the warranties given by the seller in any sale transaction (depending on the circumstances of the sale and the parties' relative negotiating position) are likely to be for periods between 8 and 24 months, and are also likely to be quite considerable in their range.

How is the price to be paid?

If you are in a selling position, you will invariably want to receive all your cash upon completing the sale. If you are a buyer, you will often want to pay part of the price in deferred instalments. However, a deferred consideration can often result in the sellers receiving a greater price. Particularly for businesses in the service sector which are not asset-rich, it can often be attractive for a seller to request an earn-out in circumstances where it believes the business will continue to show strong growth but the buyer is not prepared to pay for those prospects. (In other words, the deferred price payable for the business will vary depending on the profits of the business during the earn-out period.)

In these circumstances, however, many difficult issues can arise. The seller will want to be given sufficient scope to develop the potential of the earn-out without additional costs or restraints being put on the business by the buyer or the buyer's wider group, while the buyer will want to ensure that it is able to run the business in the manner that it chooses without undue interference from the past management. These fundamentally opposed interests lie at the heart of earn-out clauses, and before agreeing to any earn-out (whether you are a buyer or a seller), it is vital that you speak to your advisers about some of the issues that can arise and how they can be resolved.

As they have to be very carefully crafted, often the most difficult negotiations can centre round the earn-out protections to be afforded to the seller. For example, a recent earn-out provided that if the buyer (who had before the purchase been a trade customer of the seller) reduced its orders with the target below a certain level after it became part of the buyer's group, then a deemed level of custom was to be used to calculate the earn-out. (The seller was concerned that the buyer would use other parts of its group to fulfil orders in order to drive down the earn-out, which was based on a multiple of profit.) The buyer did not seek to make an exception for circumstances where the orders fell as a result of general market conditions, with the result that when over the two-year earn-out period market conditions did deteriorate, the seller had effectively managed to insulate its earn-out.

Signing on the dotted line

Once the due diligence exercise has concluded, both buyer and seller invariably look to complete the purchase as soon as possible. Typically, the negotiation process will be undertaken simultaneously with the due diligence process (although this is not always the case). In these circumstances, one issue that often arises is an attempt by the buyer to reduce the price as a result of its due diligence findings. This is often a difficult stage of the process: the seller has already spent a great deal of time, effort and money in getting to the current stage and is not attracted by the thought of having to undergo the process again with another party.

If the issue is big enough, often it can result in the deal collapsing. Some of the most recent issues that have caused deals to disintegrate in this manner include significant pension liabilities being uncovered, risks of uninsured negligence actions being pursued, fluctuations in the stock markets where shares in the listed purchaser are being offered to the seller and a downturn in the relevant target sector occurs. Many risks can now be covered by insurance policies, and the increase in the insurance products available for M&A transactions has inevitably helped to secure the conclusion of deals that might otherwise not have happened.

On occasions however, the buyer may just be looking for reasons to adjust the price downwards, knowing that the seller has already been window shopping for a Porsche and yacht. (If you are in the selling position, it is always worth endeavouring not to spend your proceeds, either actually or mentally, until you have actually received them.)

In the ideal completion scenario, all the purchase paperwork will be agreed prior to the parties turning up to the meeting, the buyer will have all the funding in place and the champagne will be flowing shortly after the meeting commences. Just as often, though, there are still numerous issues outstanding which require to be dealt with on the day, while the buyer will be trying to agree the acquisition and at the same time trying to get its funding in place.

It is worth pointing out that under Scots law, the lack of the ability to execute an agreement 'in counterpart' (where one party executes one copy of the agreement and exchanges this with a copy signed by the other party) means that even where all documents are agreed in advance of the day of intended completion, completion meetings are still very common, as each copy of the agreement has to be signed by all the parties to it.

Trying to minimize the factors that lead to delayed completions, such as sorting out the funding as early as possible, making sure all those who need to be present to sign are available, and setting realistic timescales, will help to reduce the stress that can often be felt by many during the end stages of the process.

One transaction recently was delayed when on the day of completion the seller was unable to deliver a stock transfer form of its shareholding in the target, because the solicitors had forgotten to obtain the release of the bank to whom the shares had been pledged in security. Understandably, the bank used the circumstances as a way of making sure large amounts of the proceeds were used to pay off its outstanding loans. However, this all had a knock-on effect on completion.

As it is not uncommon for there to be a number of issues in the documentation that need to be resolved at the end, having advisers around you who have been through the process on numerous occasions, and who are able to explain the issues in a clear and meaningful way, will take a lot of strain out of the ordeal. Nevertheless, if there are still issues to be resolved on the day, be prepared for a long day. It is easy to forget that once the principle of an issue has been resolved, there can be significant changes required to the paperwork to reflect the agreement.

The MBO vehicle

Any chapter on the mechanics of an acquisition needs to make at least a brief mention of one particular type of acquisition: the MBO. In situations where the existing management team are the buyers of the business, while many of the issues above can still make an appearance, many different considerations and issues also arise. For example, in relation to due diligence, there is unlikely to be an extensive exercise carried out, though whoever is funding the MBO (whether it is a bank or a private equity provider) will want to undertake their own diligence. In these circumstances, management will find they are the ones that are required to give the warranties. Again, it is important for the management team to speak to advisers who have experience of this type of acquisition and can identify and resolve the issues that will arise.

After sales

Having chosen your advisers, selected your purchase, looked under the bonnet and kicked the tyres, negotiated the deal, and signed on the dotted line, you are now free to take the wheel of your new purchase. Hopefully, in the process you will have gained a better understanding of the mechanics of an M&A transaction, so that when the time comes to sell on your purchase or to purchase a bigger and better model, you are all the better prepared. One of the key factors in any successful M&A transaction is understanding the issues and being prepared. 'Before everything else, getting ready is the secret of success' (Henry Ford).

Part Four

The process of M&A

Introduction

Peter Wood and David Stevenson, Pinsent Masons

Overview

This chapter examines the mechanical steps involved in undertaking an acquisition or merger. So what are these various stages? Traditionally, and before the advent of the 'auction sale' (which we look at below), the path that the acquisition process would take was well rehearsed. As we shall see, in simple terms, ordinarily the process will consist of:

- finding a target business;
- appointing advisers;
- negotiating terms;
- due diligence;
- exchange of contracts;
- completion.

While no single M&A transaction is the same, there are common threads that run through most. The various stages involved are fairly well defined, and it is comparatively easy for the reader to become familiar with the process itself. However, what is not so easy to define is the wealth of challenges that face those brave enough to undertake an acquisition, and particularly those entering the fray for the first time; and more to the point, how best to tackle them.

Structuring the deal

A key point to address early in the process is how the acquisition is to be structured. In this respect there is an important decision to be made: whether the deal is to be a purchase of a company in its entirety (sometimes referred to as a 'purchase of shares') or a purchase of a business out of a company (sometimes referred to as a 'purchase of assets'). There are a host of legal and commercial issues that influence which route the deal will take.

The tax consequences of either the shares or assets structure are likely to be a major consideration in determining which route is followed. Often, what is advantageous from a tax perspective for a seller is not attractive to the buyer, and whether the share capital or a business is sold may ultimately come down to which party is in the stronger bargaining position.

The pressure of time

Once the deal has been agreed in principle there are two distinct work streams: due diligence, and the negotiation and agreement of the definitive transfer documentation. In an ideal world, the due diligence exercise is completed before the parties turn their attention to the definitive sale and purchase documentation, but in reality the pressure of timing often militates against such an approach.

Once sellers have agreed to sell they will want to move with all due haste, as the longer the process continues, the greater the likelihood that there will be a breach of confidentiality which may damage the value of the business they are selling. The reason for this is, of course, that a leak of the proposed sale may unsettle staff, customers and suppliers at a time when the purchaser is still entitled to pull out. The buyer is also unlikely to want to delay, given that a leak may open the way for a competitor to trump the buyer's bid.

Balanced against this, however, will be the desire of the buyer to complete its due diligence on a satisfactory basis; and the purchaser will be aware that the faster a deal is executed, the greater the chances of something being missed. Related to this is the issue of whether and to what extent a buyer should be granted a period of 'exclusivity' within which to complete the acquisition.

In terms of timing, it is important that all relevant milestones and deadlines are established and agreed early on in the process. The timetable should be challenging but realistic. If it is unrealistic, the process can risk losing credibility, with energy becoming dissipated on allocating blame for failure to meet targets, as opposed to pushing the project forward.

Keeping the sellers onside

Unless the target is being sold out of a larger group of companies or by private equity investors only, then the business will be sold in whole or in part by individual entrepreneurs who will sometimes have been with the company for many years, and indeed may well have founded it. This can result in the sellers having an emotional attachment to the business and this introduces a number of intangible issues which need to be dealt with sympathetically. The sellers may have a number of material concerns that need to be addressed, for example about customer or supplier loyalty, and employee job security going forward. It will be important for a buyer to identify these issues early on in the process so that such concerns can be addressed.

The purchaser's future plans need to be clear so that any challenge from the sellers can be dealt with effectively. The dialogue with the sellers is critical, especially if they are to remain with the company after the sale. Differences that may exist between the sellers' and the buyer's expectations as to how the business will operate after the sale can present an interesting dichotomy that will require careful handling if the sellers' goodwill is to be maintained successfully.

When it comes to negotiating with the sellers of the business, maintaining their goodwill is important. This can be threatened when difficult issues arise which need resolving by sometimes tough negotiations. This is where a good adviser can act as a buffer between the parties in taking on the more confrontational head-to-head discussions.

Avoiding misunderstandings

A common issue that arises is the lack of understanding on either or both sides of what the process will involve and how complex and time-consuming it is likely to be. In addition, confusion over the actual terms that have been agreed can be a barrier to achieving momentum. In this respect, in the initial negotiations, it is important to identify who among the sellers is the 'decision maker' and then focus discussions on that person. To do otherwise risks uncertainty and elongating the process at a time when time may be of the essence. At this stage, a confidentiality undertaking from the acquirer is likely to be required. This is normal, but care should be taken not to sign up to anything that restricts the ability to continue to trade in the ordinary course of business.

It is all too easy for the parties to think that the deal is 'done' once non-binding heads have been signed. The sometimes fierce negotiation on the detail in the definitive documentation which can occur subsequently will at best cause frustration, and at worst threaten the successful outcome of the transaction. This is especially the case if the heads have been put together without legal input, or areas of potential conflict have been ignored or glossed over at this stage. This rarely does anyone or the success of the enterprise any favours, and should be avoided.

However, some purchasers will rate their own negotiation skills higher than their advisers and may not involve them until later in the process. Others recognize that there is sometimes no substitute for experience during the initial phases. Perhaps, however, it is the ability of an adviser (who might be a financial adviser, accountant or lawyer) to provide objectivity during what can be an emotionally charged process that is most useful.

Advisers expert in their fields have the advantage of having experienced many similar transactions, whereas for some acquirers the particular transaction will be the first they have ever been involved in. While a purchaser will often make the initial approach to a target itself, there may sometimes be merit in the adviser taking the lead. This may be especially the case where it is felt appropriate to protect the identity of the prospective purchaser and minimize the risk of the deal being leaked to the market.

Buying a company is a time-intensive exercise (the final completion meeting, in particular, can stretch out over many hours), and can test everyone's patience. The key to all of this is for none of it to come as a surprise – albeit that it often does! It is important therefore, and preferably, at the outset, that in this respect the parties' expectations are managed effectively.

Project management

Acquiring a company will involve a number of different work streams, and with this a multitude of individuals undertaking various and potentially overlapping tasks. Common complaints regarding the ease of the acquisition process revolve around uncertainty as to its outcome, risk of mistakes, missed deadlines, poor communication and a general feeling of lack of control over the process. How then does the buyer tailor its approach so as to avoid these issues?

Fundamental to the project's success is an appreciation that M&A transactions are complex, multifaceted projects which therefore need to be managed accordingly. Experience shows the important role that effective project management plays in a successful process. To achieve effective project management it is preferable that one person takes responsibility for coordinating the activities of the acquisition team. This person will have the authority and standing to be able to schedule the work that is required to bring the deal to fruition, and the work resources to carry it out. In all of this, it is vital that roles and responsibilities are allocated in a clear and unambiguous way, so that all those involved in the process are aware of what needs to be done, by whom and by when. Only in this way will everyone involved understand what is expected from them.

The project plan will only make sense if it has been prepared against the specific background of the transaction, and in this respect, team members should be briefed at the outset on certain fundamentals such as why the acquisition is being undertaken and what, if anything, are the 'must haves'. To proceed otherwise risks a lack of focus. During times in the process when the adrenalin levels inevitably rise, it is important that the acquirer does not lose sight of the reasons and assumptions that underpin the decision to proceed. Throughout, it is these that need to be validated on an ongoing basis if the ultimate success of the acquisition is not to be threatened.

Expect the unexpected

It would be unusual for something unexpected not to arise during the process. With a view to minimizing the disruption to the process that this can cause, it is important that everyone on the team understands the need to communicate potential problems to the project manager as soon as they arise. Only in this way will the issue be placed in its proper context and a solution arrived at in a timely manner.

The most effective way to deal with issues that have the potential to derail what might otherwise be a smooth process is to try to anticipate these in advance. Examples are those matters that might cause delay or threaten the availability of key people. Whatever might make completion of the project uncertain needs to be thought about and well covered.

Too many cooks ...

There is more often than not the potential for roles and responsibilities among the team, and particularly among professional advisers, to overlap. Duplication is inefficient and not cost-effective. Moreover, in the context of a process where there is already enough to do without doing the same task twice, an effective delineation of the work so as to avoid duplication is key. Again the responsibility for achieving this must rest with a single point of reference: the project manager. This area can be particularly acute in the context of due diligence.

In order to ensure the success of due diligence, the purchaser must spend time with those undertaking the review work to scope effectively what needs to be done and by whom. In particular, it is important to establish what is and is not important to the purchaser in this context, so that the work is focused appropriately. Given that there are likely to be a number of different professionals involved (lawyers, accountants, surveyors, insurance brokers, environmental consultants, actuaries and so on), there is a need for someone to manage the exercise to avoid duplication and missed reporting deadlines.

There is, of course, the other side of this: the risk that with a number of individuals working on the project, something is neglected because it is assumed by everyone involved that it is being dealt with by another member of the team. Again, having a single person to coordinate the work and responsibility should reduce this risk.

Achieving the plan

A plan is all well and good, but of little use unless progress against the plan is measured on a regular basis. Regular review meetings are necessary to achieve this. It is unlikely that project team members will be all on the same site, so a conference call mechanism is often found to be the best way of achieving this. Each call (and on some more complex and time-critical jobs the call will be daily) needs to be chaired effectively and to follow a prescribed agenda. A suggestion of what this might comprise is a rolling list of outstanding matters on the critical path, with a note of the status of such matters and who has responsibility for taking the relevant action.

Auction sales

Sales of companies by way of controlled auction are increasingly common, especially where the seller is a private equity investor. In the case of an auction sale, the process is slightly different. Typically, the seller and its advisers will prepare a document, or information memorandum, about the target and the fact of its proposed sale. Expressions of interest will then be invited in response to the information memorandum, with this leading to a short list of potential buyers being drawn up. They will then be invited to review due diligence information in a controlled environment set up for the purpose, known commonly as a 'data room'. Offers then ensue, and the field is narrowed to one or sometimes two finalists, with the route to completion being compressed into a shortened timeframe.

Participation in a controlled auction gives rise to additional challenges and risks. The process is in effect driven and run by the seller, and this has an impact on the terms of the definitive documentation. The draft contract is likely to have been prepared by the seller (where in a conventional situation the task usually falls to the purchaser). This, combined with the threat of other interested parties being able to re-enter the fray, means that the purchaser may have to settle for less cover by way of warranty and indemnity than would normally be the case. In turn, this highlights the importance of due diligence, which unfortunately may have had to have been more limited than would normally be the case. There is certainly pressure on the purchaser to 'take a view' on areas of risk and to be more robust regarding what is, and is not, material in the context of the transaction.

Conclusion

An understanding of the process and the pitfalls to be avoided is important if the acquirer is to achieve the control and certainty necessary to ensure that the acquisition is successfully implemented.

Critical issues in M&A transactions for SMEs

Gideon Nellen, NELLEN Solicitors

This chapter looks at number of critical issues that tend to arise, or should be borne in mind, in the course of a transaction:

- price and payment terms;
- completion balance sheets;
- earn-outs – seller's protections;
- warranties and indemnities;
- who gives warranties;
- limitation of seller's liability.

Price and payment terms

Clearly price is the most critical issue in any transaction, but the permutations for how it is to be paid or calculated, and in what form it is delivered, are numerous. For sellers, cash on completion understandably is king. Buyers naturally prefer to minimize their upfront commitment, and where possible pay much of the consideration in loan stock or shares, pay in stages or pay part of the consideration by reference to the future performance of the target (earn-out payments).

In people businesses where the future revenue could walk out of the door, buyers are understandably reluctant to front-load the price. A seller therefore might have to take a view whether to sacrifice some of the upside if it insists on a cash-only deal – if indeed it has a choice.

The added attraction for a buyer of paying over time or in paper is the ability for a buyer to set off warranty or indemnity claims against the deferred consideration, even if this is in breach of the agreement itself. At the very least it gives the buyer added negotiating leverage.

The result of this tension is that, particularly in the services, media and IT sector, many transactions are not structured as outright sales for an upfront cash lump sum, but comprise a mixture of an initial consideration (perhaps adjusted by reference to a completion balance sheet) and earn-out payments based on future performance milestones of the target.

A seller should of course be aware that the value of deferred consideration payments depends on the solvency or the share performance of the buyer (if based on a fixed number of the buyer's shares). It should ensure that the covenants to make the deferred payments are as secure as possible: for instance where loan stock forms part of the consideration, that it is secured, that cash is placed in an escrow account or the commitment secured by a parent company guarantee. However, escrow deposits are usually not possible where future payments can only be determined at a later date.

Completion balance sheets

Where part of the initial consideration is to be determined or adjusted by reference to the net asset value of the target (or possibly some other balance sheet calculation) as shown in a completion balance sheet, a seller should seek to minimize the areas for accounting disputes.

A seller should remember that even if, as is fairly standard, it or its accountant has the opportunity to review and comment on the draft accounts (and in the final analysis have the matter referred to an independent expert), problems can arise in areas where values, income recognition or provisions are often matters of judgment. The new directors might, for example, take a completely different view of the value of stock or plant and machinery, and seek to write it down significantly.

Sellers' protections should therefore be applied to the determination of the completion balance, so that:

■ The completion balance sheet is prepared on a basis consistent with the latest audited balance sheet;
■ departures from GAAP should either be applied or adjustments agreed;
■ values or provisions (or the absence thereof) which could be controversial should be set out.

The specialist
corporate law firm

NELLEN
s o l i c i t o r s

Mergers and Acquisitions
Private Equity
Restructurings
Management Buy-Outs
Employee Share Schemes

19 Albemarle Street
London W1S 4HS
Tel: 020 7499 8122
Fax: 020 7493 0146
info@nellen.co.uk

www.nellen.co.uk

Earn-outs

Earn-outs (most commonly related to profits or turnover or other performance measures relevant to the particular business) need to be carefully drafted to minimize the areas of uncertainty or dispute. If the earn-out is related to profits or turnover, the parties need to consider carefully how the profit or turnover figure is to be identified and calculated. Similar protections should be included in relation to the calculation of the earn-out as are applied to completion balance sheets, referred to above.

In addition various general protections should be considered, such as:

- a provision that the buyer will not do anything that, intentionally or otherwise, reduces the earn-out (such as diverting business to another group company);
- a covenant that adequate resources and human resources will be devoted to the business of the target to maximize turnover and/or profits;
- if the earn-out is profits-based, not to do anything that will reduce profits (such as inter-group charges, non-arm's length transactions, salary increases above a certain level (or ignored above a threshold).

The difficulty is always to strike a balance between protections that seek to ring-fence the target's business, and protections that the buyer maintains impose undue restrictions on the future operations of the target.

Warranties and indemnities

Warranties are statements in the share purchase agreement assuring the buyer as to a whole range of matters which are relevant to the target's business, its assets and liabilities. In practice, although the warranties form the bulk of a share purchase agreement and often cause sellers great concern, claims for breaches of warranties tend to be rare. This is because well-advised buyers normally carry out a thorough due diligence exercise prior to finalizing a deal.

If anything emerges during the due diligence process which has or might have an impact on the business of the target, the price can be renegotiated or specific indemnities sought, backed up if necessary by a retention of a suitable amount placed in an escrow account.

Warranties are intended to:

- focus the mind of sellers to disclose matters that are inconsistent with the warranties, and provide another level of information gathering in addition to the due diligence process;
- provide the buyer with a remedy – a claim in damages – if the warranty later proves to be untrue and the buyer has thereby suffered loss.

Too often sellers are confronted with a standard 40-page warranty schedule, much of which is inappropriate for the business being sold. Therefore, buyers should discuss with their lawyer which warranties are key to the target's business, and in light of this, adapt the standard schedule.

The difference between warranties and indemnities is that a breach of warranty will only give rise to a successful claim in damages if the buyer can show that the warranty was breached, and that the effect of the breach is to reduce the value of the target. The onus is on the buyer to prove the breach *and* the loss it has suffered. The buyer's loss is not always easy to prove. The principle is that the loss suffered by the buyer generally is the difference between the price paid for the target and the price that the buyer would have paid with the warranty breached. Some breaches of warranties (such as failure to disclose a litigation dispute with an ex-employee) might have little impact on the target's sustainable profits and hence its value and the price the buyer would have paid, whereas an overstatement of profits in the accounts or the failure to disclose a patent challenge might go to the heart of the company's valuation. A buyer might also have to prove that the breach had not been 'fairly disclosed' in the disclosure letter, or that it and its advisers were not aware of the matter at the time of the acquisition.

An indemnity, on the other hand, is a promise to reimburse the buyer in respect of a particular type of liability should it arise. The purpose of an indemnity is to provide the buyer with a pound for pound remedy, where a breach of an equivalent warranty may not give rise to the same level of damages and involve the buyer in establishing the level of damages it has suffered.

Indemnities are usually sought against tax liabilities of the target to the extent that they are not provided for in the warranted accounts have not arisen on profits arising in the normal course of business since the balance sheet date. Indemnities are also often sought for specific risks that have been identified in the course of due diligence. For example, if the target is involved in a dispute with a former employee who has alleged unfair dismissal and racial discrimination, it would be fairly common for the buyer to insist on an indemnity against the costs of defending the proceedings and a successful claim. In addition, the buyer might seek to withhold from the purchase price the maximum liability that could arise under the indemnity as security for payment. In these situations the seller should insist that the amount is paid into an escrow account operated on the joint instructions of its and the buyer's lawyers.

In practice, difficulties often arise in litigation over indemnities, with the buyer being keen to resolve outstanding disputes and to draw on the indemnity fund, and the seller keen to minimize the expense. Share purchase agreements ought therefore to set out precise rules as to how the litigation is to be managed, the costs and fees incurred and the mechanism for agreeing a settlement. Better still would be for the seller, if possible, to resolve outstanding litigation before a sale rather than be faced with a retention based on the worst case scenario.

Who gives warranties?

Where the target is a subsidiary company or where it is owned exclusively by the executive team, the seller or sellers will be the warrantors. However, where there are a number of sellers, some of whom might not be actively involved in the business, or trustees, institutions or charities, the position is less clear-cut.

Shareholders who have not been involved in the business might either be reluctant to give any warranties, or at the very least, insist that their maximum liability is limited to their share of the consideration and to a proportionate part of any claim.

Trustees commonly either refuse to give warranties, or limit their liability to an amount not exceeding the after-tax consideration they receive. Where there are significant trustee sellers, discussions should take place with them at an early stage to see what, if any, level of warranty liability they will agree other than as to title. Sometimes the outcome is that sellers who have been actively involved in the business have to bear a greater proportion of the liability, that liability is layered, or a proportion of the consideration is retained for a period.

Where there are multiple sellers, a buyer will usually require that the liability of the sellers be joint and several. The effect of this is that the buyer can sue any one or more or the sellers for the full amount of the damages arising from the breach of warranty, and the seller who is sued for the full amount will be entitled to seek a contribution from the other sellers under the Civil Liability (Contribution) Act 1978. However, rather than leaving the court to decide what contributions are 'just and reasonable', sellers normally agree a contribution agreement among themselves. This sets out how the liability is to be apportioned and the decision-making process for handling a warranty claim.

Limitation of seller's liability under warranties

There are various standard and accepted ways for a seller to limit its liabilities under the warranties. The main ways are the following:

- *Disclosures:* to make disclosures in the disclosure letter written by either the seller or the seller's lawyer to the buyer or the buyer's lawyer. The purpose is to disclose specific items to the buyer which qualify the warranties and which would, if not disclosed, result in a breach of warranty. The matters disclosed should be sufficiently detailed that the buyer can reasonably assess the implications of the disclosure.
- *Time limits:* a variety of time limits within which a claim must be brought are invariably included, and this is a matter for negotiation. Two to three years tends to be the norm for notification of a claim (and then a period following which a claim must be brought or the right lapses), or a date which allows for one or two audits to be completed. Tax claims tend to be for seven years.

- *Financial limits:* it is standard practice to include a variety of financial limits: minimum limits both for individual claims and the aggregate of claims (usually around 1 per cent of the consideration) below which a buyer cannot bring a claim; a cap normally equal to the consideration paid (though where the consideration is nominal and other obligations are assumed by the buyer, such as the repayment of a substantial shareholder's loan, the limit should reflect the level of commitment or risk being assumed by the buyer).

Specialists in Mergers and Acquisitions

"Star performer for mergers and acquisitions deals."

Legal Business: Corporate Review 2006

We advise UK and multinational companies at all levels within the mergers and acquisitions sector. To find out more about how we can help your business, please contact David Wilkinson on david.wilkinson@ffw.com.

"A class act from start to finish... one of the best kept secrets in the law world."

Senior corporate finance partner, 'Big Four' accountancy firm

Legal documentation: where to start

David Wilkinson, Field Fisher Waterhouse

The 'typical' transaction

A typical M&A transaction will involve either a *share sale*, when the buyer acquires the shares in a company (the target) with all of its existing assets and liabilities in place, or a *business sale*, where rather than buying the target itself, the buyer acquires assets and liabilities of the target's underlying business. The buyer might acquire all of the assets and liabilities associated with the target's business, but more typically it 'cherry picks' only those assets and liabilities that it wants to take on.

In putting the deal together, it will be important to agree early in the negotiations on which structure is to be adopted, as this can have a significant effect on the willingness of either party to do the deal. Various factors will need to be taken into account. These will include:

- *Existence of unknown/unquantifiable liabilities*. If the buyer perceives that there is a significant risk that the target company has significant unknown, and perhaps unquantifiable, liabilities, the buyer is more likely to want a business sale. This will then allow the buyer to limit the extent to which it will take on liabilities associated with the target's business.
- *Tax consequences for the buyer*. The most significant of these relates to the amount of stamp duty/stamp duty land tax that is payable on the sale. For example, in the UK, stamp duty on the purchase of shares in a company is 0.5 per cent of the consideration, whereas stamp duty land tax on the purchase of a property ranges from 0 per cent to 4 per cent. Thus, at its simplest, if a company

is worth say £10 million and one of its assets is a freehold property worth £10 million, the stamp duty on the purchase of the shares in the company will be £50,000 whereas on a business sale the stamp duty land tax on the purchase of the property element of the assets will be £400,000. (For further details see Chapter 3.6.)

■ *Tax consequences for the seller.* Often a business sale is much less tax efficient for a seller than a share sale. (For further details see Chapter 3.6)

■ *Disentangling the business from other businesses.* If the business to be acquired is owned by a company that also carries on other business activities, it might be necessary for the buyer to acquire just the target business. Otherwise, if the buyer were to acquire the company, the seller would need to strip out the other activities prior to the sale taking place.

While there are some similarities between the issues that each type of transaction raises, there are also differences. Each type of transaction is therefore considered separately in the following two chapters. However, regardless of the type of transaction, before getting to the point of documenting the deal, it is likely that two key documents will need to be prepared, namely a 'confidentiality letter' and a 'heads of terms'.

Confidentiality letter

No seller should proceed very far with any discussions concerning a possible sale until the buyer has signed a confidentiality letter (also known as a non-disclosure agreement or NDA). As part of the discussions, the buyer is likely to want to see a lot of confidential information relating to the target. The seller will want the buyer to undertake to keep this information confidential.

Although a confidentiality letter should always be put in place, a seller should not over-estimate the value of the protection which it affords. If the buyer breaches the restrictions in the letter, it may be very difficult for the seller to prove this or to show any quantifiable loss. Even if this is possible, it might be very costly to pursue the buyer through the courts. For this reason sellers should always think very carefully about the nature of the information that they disclose to any potential buyer. Any 'crown jewels' type information, such as pricing of customer contracts, should either: be withheld from the buyer until the deal has been done, or at least until the buyer has convinced the seller that the deal is going to happen; or made anonymous so that the buyer obtains the information it needs to consider whether to proceed with the deal, but does not gain enough information to enable it to poach the seller's customers.

The typical elements of a confidentiality letter and the issues which arise in relation to them are as follows.

The obligation of confidentiality

This will normally only be imposed on the buyer, as it is the seller that will be providing information about its business to the buyer. However, if the buyer will be disclosing detailed information about its business to the seller (perhaps because the seller will also be becoming a shareholder in the buyer on conclusion of the transaction), then the confidentiality obligation should cut both ways.

When drafting the confidentiality obligation, it is normal to ensure that it covers all information provided to the party accepting the obligation (regardless of when it is provided). In reality some information will often have passed between the parties in advance of the confidentiality letter being signed.

Typically there will be a number of carve-outs from the confidentiality obligation so that it will not apply to:

- information already in the recipient's hands prior to its receipt from the other party;
- information that is already in the public domain, or that subsequently comes into the public domain other than as a result of a breach of the confidentiality obligation;
- information required to be disclosed by law (for example as a result of a court order or in the course of a regulatory investigation),or under the rules of some regulatory body to which the relevant party is subject (such as the rules of the London Stock Exchange).

Non-disclosure of the discussions

Typically neither party will want the existence of the potential deal to be made public until formal sale documents have been entered into. Thus both parties will normally agree to keep the existence of the discussions confidential.

No poaching of staff

If the seller discloses employee information to the buyer, the seller will be concerned to ensure that the information is used solely for the purposes of considering the potential transaction and not for identifying employees that the buyer can then seek to poach. Thus it would be normal for the seller to impose some form of restrictive covenant on the buyer to prevent it from employing the seller's staff during the period of any discussions and for a further period thereafter. Typical points that are up for debate in any such restrictive covenant are for how long the restriction should last in the event of the discussions breaking down, and whether the buyer should be prevented from employing an individual who independently approaches the buyer or responds to a general job advert.

Heads of terms

Once the parties have agreed the key elements of the deal, it is usual for them to enter into heads of terms. These are intended to be a short written document outlining the main terms of the transaction that the parties have agreed upon 'in principle'. They are also known as 'letters of intent' and 'memoranda of understanding', and typically, in addition to setting out the main terms, will set out the proposed timetable for the transaction. The form of these heads of terms varies considerably, from a simple letter to a detailed document.

Normally the heads of terms are not meant to have any legal force. Therefore, they do not prevent either party from changing its mind later in the sale process. Nevertheless, the fact that each party will have signed up to the document does provide the heads of terms with a degree of moral force.

Although the heads of terms are not meant to be legally binding, they are sometimes structured so that they do include a few legally binding provisions which apply to the way in which the sale process will be conducted (as opposed to the terms of the eventual deal). These terms might cover, for example, the grant of a period of exclusivity for the buyer, during which the seller will agree not to negotiate or conduct talks with any other person in connection with an alternative deal, and the payment of a break fee to cover the other party's wasted costs, if one party pulls out of the transaction for no good reason.

The key issues to consider when drafting the heads of terms are as follows.

Subject to contract

The nature of the heads of terms is that they only set out the key elements of the deal, and they are not supposed to bind the parties to proceed with it. Although putting 'subject to contract' at the start of the document can help in this regard, it is not the best approach. This is because there may well be provisions in the heads of terms (such as any provisions as to confidentiality, exclusivity and break fees) which the parties do want to be legally binding. Thus the words 'subject to contract' can create confusion because some parts of the document are not 'subject to contract'. By far the best approach is to have a paragraph at the end of the heads of terms, which states specifically which paragraphs are legally binding and which are not.

Focus only on key terms

It is very easy to get bogged down in the detail when agreeing the heads of terms. This should be avoided because, unless points are to be negotiated to their final conclusion, you will only find that you end up negotiating the points again once you start negotiating the formal sale documents. It is better to try to keep to high-level key principles. In short, anything that is fundamental to either party's willingness to do the deal should be included. In the context of a typical deal these might encompass:

- what is being sold;
- the consideration and the form that this is to take (such as cash, shares, loan notes);
- the timing of when the consideration is to be paid;
- any price adjustment mechanisms;
- whether there are to be any warranties/indemnities, and if so, who will give them and whether they are to be those that are usual for the type of deal;
- any retention from the purchase price that is to be held back by the buyer to cover potential warranty and indemnity claims;
- whether there are to be any restrictive covenants, and if so, who they will apply to and whether their period or scope is to be different from the norm;
- the terms of any exclusivity that is to be granted to the potential buyer;
- the terms of any break fee;
- any key issues that are departures from the norm for a business/share sale;
- the timetable for the transaction.

Exclusivity

Many buyers will insist that once they have signed the heads of terms, they are given a period of exclusivity in which to conduct negotiations and due diligence. Their argument is that at this point they will start to incur substantial costs, and they are not prepared to do this if it is easy for the seller to walk away from the deal.

Any seller should be wary about granting exclusivity. As soon as it is granted, the balance of the negotiating advantage tips towards the buyer. Other potential buyers that the seller has been talking to are likely to notice that the seller is no longer talking to them. If the seller starts talking to them again, they will guess that this is because there has been a problem with the seller's preferred deal. This is likely to cause the other potential buyers to harden their negotiating stance because they will realize that the seller no longer has as many potential buyers available to it, and they will fear that there must have been something wrong with the business to cause the preferred buyer to pull out.

If a seller is going to grant a period of exclusivity to the buyer, then from the seller's perspective the period should be kept as short as possible. This will then limit the ability of the buyer to exploit its new-found negotiating advantage, and also keep the buyer focused on doing the deal as quickly as possible.

Break fees

Neither party wants to incur the costs of trying to formalize a deal only to find that it collapses because the other side has changed its mind. Thus the buyer may ask the seller to agree that, if the seller withdraws from the transaction or the buyer finds out anything untoward during due diligence that causes the buyer to terminate the negotiations, the seller should pay the buyer a break fee to cover its wasted costs. Equally a seller may ask the buyer to show its commitment to the process by agreeing that, if the buyer withdraws from the negotiations, the buyer will pay the seller a break fee to cover the seller's wasted costs.

The idea sounds simple. The reality is very different. A well-advised seller would want to ensure, for example, that it is not tied in to the buyer in the event that the buyer seeks to change the terms of the deal, and that the buyer cannot claim a break fee after walking away from the negotiations for a spurious reason. Equally, if the buyer walks away from the deal after finding out something during due diligence that the buyer considers to be important, but the seller considers spurious, the buyer will not want to find that it has to pay a break fee to the seller. The end result is that break fee provisions are very difficult to draft with certainty, and are not the norm in private company M&A transactions.

The next step

Once the confidentiality letter and the heads of terms have been put in place, attention will then move to detailed due diligence (See Chapter 4.6) and agreement of the formal sale documents. Those required for a share sale are considered in Chapter 4.4, and those for a business sale in Chapter 4.5.

4.4

Legal documentation: purchase of a company (share sale)

David Wilkinson, Field Fisher Waterhouse

Deal structures

There are two main ways of acquiring a company: via a takeover offer or via a share sale agreement. The former is used in the context of companies that have a large number of shareholders (generally these will be quoted companies), where it is not practical to expect that the shareholders will come together to sign an agreement for the sale of the company. By contrast share sale agreements involve a contract between the existing shareholders and the buyer, under which the latter agrees to acquire the relevant shares.

The issues that arise on each type of deal are quite different. As most companies are sold by way of a share sale agreement, this chapter will focus on the issues raised by transactions involving such an agreement.

The 'key' documents

The documents for a share sale are built around three key documents, namely:

- *The share sale agreement.* This sets out the obligation of the seller to sell and the buyer to buy at the price set out in the agreement. Normally the share sale agreement will also include one or more schedules of warranties which are given by the seller to the buyer about the state of the company to be acquired (the target).
- *The tax deed.* This provides that if the target has any unexpected tax liabilities which arise as a result of pre-completion activities, then the seller will compensate the buyer for these.
- *The disclosure letter.* This is the buyer's opportunity to point out those issues relating to the target that it wants the seller to be aware of and that, by virtue of them being included in the disclosure letter, cannot later form the basis of a claim under the warranties included in the share sale agreement.

Each of these documents is considered further in this chapter.

Ancillary documents

In addition to the key documents referred to above, there can be a long list of other documents required to implement a share sale transaction. Many of these are standard and uncontroversial. Examples of these additional documents include:

- New employment agreements for the sellers/key employees.
- An ongoing supply of services agreement between the seller and the target. These are particularly common where the target is part of a larger group of companies and its business has relied on certain support provided by other group companies (for instance for IT support/maintenance, HR management, payroll management, sales distribution). In this case, the buyer may want this support to continue for a period of time to enable it to prepare the target for operating on a stand-alone basis or for being absorbed into the buyer's group.
- A new lease which might need to be granted to the target, where it occupies a property owned by the seller or another member of its group, and the buyer wishes to remain in occupation for a period of time. Alternatively the buyer might simply buy the freehold of the property or take over the existing lease at the same time as it acquires the shares in the target.
- Administrative documents required to implement the transaction. These will include board minutes approving the transaction and appointing the buyer's nominees as directors, secretary, auditors etc; resignation letters from those of the existing directors, secretary and auditors of the target who are standing down on completion of the sale; stock transfer forms for the actual transfer of shares; and any necessary forms that need to be filed at the Companies Registry as a result of changes that occur on completion of the sale.

The share sale agreement

What does it involve?

The share sale agreement is quite a complex document. In addition to setting out the basic obligation of the seller to sell and the buyer to buy the shares in the target, the agreement will typically include some or all of the following elements:

- details of the shares being sold;
- details of the price to be paid for the shares and any price adjustments that might occur after completion of the deal;
- restrictive covenants by which the seller agrees not to compete with the buyer once the target has been sold;
- any warranties that the seller gives to the buyer;
- any conditions (for example the obtaining of tax or competition law clearances) that need to be satisfied prior to completion of the deal;
- arrangements for the transfer of pension funds where the employees of the target are part of a final salary pension scheme and will be transferring over to the buyer's pension scheme following completion of the deal (this is a complex area which is considered further in Chapter 1.6).

The shares being sold

It is self-evident that the share sale agreement will need to specify exactly what shares are to be sold by the seller to the buyer. This is normally a simple part of the agreement. However, the buyer will want to ensure, through its own investigations and through appropriate protections in the agreement, that:

- where the buyer is supposed to be acquiring all of the shares in the target, there are no other shares in issue nor any options which bind the target and would entitle any person to subscribe for further shares in the target after completion of the deal;
- where the buyer is only acquiring some of the shares in the target, none of the remaining shareholders in the target will have any rights of first refusal to buy the shares being sold, and that the buyer has certainty as to the proportion of shares in the target that it will end up with after completion (after taking into account any options which may have been issued for others to subscribe for shares in the target);
- the shares in the target are owned by the seller and that it is not restricted from selling the shares, for example, as a result of their being used as security for any borrowing by the seller;
- the share sale agreement makes clear whether the shares are being sold with any accrued but unpaid dividend entitlement.

The price

The pricing provisions in the share sale agreement are crucial, and often raise issues far beyond answering the question of 'How much?' In addition to this question, it is necessary to consider the following.

What form will the price take?

Will the price all be paid in cash? Sometimes buyers may seek to pay for their acquisitions using a mixture of cash and shares in the buyer. From the seller's point of view, the possibility of part of the price being satisfied in shares raises numerous other issues, including:

■ *How easy is it to turn any shares into cash?* If the buyer is an unlisted company, this might be very difficult. If it is listed, it might be a bit easier provided that there is sufficient liquidity in the shares. However, even then, depending on the size of the shareholding that the seller will receive, the buyer may impose certain restrictions on the seller's ability to sell the shares (at least in the short term). A one or even two-year restriction would not be unusual.

■ *Do the shares represent sufficient value for the seller?* If the seller is taking shares instead of cash, then it will want to know how much these shares are likely to be worth. For listed companies this is relatively simple to work out, as the shares will have a quoted market price. However, for unlisted companies, and indeed smaller listed companies, the seller will want to do its own due diligence into the buyer to check that there are no hidden problems with the buyer which may affect the value of the shares. The seller may also seek certain warranties from the buyer, or the shareholders in the buyer, about the buyer's financial standing.

■ *What influence will the seller have over the buyer going forward?* The seller may go from being in control over the target to being a minority shareholder in the buyer. Unless the buyer is a listed company, the seller may want a shareholders' agreement to be put in place. Under this the seller and the existing shareholders in the buyer would agree certain matters regarding the ongoing management of the buyer, and certain rights in favour of the seller to ensure that its position as a minority shareholder is not abused.

■ *Does the buyer have necessary shareholder approvals in place to enable it to issue shares?* While it is easy to obtain these quickly in the case of private companies owned by a small number of shareholders, there is a time-consuming process to go through in the case of listed companies. This would need to be established in the course of agreeing the timetable for the transaction.

When is the price to be paid?

Often the whole of the price is paid to the buyer on completion of the deal. However, in some cases, the price will be paid in instalments. The latter is preferable from a buyer's point of view, because payment by instalments helps to smooth the cashflow impact of the transaction. If instalments are proposed, it will be important for the seller to satisfy itself over the ability of the buyer to pay the later elements of the price as they fall due. In extreme cases, a seller might consider asking for some sort of security (such as a charge over the shares in the target) to protect itself from the credit risk in the buyer.

Is the amount of the price linked to future performance of the target?

If the price is to be paid in instalments, the buyer will want to establish whether each instalment is fixed or will fluctuate by reference to the future performance of the target. If linked to performance, then the future instalments are often referred to as 'earn-out consideration'. Drafting and negotiating provisions relating to an earn-out is a complex task, and various questions will need to be addressed including:

■ *What will be the targets against which the earn-out consideration will be assessed?* Often, they will be set by reference to the profitability or turnover of the target in a set period following completion. In either case, it will be important to establish the accounting policies that will be used to determine whether profitability/turnover targets have been met. This is a crucial area. Slight changes in the policies for depreciation, bad debt provision, income recognition and so on could have a dramatic effect on the level of profitability/turnover of the target, and therefore whether or not the earn-out consideration is payable.

■ *What control will the seller have over whether or not the targets are met?* No seller is likely to agree to an earn-out arrangement unless the seller will remain involved (for instance, as managing director) in the ongoing operation of the target and will be in a position to influence whether targets are met. In addition, sellers are likely to seek to impose restrictions on the buyer to ensure that it does not seek to manipulate the target's performance so as to reduce the amount of the earn-out consideration. These restrictions, which will often run to a number of pages, will be a sensitive area of the negotiations, as the buyer will not want to be restricted in how it can run the target after completion.

■ *Is the earn-out consideration really disguised remuneration for the services of the seller?* Where there is an earn-out consideration, the seller will often remain employed by the target after completion of the deal. HM Revenue & Customs will therefore be keen to establish whether the earn-out consideration is truly consideration for the sale of the shares in the target or whether it is in fact remuneration for the services provided by the seller after completion.

In the UK remuneration is taxed at the seller's marginal rate of tax (normally 40 per cent, at 2006/7 rates) and also attracts national insurance. In contrast, consideration on the sale of shares is taxed at capital gains tax rates (for individuals this will often be an effective 10 per cent at 2006/7 rates, assuming that the seller is entitled to full taper relief). Accordingly, there is a large incentive for the seller to have the earn-out consideration taxed as consideration, and even to structure the seller's post-sale remuneration so that it is expressed to be payable in connection with the sale of shares in the target.

HM Revenue & Customs are alive to this sort of 'tax planning' and retain the right to tax any 'remuneration' element of the earn-out consideration as if it were normal remuneration. Factors that they will take into account in deciding whether the earn-out consideration is actually disguised remuneration are:
- whether the payment of the earn-out consideration is dependant upon the seller remaining employed by the target post-completion;
- whether the level of the seller's salary post-completion is less than the level of the seller's salary prior to completion.

This is a complex area and one in which tax advice will need to be obtained.

Will there be any 'post-sale' adjustments to the price?

To avoid the risk of material changes in the business since its last audited accounts, or of the seller 'asset-stripping' the business immediately prior to the sale, a buyer will normally agree to pay a certain price based on the target having a certain level of assets at the time of completion of the deal. Accordingly, after completion a balance sheet for the target will be drawn up and the level of assets assessed. If they are less than the target figure, the price will normally be adjusted downwards on a pound for pound basis. If they are greater, then normally a seller will insist that the price is increased on a similar basis. However, not all buyers will agree to this. They will argue that the adjustment mechanism is a protection for the buyer and not a means of earning additional consideration for the seller.

Restrictive covenants

No buyer will want to acquire the target and then find that the seller immediately sets up a new business competing with the target. To prevent this, buyers will often insist that the seller agrees to comply with certain restrictive covenants for a fixed period after completion of the deal. While some buyers will instinctively ask the seller to agree to quite onerous restrictive covenants which last for a long period after completion, this is not a sensible approach.

In the UK restrictive covenants are seen as anti-competitive. They are only enforceable if the buyer can show that they are reasonable and no more onerous than is reasonably necessary to protect the goodwill of the target in the period of transition of ownership to the buyer. This is a complex area. What is acceptable will depend on the facts of a particular case. However, as a general rule restrictive covenants that last for up to two years after completion are considered to be acceptable.

Warranties

This is one of the most hotly negotiated areas of the share sale agreement. A buyer will set its price based on certain assumptions about the state of the target's business and the information that the seller has shown to the buyer during due diligence. As only the seller will be able to say conclusively whether these assumptions are correct and the information is accurate, the buyer will only be prepared to pay the price if the seller warrants that they are correct/accurate. The warranties will cover all aspects of the target's business including:

- accuracy of financial information;
- ownership of assets;
- nature and extent of contracts;
- absence or otherwise of any disputes;
- employment and pensions arrangements;
- extent to which there have been any recent material changes to the target's business;
- intellectual property;
- existence of appropriate licences;
- share structure and ownership of the target.

If any of the warranties turn out to be untrue, and the relevant facts were not disclosed in the disclosure letter (see below), then the buyer will have a financial remedy against the seller and the price will be reduced to take account of the fact that the target is not worth as much as the buyer had thought. If a seller is not prepared to give the warranties (and some sellers, such as liquidators, are not), then the buyer will discount its price to take account of the increased risk of the deal.

The extent and scope of the warranties will depend on the circumstances of the deal. However, a seller would normally only expect to give warranties about the state of the target's business at the time of completion of the deal, and not about what might happen in the future. It would also expect that there are certain limitations on the buyer's ability to bring claims. These limitations might include:

- A restriction on the time period within which claims can be brought. Seven years for tax matters and between one and three years for other matters is not unusual.
- A cap on the amount the buyer can claim. This is usually set at the amount of the price (paid for the target) but there are circumstances where the seller might be able to negotiate a lower figure.
- Limitations so that claims cannot be brought for trivial amounts and so that the aggregate value of all claims must exceed a set threshold before any claims can be brought.
- Exclusions so that claims cannot be brought where they arise as a result of things that the buyer has done after completion, or as a result of changes in law, tax rates and/or accounting policy of the target.
- The right for the seller to step in and try to mitigate the consequences of any breach of warranty. For example, if, as a result of the circumstances giving rise to the breach of warranty, the target has a claim against any third party, the seller will want to have the right to take over control of that claim. This is because any amount recovered from the third party is likely to reduce the amount payable by the seller.

■ An exclusion so that no claim can be brought where there was a provision for the subject matter of the claim in any balance sheet that was used for the purposes of setting the price.

While a buyer might feel very pleased with itself for negotiating a very extensive set of warranties, it should always bear in mind that these warranties only have any value if they provide a meaningful remedy. The warranties will be worthless if the buyer cannot find the seller or if the seller, at the relevant time, does not have the necessary financial resources to meet the claim. This is a particular risk area where the seller is an individual or a small company.

To protect the buyer against this risk, the buyer will often insist that a certain proportion of the price is retained on completion of the deal for a sufficient period of time to allow the buyer to assess whether the warranties are true or untrue. The period of such a retention will vary from deal to deal. As a general rule, a period of 6 to 18 months is not unusual.

The retention of part of the price creates a credit risk for the seller. It will want to ensure that the necessary funds are available for payment to the seller in the event that no warranty claims materialize. To protect itself in these circumstances, the seller will often insist that the retained element is paid into an account (often referred to as an 'escrow account') in the joint names of the solicitors for both the buyer and the seller. This will ensure that the funds will be available for meeting any warranty claim, but will also be available for payment to the seller in the event that there are no such claims within the period of the retention.

Conditions to the deal

Often deals will complete immediately after the share sale agreement is signed, so the shares in the target pass immediately from the seller to the buyer. In other cases, there will be a gap while certain conditions are satisfied. This is particularly common on larger, more complex deals.

The conditions to a deal will depend on the circumstances of that particular transaction. Examples might include obtaining of competition or regulatory approvals, tax clearances, obtaining approval of the shareholders of the seller and/or the buyer, or obtaining approval to the transfer of certain licences which are needed for the ongoing operation of the target's business.

If conditions are proposed, then the parties need to be aware of the risks that they pose. Prior to signing a conditional sale agreement, the seller has complete discretion over whether or not to sell the target and to whom. However, once the deal has been signed, the seller has tied itself to the buyer and will want to ensure that any conditions are satisfied as quickly as possible, and that the conditions are not framed in such a way as to give the buyer an opportunity to walk away from the deal after signing.

To protect against this risk, both parties are normally contractually required to take such steps as are within their power to ensure that the conditions are satisfied as soon as is reasonably practicable, and the conditions will normally be framed in such a way as to ensure that the seller and the buyer have no or limited discretion to decide whether or not they have been satisfied.

Although a conditional agreement poses risks for the seller, it also poses risks for the buyer. It will have agreed to acquire the target on the basis of the facts existing at the time that the agreement was entered into. The buyer will be keen to ensure that the seller does not do anything to change these in the gap between exchange of the share sale agreement and completion of the deal. Accordingly, the seller will normally be required to agree to various restrictions on how the business is operated in the intervening period. The buyer might also seek to require the seller to repeat the warranties at the time of completion. However, while this is common in some jurisdictions, it is not so common in the UK.

The tax deed

The tax deed is a very complex document which is normally negotiated by tax lawyers, and which many sellers either do not read or find too complicated to understand. However, the principles behind the tax deed are not that complicated.

If there are any unexpected tax problems associated with the target, the buyer will, quite fairly, expect that the price is reduced by an amount equal to the consequential tax liability. The complications arise around the definition of when a tax problem is unexpected, and also in quantifying the extent of that problem. In general terms, the problem will be unexpected where it was not provided for in the last set of statutory accounts for the target, or where it has arisen as a result of transactions outside the ordinary course of business of the target following the preparation of those accounts.

On one analysis, assessing the extent of any tax problem is simple. It is whatever amount the target has to pay to HM Revenue & Customs as a result of the problem. However, tax problems will not necessarily involve any payment having to be made. For example, the tax problem might be:

■ the failure to recover a tax rebate which had been assumed in setting the price;
■ the failure to obtain some tax deduction or tax relief as a result of things which have happened prior to completion of the deal;
■ the use of tax reliefs or tax deductions available to the target as a result of the operation of the target after completion, and which the buyer would expect would be available for setting off against post-sale profits and not pre-sale problems;
■ the unavailability of pre-sale tax losses which the buyer had assumed would be available for setting off against future profits.

The tax deed will therefore contain various provisions for assessing the extent of the tax problem in all of the circumstances in which a tax problem might be considered to arise. As with the warranties, the tax deed will also contain lengthy provisions limiting the ability of the buyer to bring claims under the tax deed. These are likely to be similar in nature to those that apply for the purposes of limiting claims under the warranties.

The disclosure letter

Normally the warranties will be expressed as certain absolute statements, for example, 'The target is not involved in any litigation', 'The target owns all fixed assets used in the operation of its business', or 'All long-term or onerous contracts that the target is a party to have been disclosed to the buyer'. These statements may not be true in a given case. Rather than insert suitable qualifications in each warranty, the transaction will normally be structured on the basis that the seller will write a letter (known as a 'disclosure letter') to the buyer to disclose facts that exist in relation to the target and that contradict any of the warranties. No claim can then be brought under the warranties in respect of any matter disclosed in the disclosure letter.

As far as the seller is concerned, preparation of the disclosure letter is one of the most boring, yet important, aspects of the sale process. It involves a line-by-line analysis of each of the warranties (which often run to more than 50 pages) to consider what needs to be disclosed to the buyer. This is because it is only by including something within the disclosure letter that the seller can be sure that the buyer cannot subsequently bring a warranty claim in respect of that matter.

The buyer will need to study the disclosure letter carefully to ensure that the seller is not using the disclosure letter as a 'back door' means of qualifying the warranties. Buyers should therefore insist that any 'disclosures' in the disclosure letter are such that the buyer can properly understand the nature of the disclosure and also the financial consequences of whatever is being disclosed.

Closing the deal

The completion of a share sale is normally a fairly mechanical process, although many buyers and sellers are often surprised by the number of documents involved. This is because they forget the need for other documents including stock transfer forms, share certificates, board minutes for the buyer, the seller and the target, resignation letters for any people who will cease to be directors/the secretary/the auditors of the target, forms for filing at the Companies Registry, and new bank mandates for the target. Indeed it would not be unusual for there to be over a hundred of these extra documents on a more complicated transaction!

Legal documentation: purchase of a business (business sale)

David Wilkinson, Field Fisher Waterhouse

The nature of a business sale

A business sale involves the sale of assets and liabilities relating to the business to be sold (the 'target'). This contrasts with a share sale which involves the transfer of the shares in the corporate vehicle which owns the assets and liabilities of the target. Although what is being sold under each type of sale is very different, there are a number of similarities between the legal documents used. For this reason it is useful for readers also to read Chapter 4.4 (Legal documentation: purchase of a company (share sale)), as this chapter will cross-refer to that chapter where the issues are the same.

The 'key' documents

The key documents for a business sale will be:

■ *The business sale agreement.* This sets out the obligation of the seller to sell and the buyer to buy the business at the price set out in, or determined in accordance with, the agreement. As with a share sale agreement, the business sale agreement will normally include one or more schedules of warranties which are given by the seller to the buyer about the state of the business to be acquired (the target).

■ *The disclosure letter.* This performs the same function as the disclosure letter in a share sale, and is the seller's opportunity to point out issues about the target so that these cannot later form the basis of a claim under the warranties.

The business sale agreement is considered further below. The issues arising in relation to the disclosure letter are similar to those set out in the relevant section of Chapter 4.4 in relation to share sales.

How does a business sale agreement work?

The target will be made up of a collection of assets and liabilities. These will include:

■ tangible assets, such as land, buildings, machinery, plant, tables, chairs, equipment and vehicles;

■ intangible assets, such as goodwill, customer and supplier contracts, employment contracts, book debts, intellectual property (such as copyright, patents and trademarks), licences for the operation of the business and rights to bring claims against third parties for wrongs done to the business prior to completion of the sale;

■ liabilities such as obligations under contracts, borrowings, amounts payable to suppliers and liabilities for wrongs done by the business prior to completion of the sale.

In drafting the business sale agreement, it is necessary to consider each of these and to decide whether or not they are to transfer to the buyer. This makes the business sale agreement much more complex than a share sale agreement, which has to concern itself with the transfer of only one thing, namely the shares in the target company.

Similarities between a business sale agreement and a share sale agreement

Although a business sale agreement is a more complex document than a share sale agreement, there are a number of similarities in the issues that will need to be dealt with. For example, broadly similar issues will arise in relation to:

■ the nature and structure of, and possible adjustments to, the price;

■ any restrictive covenants that are to be given by the seller;

■ any warranties that are given by the seller to the buyer about the business being sold;

■ any conditions to the deal being done.

Each of these issues was considered in detail in Chapter 4.4 in relation to a share sale agreement. The legal considerations highlighted there apply equally in relation to a business sale agreement and are not explored further in this chapter.

Deciding which assets and liabilities are to be transferred

With a share sale agreement, all assets and liabilities associated with the target company remain with the company when it has been sold. In contrast, on a business sale, it is possible for a buyer to 'cherry pick' only those aspects of the target that the buyer wants to take on. In practice, this tends to lead to a desire to take all the assets but to leave behind as many of the liabilities as possible.

As even the best-run target is unlikely to have a list of every asset and every liability in the business, it is unlikely to be possible to identify what is to be sold by simply attaching a list to the business sale agreement. Instead, those items being sold will normally be identified by a combination of a specific list backed up by a generic description. From a buyer's point of view it is important to check the generic descriptions carefully, particularly the extent to which they describe (in detail) the liabilities that are to be transferred.

Transferring tangible assets

Ownership of many tangible assets will be transferred to the buyer simply by the buyer being given physical control of them on completion of the deal. However, further formalities are required in relation to some assets such as land, where it is necessary to prepare formal written transfers of the land, and in most cases register that transfer with the Land Registry. Accordingly, one of the completion obligations of the seller will be to deliver these formal transfers to the buyer on completion of the deal.

Transferring intangible assets

Generally, there will need to be formal written transfers in relation to the transfer of intangible assets. Where ownership of the relevant asset is not registered at any public registry, the formal transfer will normally be included in the business sale agreement. Nevertheless, additional documents will be needed for certain intangible assets. For example:

■ *Registered trademarks, patents and design rights*: a formal transfer agreement will be required and this must be registered at the appropriate registry.

■ *Book debts*: there will need to be a written agreement transferring the debts and (if the buyer wants to be able to sue for payment of the debt) notice of the transfer must be given to the person who owes the debt.

The target's contracts are an intangible asset that are not easy to transfer formally. Contracts are made up of both rights and liabilities or obligations. Depending on the terms of the contract, the seller may have an ability to assign the rights to the buyer. However, to transfer the liabilities or obligations, it will be necessary to obtain the consent of the counterparty to the contract. This means that to transfer the whole of the contract, it will be necessary to obtain the consent of the counterparty. The contract would then be transferred by way of an agreement (known as a 'novation agreement') to which the seller, the buyer and the counterparty are all signatories.

Many targets have hundreds, if not thousands, of contracts. These range from major customer and supplier contracts to smaller contracts for the purchase of office supplies and equipment. To transfer each of these contracts by way of a novation agreement would be extremely time-consuming and costly. Instead, buyers normally only seek to obtain a formal novation of particularly key long-term contracts. For other contracts, a buyer, while reserving the right to require the seller to cooperate in obtaining a novation agreement, will instead agree with the seller in the business sale agreement that, until such time as a novation agreement has been entered into, the seller will pass all benefits under the contract to the buyer, and the buyer will perform the relevant contract as the subcontractor of the seller and will indemnify (that is, compensate) the seller for any failure by the buyer to do this.

Transferring liabilities

Most liabilities of the target will arise out of its contracts. However, some will simply exist, for example those that arise as a result of negligence by the seller. Either way, the liability cannot be transferred without the consent of the person to whom the liability is owed. Where the liability forms part of a contract, it will be dealt with in the way described in the previous section. In other cases the buyer will, if the liability is to be transferred to the buyer, agree to satisfy the liability on behalf of the seller and indemnify the seller for any failure by the buyer to do this.

It is important that a seller understands that this indemnity arrangement does not release the seller from responsibility for the liability. The person to whom the liability is owed (the third party) can still sue the seller. The seller would then have to look to the buyer to satisfy the claim. However, if the buyer fails to do this, the seller will remain responsible to the third party. Sellers should not lose sight of this technicality. They should ensure that any buyer to whom they transfer liabilities as part of a business sale has the financial resources to meet its obligations under any indemnity. In cases of doubt, the seller might want to look for some form of security, such as a parent company guarantee.

Transferring employees

The position of employees in relation to a business sale is governed in the UK by the Transfer of Undertakings (Protection of Employment) Regulations 2006 (the 'Regulations'). The issues which arise out of the Regulations, and other related pieces of legislation, are extremely complex and could form a book on their own. Nevertheless the key issues are set out below.

When a business is sold, the Regulations will automatically transfer all of the employees engaged in that business to the buyer. The employees will transfer together with their contracts of employment and all rights and liabilities arising out of the employment relationship. This could include some claims that the employees may have had against their former employer. It is not possible to contract out of this, as it occurs automatically by operation of law. This creates a big risk area for the buyer. It will take on any employees and any liabilities to them (including liabilities for sex and race discrimination, personal injury and so on) regardless of whether the buyer knows about them.

To protect the buyer, a business sale agreement will normally include provisions that seek to apportion the liabilities and risks associated with the employees between the seller and the buyer. This will not affect the extent of the obligations assumed by the buyer. However, it will provide the buyer with a degree of financial remedy against the seller. Of course, the buyer will need to satisfy itself that the seller will have the ability to meet these financial obligations, and should if necessary consider withholding part of the purchase price while the relevant obligations are satisfied.

The way in which the employment-related provisions work is typically as follows:

■ The buyer agrees to assume responsibility for those employees that the seller specifically identifies to the buyer.

■ Although the buyer accepts responsibility for identified employees, the buyer normally expects the seller to agree to ensure that all pre-completion liabilities to these employees (for instance, for arrears of salary) are settled prior to completion, and to indemnify the buyer for pre-completion liabilities that come to light after completion.

■ The seller agrees that, if the buyer finds that the Regulations transfer more than just the specifically identified employees, the seller will indemnify the buyer for the liabilities that the buyer assumes in respect of these additional employees and any costs incurred in dismissing them.

The Regulations also seek to provide certain protections for the employees who may be affected by the transfer to the buyer. They do this in a number of ways, including:

■ *Continuity of employment*. The Regulations provide that the employee's period of continuous employment (which is relevant when calculating any redundancy pay, notice periods and the like) is unbroken, so that periods of employment with the seller will count towards the period that the employee is considered to have been employed by the buyer.

■ *Consultation with appropriate representatives.* The Regulations impose an obligation on both the seller and the buyer to provide information about the transfer to appropriate representatives of those of their respective employees who will be affected by the transfer. Appropriate representatives are a trade union (where one is recognized), pre-existing representatives (if appropriate) or representatives elected by the affected employees by secret ballot. There is an additional obligation to consult those representatives where 'measures' (actions, steps or arrangements connected with the transfer that may impact on the employees) are envisaged. Consultation must be 'with a view to seeking agreement'. If these obligations are not observed, a claim can be made in the Employment Tribunal for up to 13 weeks' pay for each affected employee.

■ *Provision of information.* To enable the buyer to manage the transferring employees properly, it is necessary for it to have certain information about them. The Regulations impose certain obligations on the seller to provide designated 'employee liability information' to the buyer at least two weeks in advance of the transfer taking place.

Pensions considerations

The use of a business sale instead of a share sale makes a big difference for the pension rights of transferring employees, and in some cases the pensions obligations of the employer. The easiest way to analyse pension arrangements for this purpose is to look at the implications of three different types of pension scheme:

■ *Final salary (or 'defined benefit') pension schemes sponsored by the employer*: these sometimes include generous early retirement or redundancy pensions;

■ *Money purchase (or 'defined contribution') pension schemes sponsored by the employer*: many of these were set up in the 1990s but they are a lot less popular now.

■ *Insurance-based pension arrangements*: these are always money purchase schemes, and include 'stakeholder' pension schemes, 'group personal pension plans' and individual pension plans. Employer contributions might be made to these schemes although there is no legal requirement for this.

Where employees are in either of the employer-sponsored schemes referred to above, the right to be in such schemes does not transfer (together with the employee's contract of employment) to the buyer under the Transfer of Undertakings (Protection of Employment) Regulations 2006 (the 'Regulations') as described above. Instead, pensions legislation provides that after the business sale, the employees will have rights under their employment contracts to pension contributions from their new employer of up to 6 per cent.

However, the employer can require that the employee matches any employer contributions, in which case if the employee wants to obtain the benefit of the full 6 per cent from the employer, the employee will also have to contribute 6 per cent of his/her own salary, thus giving total contributions of 12 per cent. Unlike employment rights protected by the Regulations, the employee and employer can contract out of this statutory right, for instance by providing the employee with higher pay in lieu of the employer pension contributions.

Rights to membership of, and contributions to, an insurance-based arrangement as set out in the third bullet point above are protected by the Regulations. The obligations on the seller to provide these will automatically transfer to the buyer under the Regulations.

There are special problems with early retirement and early redundancy pensions, as these are treated as employment rights protected by the Regulations and not pension rights. This is particularly difficult, as the pensions are usually provided through the employer scheme which will not transfer to the new employer. Further details are set out in Chapter 1.6.

Tax

With a share sale, the target company is acquired with all of its tax liabilities in place. On an asset sale things are simpler, as tax liabilities tend to be left behind for the seller to satisfy. Thus there is no need for the tax deed which is often a feature of a share sale transaction.

There are, however, two particular tax issues which often need consideration on a business sale. The first of these relates to how the consideration is to be apportioned across the assets being sold. This can be important for a variety of reasons, including the buyer's ability to claim capital allowances going forward, the extent to which the seller will be liable to repay any capital allowances already claimed and the amount of stamp duty that is payable.

On a share sale, stamp duty will normally be payable on the consideration paid for the shares at the rate of 0.5 per cent. On a business sale, the amount of tax/stamp duty paid for each asset that is transferred needs to be considered separately. If shares are included in the assets transferred, stamp duty will be payable at 0.5 per cent on the amount of the consideration apportioned to the shares. If land is transferred, stamp duty land tax of up to 4 per cent will be payable on the consideration apportioned to the land.

The second tax issue to remember relates to VAT. VAT is not payable on the consideration paid on a share sale. However, VAT is potentially payable on an asset sale, unless it is considered to be a 'transfer of a business as a going concern' (also known as a TOGC). Essentially, this means that there has to be a transfer of a clear business unit. If there is a TOGC, and the buyer is registered for VAT and will, immediately following completion, use the assets transferred for carrying on the relevant business, then no VAT will generally be payable. In most business sales the rules will be satisfied so that no VAT is payable. However, this should always be checked.

Closing the deal

As with a share sale, the completion of a business sale agreement is often quite a mechanical affair, and there will be a need for various ancillary documents. The number of these can be significantly more than in a share sale because of the need to prepare individual forms of transfer for particular assets. Additionally, while after a share sale the only task remaining is to pay stamp duty on the share transfer, on a business sale, stamp duty/stamp duty land tax may need to be paid on certain assets and the buyer will also need to set about registering the transfer of any assets (such as property, trademarks and patents) with the appropriate registry.

Due diligence

Peter Guinn, Alliotts

What due diligence is

Thorough due diligence answers the question of whether a deal is being done at the right time at the right price for the right reasons. It involves an investigation into the affairs of an entity (which may be a division, a company, a group of companies or some other form of business entity). It results in the production of a report detailing relevant data and points. The investigation is performed prior to the business's acquisition, flotation, restructuring or other transaction. The report will highlight key data in an executive summary to provide an overview of the entity's affairs, before then going into detail on the relevant aspects of the entity.

Due diligence is performed by many advisers on the team. For example there may be separate legal due diligence, financial due diligence, tax due diligence, environmental due diligence, commercial due diligence and information technology due diligence. Alliotts finds that although its key role is financial due diligence, items identified during our work are passed on to the other team members to assist them with their work. This then enables us to 'project manage' the assignment, keeping all team members on track to meet the timetable deadlines and minimize the risk of repetition of work.

From an Alliotts viewpoint, we see financial due diligence as a vital part of the deal process. It provides a wealth of information on the target business, some of which may have been totally unforeseen by the parties to the transaction. An unexpected synergy may be found, or a major problem in the accounting records may be uncovered.

Often a problem found during financial due diligence raises points to be dealt with by others involved in the deal process. For example, a review of the payroll systems may reveal a compliance problem that feeds into the warranties and

ALLIOTTS
CHARTERED ACCOUNTANTS
BUSINESS ADVISORS

Alliotts Corporate Finance

Driving Deals Forward

We are A team of dynamic, multi talented corporate finance experts with a proven record of achieving successful deals

Our portifolio UK SMEs through to international businesses

Our services

- Raising finance
- Buying businesses
- Selling businesses
- Due diligence
- Exit strategy and planning
- Mergers and Acquisitions

Our results tell the story of our success

Ian Gibbon/Peter Guinn

020 7759 9393

corporatefinance@alliotts.com

www.alliottscorporatefinance.com

Alliotts Chartered Accountants and Business Advisors

9 Kingsway, London WC2B 6XF
(other offices in Guildford and Harrow)

disclosure letter the lawyers draft. Or we may uncover an unusual lease obligation which then feeds into the legal due diligence. Certainly a good financial due diligence report helps buyers understand exactly what they are buying into, which may or may not be different from the picture they had formed of the deal.

What due diligence involves

Each transaction is different, and the extent and scope of the financial due diligence has to be tailored to fit the needs of the buyer. For example, a MBO may entail less due diligence in certain areas as the management have a full knowledge of the financial area concerned. By contrast, an MBI or venture capital investment may entail very thorough due diligence as the investing team will require full information on the target's financial affairs. However, broadly the work should cover:

- the history and commercial activities of the business;
- its organization structure and employees;
- its accounting policies;
- the information systems;
- a detailed review of financial statements;
- a review of the financial projections;
- anything else the team may uncover that is of relevance to the transaction.

History and commercial activities

The history and commercial activities review covers such things as historic milestones of the business, details of its shareholders and trading characteristics, and the influence of particular features of the industry sector. Such features may include legislative restrictions or freedoms, details of key competitors, the presence of any competitive technologies that may affect the business, and the need for any licences and the like. It also covers a review of the customer and supplier base, including identifying the key customers and suppliers, discovering pricing influences, trading seasonality, strength of contract terms and credit worthiness.

When they are on site reviewing these areas, the due diligence team will reveal the key customers and suppliers who do not have good contracts, or have pricing peculiarities, or have significant seasonality. Such features may not have been previously identified by the buyer. Problems with retention of title clauses on stocks, or extended credit afforded to certain customers, can all be uncovered. In some industry sectors customers may have retrospective discount clauses whereby the turnover threshold is exceeded post-deal with no provision having been made for the cost pre-deal.

The commercial activities review will also identify such things as key production processes, quality control issues, stock control issues and production planning issues. The review should highlight whether there are capacity problems, and whether efficiencies can be achieved post-deal.

The organization structure and employees

The organization structure and employees aspect of the review can identify management 'holes' where either pre- or post-deal a hole will appear that the buyer must plan to plug. Dependencies on key staff may become apparent, any problems in recruitment or training may be picked up, and unexpected trends in staff turnover may be uncovered. These days, pensions are a crucial aspect of any acquisition, and valuable financial information on pension commitments and other employee reward structures can be found and confirmed. Overall, the report will highlight the corporate culture and working environment, so the buyer can see whether there is a good fit between the parties, or get advance notice of a major culture clash.

Accounting policies

A through review of the application of accounting policies is vital. A trend of reducing gross margins could be masked by a change in the application of stock provisioning policies. A rising gross margin could be the result of a reallocation of costs to distribution or administration cost centres instead of cost of sales. Even a simple change in the level at which a fixed asset becomes capitalized instead of written off to repairs and renewals can have an impact on the trend shown by the accounts. For some service industries there is a major impact of new generally accepted accounting policies for turnover recognition. A rise in turnover between this year and last year for a professional services company could be entirely caused by a change in turnover recognition policy or milestone billing policy rather than a true increase in the underlying trade.

A buyer diversifying into a different industry sector may be unaware of the risks presented by such legitimate accounting policy factors. It's the job of the financial due diligence team to tailor their report to suit the buyer and cover the areas it needs to know about, as well as just the areas it thinks it needs to know about!

Overall the report should identify the consistency of application of the accounting policies, compare these with industry practice, and highlight unusual items and recent changes. Crucially, it should also identify those areas where the policies of each party to the deal differs; otherwise what one party understands to be a measure of financial performance may in fact be a very different measure when its own accounting policies are applied to the item.

For example, one party to the deal may make a general provision for warranty claims and returns, whereas the other may only recognize these as and when they arise. Each party would therefore have a different turnover and gross margin figure in mind even when looking at the same basic sales data. If there is an earn-out linked to turnover or margins, such misunderstandings over accounting policies may prove expensive. Earn-outs are a key area where the input from the financial due diligence team into the wording of the sale and purchase agreement contract is vital.

Information systems

Good information systems are vital to any business. The due diligence review may find that there is a need to budget for the replacement or major improvement of a business's systems. There may have been historic underinvestment that the buyer will need to make good. There may be major shortfalls in the systems, which mean that key information such as the order book or stock records are found to be unexpectedly unreliable, which may impact on the whole rationale of the deal.

A classic information system problem is stock control. The information system might tell the user that the stock is current and saleable, but an inspection of the depot shelves then reveals that some stock is damaged or past its 'best before' date. In manufacturing businesses some goods recorded as valuable 'stock' may be found by the team to be in fact overruns of production with no current marketplace. A review of the sales information system may reveal that although sales are being recorded for a customer, there might not be any new orders in the pipeline to provide sales for next year. A poor information system may mask this valuable information.

Detailed review of financial statements

The detailed review of financial statements has the aims of identifying hitherto unnoticed financial trends, of fleshing out the trend in numbers into an analysis of how the business is actually performing, and identifying whether the facts and figures as presented by management tally back to what the financial statements are actually saying.

The review should include cashflow analysis, adjusted for any changes caused by the inconsistent application of accounting policies. Such cashflow analysis may then feed into assumptions behind the projections that the buyer has prepared.

The review will analyse each key area of the accounts to glean useful information for the buyer. For example a review of fixed assets may reveal a trend of underinvestment in plant and equipment that the buyer will need to reverse. A review of debtors and creditors may reveal certain 'sundry' debtors or creditors which are in fact really bad debts or hidden liabilities. The review would also include comparison with budgets and industry trends. Related party transactions would also be identified, and in some situations post-deal changes to the pricing or occurrence of related-party transactions could be crucial.

Review of the financial projections

The due diligence team are placed in a key position to assess the reliability of any financial projections prepared by either of the parties to the deal. The detail they will have uncovered by being on-site during the assignment allows them to both perform a high-level credibility review of the projections, and pinpoint areas of the projections that do not tally with actual recorded performance. At present the Financial Assistance regulations of the Companies Act 1985 affect many bank-backed buy-outs, and the accuracy of the financial projections is essential when it comes to directors signing their Statutory Declarations under section 155 of the Companies Act 1985.

Anything else?

The 'anything else' category is where good advisers earn their fee and the thanks of the buyer. It is impossible to foresee what the due diligence team may uncover, but on almost every assignment that Alliotts has been involved with, there has been an element of the unexpected that has been found purely due to the skill and experience of the on-site team.

An example is the identification of a technology change that would seriously impact the business post-deal. Alternatively, the buyer may believe it is buying in at the bottom of the trading cycle, but the due diligence team may uncover facts and operational trends which reveal that the cycle has in fact peaked already. Or the buyer may be unaware that the workforce of the target company works entirely different hours and shifts from its own workforce, and any attempt to merge the workforces could result in an increase in costs and not the reduction that it was hoping for. With tougher environmental and employment regulations almost every assignment leads to an unforeseen legal or environmental compliance issue that has to be remedied pre-deal.

Conclusion

Received wisdom suggests that post-deal, one half of corporate finance transactions succeed and one half fail. A cynical view would suggest that in fact one-third succeed, one-third fail and, because of a lack of information, the management of the other third are unsure whether they succeeded or not. Good due diligence before a deal can go a long way to ensuring that the deal fits into the first category and not the second or third.

Acquisitions of smaller, owner-managed businesses

Philip Wild, Kidd Rapinet

Introduction

This chapter looks at some of the issues that commonly arise on acquisitions of smaller businesses, where the purchase price can be anything from a few thousand pounds up to about £20 million or so. At Kidd Rapinet, Solicitors, we have considerable experience of this market sector as well as of larger transactions, and so are well placed to compare the different sizes of deals.

Businesses of this size are typically owner-managed or family businesses, founded by an entrepreneur or small management team, who are selling out in order to realize their investment or retire. Typically, the buyer is a larger company seeking to grow by acquisition. It may also be owner-managed, but the issues arise from the nature of the target company, rather than the buyer. This chapter is not specifically concerned with management buy-outs (MBOs) or management buy-ins (MBIs), but where they fall within the above price range or share some of the above features, many of the considerations discussed below can arise.

Kidd Rapinet acts for both sellers and buyers in this type of transaction, and the issues are considered from both the perspective of the sellers and their solicitors, and the perspective of the buyer and its solicitor.

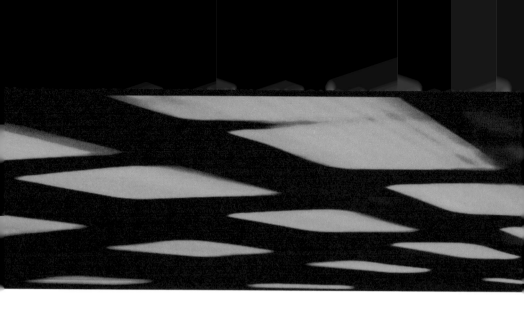

KIDD RAPINET
SOLICITORS

Specialists in Mergers & Acquisitions

Providing a competitive service to owner-managed businesses

Contact:

Chris Henniker
020 7024 8044
chenniker@kiddrapinet.co.uk

Philip Wild
020 7024 8029
pwild@kiddrapinet.co.uk

Phil Astles
020 7024 8074
pastles@kiddrapinet.co.uk

www.kiddrapinet.co.uk

Deal structures

The acquisition may be either of the shares in the target or of its business and assets. Nowadays sellers usually prefer a share sale, because of the availability of business asset taper relief, which can reduce their liability to capital gains tax to 10 per cent after holding the shares for two years. Buyers are often willing to accommodate this, provided there are no major concerns about liabilities of the target that cannot be addressed by indemnities. It is also common for sellers to ask for any deferred element of the purchase price to be payable in loan notes, so that they can roll over the capital gain, and buyers are again more than happy to accommodate them in this.

Property-based deals are becoming increasingly common. With stamp duty land tax at 4 per cent but stamp duty on shares at 0.5 per cent, where a property is held by a single-purpose-vehicle company it can be very attractive for the buyer to acquire the shares rather than the land. Many of the same considerations can apply in these cases.

Deals within this price range can sometimes be distressed sales, where the target has insolvency issues. In these cases, both sides need to take care that the deal is not open to challenge on a subsequent liquidation. The solution is to involve an insolvency practitioner. Where a deal of this sort is agreed in advance, the target put into administration and the administrator then sells the assets to the buyer, it is commonly referred to as a 'pre-pack'.

The structure of a smaller deal, whether for shares or assets, is no different from that of larger deals (as discussed elsewhere in this book). However, with smaller amounts involved, both parties are naturally more sensitive to the level of fees, and commercial decisions need to be taken on how much effort is devoted to dealing with each aspect of the transaction. Both parties' solicitors need to be sensitive to this.

The key document is the sale and purchase agreement. Acquisitions by means of offer letters are rare, because of the small numbers of shareholders involved. It is rare for buyers to rely on section 429 of the Companies Act 1985 or 'drag along' articles of association. They are wary of dissident minority shareholders, and want all the shareholders to give the warranties.

Due diligence is carried out by written enquiries and replies, rather than a data room, partly because auctions between competing buyers are rare and partly because the buyer tends to have the stronger negotiation position and therefore more control over the process. The buyer will expect all shareholders to be parties to the share sale and purchase agreement, and to give warranties and indemnities. On an assets purchase, it will expect the shareholders to guarantee the warranties and indemnities given by the seller company.

Deals of this size are mostly handled very professionally, but sometimes one comes across a client or (even worse) a solicitor who is inexperienced in corporate acquisitions.

CASE STUDY 1

Kidd Rapinet was acting for the buyer on the purchase of a property special-purpose-vehicle company, where the sale was handled by a property solicitor in a small firm. The first draft disclosure letter dealt solely with a potential third-party claim against the target for commission on the deal, which had not previously been disclosed to the buyer, and then went on to include an indemnity against the claim from the seller (which was good, but should have been in the sale and purchase agreement, not a disclosure letter – the sole purpose of which is to qualify the warranties) and a purported cross-undertaking by the buyer to carry on any resulting litigation, which the seller obviously felt strongly about.

From the disclosures made, it appeared to us that the company would be at serious risk of losing the litigation, as although the seller's account appeared genuine, the written documents tended to support the other party's version of events. We therefore advised our client against such an undertaking, as it might be necessary to settle the claim in order to minimize losses. No other matters were disclosed (which is unusual, even in a special purpose vehicle) and the sellers' solicitors had failed to negotiate any limitations on their client's liability in the sale and purchase agreement.

Although it may appear there are opportunities to take advantage of such a situation, invariably it just results in delay and therefore increased costs, as one finds oneself arguing over points which experienced parties take for granted, while points that should have been taken are missed. Inexperienced clients may need some guidance through the process by their solicitor, but with an experienced solicitor acting for them, this should not be such a problem.

The buyer's concerns

The management team

The value in many smaller businesses can be in the management team, rather than in assets or goodwill/the brand. Where key members of the team are to be retained, they need to continue to be motivated to succeed now they are working for someone else. The usual method of achieving this is an earn-out, where part of the purchase price is deferred and varies depending on results achieved by the business after the purchase. This helps the buyer to defer payment and to ensure that it is paying based on what it is actually getting. An earn-out can also be attractive to sellers, who will invariably believe they can achieve the higher end of the targeted results. Restrictive covenants are also important here, as whether a manager leaves on the sale or departs afterwards, the last thing the buyer wants is him or her setting up in competition.

Due diligence

As in any deal, due diligence is vital. In the past on smaller deals this was often limited to the disclosure process against the warranties, but today the process invariably starts with written due diligence enquiries and replies, which then form the core of the disclosure letter. In smaller businesses in particular, there can be a lack of compliance with legal requirements; for example failure to give all employees written particulars of their terms, failure to notify processing of personal data, or failure to write up the company books or keep minutes. A commercially-minded buyer may consider such issues immaterial, but they can be indicative of administrative shortcomings, which may hide more serious problems. The best management teams often include an entrepreneur, who grows the business, and an administrator, who manages it. Due diligence replies can vary in quality (despite the best efforts of the sellers' solicitors) where the person dealing with the administration and providing the due diligence replies is more of an entrepreneurial type.

Among the issues the buyer's solicitors will be on a particular look out for in due diligence are change of control clauses (as third parties are more likely to have requested these with owner-managed businesses), non-arm's length arrangements (which will need to be terminated) and ownership of intellectual property rights (IPR). In the technology sector, IPR will be a key asset. IPR may have been created by the sellers themselves (not necessarily working under a contract of employment) or they may have used subcontractors, without tying up the legal niceties of taking an assignment of copyright. The buyer will require written assignments of IPR in any case where there is doubt over ownership.

The sellers' concerns

Disclosure

Given the potential for serious issues that may emerge from due diligence, especially in a business with a more entrepreneurial culture, it is important when acting for the sellers to seek to identify any such issues at an early stage. If a potential problem issue is discovered, the sellers' solicitors should always urge their clients to make full and frank disclosure, preferably at the heads of terms stage. The sellers may be tempted to wait for the buyer to discover the issue, and to see if they can get away with it, but a diligent buyer who is properly represented will almost certainly discover any problems.

Even if a problem is missed in due diligence, if it was knowingly omitted from the disclosure letter, this would be fraud. No sellers' solicitor could be party to a fraud, and the limitations on the sellers' liability do not apply where there is fraud. On the positive side, if the sellers are frank about a major problem from the beginning, it can become much less of an issue and help engender trust in the negotiations. If it comes out later in the process, such an issue can become a deal breaker, at a point where both parties have incurred substantial costs.

Sometimes an issue is identified which the sellers are anxious not to highlight, and is not an obvious claim that it would be fraudulent not to correct. Such situations need to be handled carefully, to ensure the clients' interests are protected and that advisers act ethically throughout.

CASE STUDY 2

Kidd Rapinet acted for the sellers on a software business, which was faced with an increasing challenge in adapting to the latest operating systems and web-based technologies. Our clients had already noted a drop in turnover, and particular care therefore needed to be taken about the wording of the warranty about trading since the accounting date, and any disclosures made against that warranty. It was important that no misrepresentations were made, fraudulent or otherwise. We were successful in this, but the buyer discovered a separate warranty claim after completion on an unrelated matter of which the sellers had been unaware. An amicable settlement was reached, in which the sellers admitted liability on this warranty claim, but we were able to resist any significant concession on the downturn in business.

Limiting liability

As well as ensuring proper disclosure has been made, the sellers' solicitors' main concern will be to negotiate proper limitations on their clients' liability. Issues can arise here where different sellers have different percentage shareholdings, and where some are managers who have been active in running the business and others are passive shareholders who may have no knowledge of the matters covered by the warranties.

The buyer and its solicitors will insist upon joint and several liability, so that any seller can be sued for breach of warranty up to the agreed aggregate cap on liability (usually the amount of the purchase price). A seller who is only receiving a small percentage of that amount may understandably have some difficulty with this concept. The sellers will normally agree between themselves to share contributions to any claim in proportion to their original shareholdings and the percentages of the total purchase price each receives. But this will not help them if one of the sellers has become insolvent, which is exactly what the buyer is seeking to protect itself against by insisting upon joint and several liability.

Where this is a concern, the sellers' solicitors will sometimes seek to negotiate an individual cap on each seller's liability equal to the amount of the purchase price received by him or her. Although most solicitors will deny (when they are acting for a buyer) that such limitations are ever agreed, the fact is that they can sometimes be successfully negotiated, especially where the sellers feel sufficiently strongly about it and the buyer is less concerned about their solvency or the risks of a claim.

Sellers who have not been involved in the management will be reluctant to give warranties about matters of which they have no knowledge. Some warranties are qualified as being given 'to the best of the sellers' knowledge and belief' or 'so far as the sellers are aware'. But this will not help the non-management shareholder, as there is inevitably a clause that says this is to be determined by reference to the knowledge of named members of the management team. Usually, the sellers' solicitors have to explain to their clients that the warranties are a means of apportioning risk as much as they are of identifying what the sellers know, and that if the sellers want to receive their money they will have to continue to trust their management team, as they presumably did when they were running the company. The only sellers who may be able to negotiate limitations based upon their personal knowledge are trustees or venture capitalist investors, and this will probably result in the management team having to assume a greater share of the potential liability.

Protecting the earn-out

When considering earn-out provisions, the sellers' solicitors will be concerned to protect the earn-out entitlement against manipulation by the buyer, who will now be in control of the finances. It is normal to insert some protections to ensure the business upon which the calculation is based is conducted on an arm's length basis, especially when trading with other members of the buyer's group, and that the buyer cannot evade liability by stripping the business out into another group company.

Personal assets and liabilities

Any personal assets held by the target will need to be identified, and transferred out of the company into the sellers' individual names, to avoid giving the buyer more than was intended. This may seem simple, but it can be a company law minefield, involving potential issues of financial assistance and unlawful distributions. The sellers' solicitors may need to question their clients carefully about any personal assets, as managers can forget they have put an asset in the company's name and buyers do not always ask in due diligence about factors which only have an upside for them.

CASE STUDY 3

Kidd Rapinet was acting for the sellers of a successful family business founded by the managing director. As part of due diligence we were provided with fully written-up company books and a minute book with board meetings minuted back to incorporation. Before handing these over to the buyer's solicitors, we had a quick read through the minute book as part of our usual process of checking due diligence before disclosing it. We found a board minute approving the purchase of a property in France, which had not been mentioned in replies to property enquiries.

When we asked the managing director about this, he explained that it was his personal chalet for skiing holidays, and he had forgotten that it had been put in the company's name. We disclosed the position to the buyer, and were able to arrange the transfer of the chalet into the managing director's name. This could have caused problems if it had not been discovered that the chalet was still in the company's name until many years after the sale.

In smaller businesses, personal guarantees may have been required by the bank or landlord, and the sellers will need to be released from these, so that they are not guaranteeing the buyer's business. As a third party needs to agree to the release of the guarantee, and is unlikely to do so within the timetable set for the sale, the usual formulation is that the buyer will use best or reasonable endeavours to secure the release, offering its own guarantee in substitution if need be, and will in the meantime indemnify the sellers against any calls on the guarantees.

After completion

In the earn-out situation, issues can continue to arise after the deal has been completed. Former owner-managers can have difficulty adjusting to a larger company culture. This can be a difficult step for entrepreneurs growing their company under their own management, even without a sale, and it can be a sudden culture shock on making the step up in one go after selling out to a larger company.

Warranty claims are rare, but if they do arise, especially in an earn-out where the parties have to continue to work together, it is important to seek to resolve them amicably.

Conclusion

In most respects the mechanics of an acquisition of a smaller, owner-managed business are no different from those of a larger, unlisted company. However, the particular characteristics of owner-managed businesses and the relationships between the shareholders can give rise to some unique problems. The experienced adviser in this sector will have seen these many times before, and where his or her clients have less familiarity, he or she will be able to guide them smoothly through the process.

Cautionary tales

Duncan Taylor, Nelsons

After years of hard work, your entrepreneurial instincts are about to reap their reward. Someone wants to buy your business. The price is right, you feel comfortable that the buyer will look after your employees, some of whom have been with you for years, and the integrity of the company's identity will be respected. Mentally, you have banked the money and are wondering how quickly you can get your handicap down to single figures on those forgiving Spanish golf courses. It's just a matter of sorting out the paperwork; nothing can go wrong, right? Wrong!

Does everyone want to sell?

It is a common misconception that, in the case of a sale of a private company, if the majority shareholder wants to sell, then all of the shareholders must sell. That may not necessarily be the case.

CASE STUDY 1

ABC Limited was a successful manufacturer and distributor of car care products. It had a national reputation and while it had seen some tough times, was well run and profitable. Founded before the Second World War, the founder had left his shares to his three sons, only two of whom worked in the business.

An unsolicited offer was received which the two brothers who worked in the business were keen to accept. They took the view that, as they worked in the business and were the only directors of the company, it was their decision

your future is our number one priority

When your business has important decisions to make, there's one firm that can answer all your questions.

The Legal 500 recognises Nelsons as a Regional Heavyweight and one of the most comprehensive law firms in the East Midlands. In the 2006 edition, it was noted that our corporate practice has become the firm's "main driving force".

So if you need advice on any aspect of corporate finance, including mergers, acquisitions, management buy-outs or buy-ins and disposals, we can offer tailormade, practical solutions that will add value to your business.

We are experienced in giving pragmatic advice on all aspects of equity and debt funding and can also advise you on company re-organisations, joint ventures, share sales and purchases, and issues of corporate governance.

If you're looking for a firm that will make you their number one priority, you know the one to call.

one team to contact

Derby
Clare Vickers
01332 372372
clare.vickers@nelsonslaw.co.uk

Leicester
Pip Dawkins
0116 222 6666
pip.dawkins@nelsonslaw.co.uk

Nottingham
Duncan Taylor
0115 958 6262
duncan.taylor@nelsonslaw.c

whether or not to proceed with the sale. They approached the third brother and told him that the company was to be sold: it was a good deal with a fair price being paid. The third brother, however, took an entirely different view; he considered that the price on offer was unacceptably low. The best efforts of the other two brothers failed to convince him.

The shares were held in equal proportions. The brothers who worked in the business were not in a position to amend the articles of association of the company to insert a drag-along, tag-along provision which would have enabled them to achieve their goals by allowing them, as majority shareholders, to compel the dissenting brother to accept an offer that the majority wanted to accept, provided that the price payable per share was the same for all the shareholders. The directors did consider offering to sell the company's business, rather than shares, but the taxation implications of doing so were unattractive.

The purchaser simply became disenchanted; unable to achieve the quick clean deal that it was looking for, it simply walked away.

Moral

Where a target company has multiple shareholders, be sure that they all want to sell, and if so, that there is a clear agreement over the deal parameters that will be acceptable, most importantly in terms of price but also in relation to other aspects of the transaction: responsibility for warranties and indemnities, arrangements for the protection of the interests of the staff and so on. This is likely to be of particular relevance in family companies, where emotions can run high.

Not buyer beware, but beware the buyer

Due diligence may not simply be the prerogative of the buyer, but also that of the sellers. You're selling your business but what do you know about the buyer?

CASE STUDY 2

The target was an IT software company, run by a husband and wife who were both shareholders and directors. In the course of discussion with a customer, they happened to mention to him that they were contemplating selling with a view to pursuing unrelated business opportunities. The customer mentioned that he knew of someone who might be interested, with a background in the same industry. While the 'friend of a friend' was still employed by a major international business he was, apparently, keen to go into business in his own right.

Introductions were made and the prospective purchaser met with the shareholders. The sellers instructed their solicitor to prepare a confidentiality undertaking, incorporating provisions as to exclusivity; it was signed and negotiations progressed. It was agreed that the seller's solicitors should produce a draft sale and purchase agreement while due diligence progressed. Limited legal due diligence was undertaken by the solicitors instructed by the prospective purchaser, who dealt with business and accounting due diligence himself, asserting that he knew more about software businesses than any advisers he might use.

The sale and purchase agreement and ancillary documentation were in all but agreed form when the purchaser informed the sellers that he was struggling to raise the necessary funding to proceed. He asked the purchasers to consider accepting only part of the consideration in cash and the balance by way of deferred consideration. The sellers declined to do so, confirming that they were willing to proceed but only if funding was available to satisfy the purchase price in cash in full upon completion.

The transaction went on hold while the purchaser attempted to raise funding but after some weeks indicated that he would be unable to proceed and was therefore withdrawing.

Result

No sale and therefore no funds available to the sellers to meet the fees of their professional advisers.

Moral

As a seller, undertake buyer due diligence. At the lower end of the mergers and acquisitions market in particular, time wasters abound. Make sure that you are comfortable that the buyer is genuine, and in particular that it has the financial means to do the deal.

Don't neglect the housekeeping

No purchaser will want to proceed if there is any evidence of inappropriate business practice or unlawful behaviour in the way that the target business has been run.

CASE STUDY 3

ABC Limited was a successful double-glazing company, operating across the north of England. It had a good reputation, in terms of being price competitive, the quality of its products and installation, and customer care. It was approached by an existing broad-based company with interests in the sector, looking to improve its geographical footprint. The price was a full one and therefore attractive to the selling shareholders even though the company had been profitable and cash generative for a number of years, enabling the shareholder directors to enjoy a good standard of living.

All went well in the preliminary discussions; heads of terms were agreed and signed without significant argument, due diligence commenced and the preliminary findings from a tax, accounting and legal point of view were positive.

A draft sale and purchase agreement was prepared and put into circulation. The sellers' solicitors arranged to meet with them with a view to running through the agreement, in particular focusing on the warranties and upon issues relevant to be disclosed against them in the disclosure letter, thus qualifying the warranties to be given. Having reached the end of the warranty schedule, the solicitor asked his clients whether they were aware of any other issues that would not have been specifically caught by the warranties but that might be of concern to a prospective purchaser.

There was a pause. The selling shareholders looked at one another. There was an embarrassed shuffling of papers. Then the principal shareholder said, 'There's the flat in Spain ...'.

It transpired that a flat in Spain had been purchased for the use of the shareholders. Although the company's money had been used, the flat was registered in the name of the shareholders. Effectively, the transactions had been 'lost' in the books and records of the company. Unsurprisingly, the purchaser withdrew.

Moral

Do not be tempted into improper business practice – you are likely to be found out. If you have been or are contemplating a sale, get advice on any issues before you start the process, and establish what, if any, remedial action can be taken.

Due diligence and disclosure

Due diligence issues are fundamental to the process. They are important to the purchaser, in terms of confirming its understanding of what it is buying, but are important also to the sellers on the basis that the work done on responding to the due diligence enquiries will provide the basis of disclosure.

CASE STUDY 4

ABC Limited was a thriving office supplies business based in the south-west. Its shareholders were a husband and wife who, having reached their middle fifties, had come to the conclusion that now was the time to dispose of the business and retire on the proceeds. Having done so, they instructed their accountants to market the business. A number of potential purchasers expressed an interest, and ultimately an offer was received from a purchaser offering cash consideration and looking to proceed to an early completion.

Given that it was looking to work to a tight timescale, the purchaser undertook only limited due diligence, making it clear that it anticipated that the warranties contained in the sale and purchase agreement would prompt disclosure so that it would still receive information in relation to the company and its business in advance of completion. It could then take a view whether or not any issues that arose would cause it either to walk away from the transaction, or alternatively reduce the price. The draft sale and purchase agreement contained a full set of commercial warranties, including in particular a warranty to the effect that the execution of the agreement and the completion of the transaction would not entitle any person to terminate any contract to which the company was a party.

The sellers struggled to maintain interest or concentration on the detail of the warranties, much as their solicitors tried to impress upon them the importance of a full disclosure exercise. In consequence, they failed to raise with their lawyers issues relating to contracts containing 'change of control provisions' which should have been disclosed. The transaction proceeded to completion. A number of customers, becoming aware of the change of control, exercised their right to terminate. The purchaser duly claimed for damages under the warranties.

The result

This was an unsatisfactory transaction for both purchaser and sellers. While the purchaser did succeed in its warranty claims, it ended up having acquired a business that was something other than what it had contemplated. For the sellers, the dream of walking away and counting their money was compromised: they still had money to count but rather less than they had anticipated.

Moral

For the purchaser, don't cut corners on due diligence. Be clear that what you are buying is what you think you are buying. For the sellers, do not cut corners on disclosure. A full and detailed disclosure exercise, on which time and effort has been spent, should mean a well-written and effective disclosure letter which, in turn, should obviate future warranty claims.

Choose your advisers carefully

Legal, taxation accounting and other issues will arise throughout the transaction; be sure that your professional advisers have the appropriate experience.

CASE STUDY 5

The target was an equipment hire business. The principal shareholder and managing director was in poor health. The only other shareholder was his wife. He was the sole director but the next tier of management was interested in pursuing an MBO. The principal shareholder was unenthusiastic about selling to management, but the management team engaged a national firm of accountants to prepare a business plan and advise them in relation to funding and price. With the benefit of that advice, they were able to make a well-argued approach to the principal shareholder, who in the absence of any offers at the same sort of level, decided to proceed by way of a sale to management, and to their funders.

Difficulties were encountered in relation to the financial, tax and accounting due diligence. Historically, the business had employed an accountant who was a sole practitioner and not qualified to give audit reports; he effectively farmed out the draft accounts to another local accountant who was apparently happy to sign the audit report given that he had known the unqualified accountant for a number of years. In consequence, additional work on financial and taxation due diligence issues had to be undertaken by advisers to the management team and to the funders.

Things went from bad to worse as the legal process got under way. The management team's solicitors produced a draft sale and purchase agreement. The seller's solicitors, upon receipt, replied asking when they could expect to see the draft disclosure letter. They had failed to understand that it was an exercise that they, as the seller's solicitors, should undertake. In consequence, the solicitors acting for the management team had not merely to negotiate the disclosure letter on behalf of their client, but in the interests of facilitating the progress of the transaction, effectively provide the seller's solicitors with a template for the disclosure letter itself – a less than satisfactory position.

Ultimately the transaction did proceed to completion, but not without further difficulties and clear gaps in expertise and understanding between the advisers to the management, experienced in the field, and advisers to the seller, who regrettably were not.

Moral

A smooth and swift transaction will only be achievable with experienced professionals instructed on both sides. If in doubt, ask other people whose business expertise you trust whom they would recommend. Beauty parade the advisers, and be sure that you are comfortable with the firms that you engage, and the people that will be working on the transaction, even if they may not be the cheapest option.

Aquila, established in 2002 and based in central London, provides strategic financial communications and public relations advice – two parallel communication streams that we tailor to the needs and aspirations of our clients.

Our consultants bring together a blend of **financial communications, journalism, public relations**, and **hands-on city experience** – from in-house and consultancy-based roles.

This combination of skills allows us to understand and cater for the needs of our clients and reach their key audiences.

www.aquila-financial.com
Telephone +44 (0)20 7202 2600

Aquila Financial Limited
Aquila Public Relations Limited
181 Union Street
London SE1 0LN

Part Five

Shareholders' and directors' considerations

Which way forward?

Sooner or later every organisation looks at acquisitions. But while the rewards of making the right deal can be tremendous, the cost of getting it wrong can be far greater.

And getting it wrong is all too easy if there is any lack of clarity over exactly what is to be achieved. Or how. Or if the deal itself is poorly executed. Or if management becomes distracted from running its existing business.

We can help you get it *right*.

We will work with you through all aspects of the complex and technical deal process from inception to completion - and beyond. Ensuring *you* are in control.

We can also manage the process on your behalf and coordinate the activities of all personnel involved - both internal and external specialist advisers - to ensure that everything that needs to be done *is* done. And done well. Leaving you free to run your business.

Offering you substantially increased likelihood of success, and the opportunity to save time, effort and money.

So why not give us a call right now, and ensure that *your* move is in the right direction?

H&Co Howles & Company Ltd

ACQUISITION & MERGER CONSULTANTS

HOWLES & COMPANY LTD • 95 HAMPSTEAD WAY LONDON NW11 7LR
TEL: +44 (0)20 8731 7182   FAX: +44 (0)20 8731 7633
email: geoff@howles.co.uk   *web:* www.howles.co.uk

AUTHORISED AND REGULATED BY THE FINANCIAL SERVICES AUTHORITY

The acquisition process, from start to finish – and beyond

Geoff Howles, Howles & Company

Introduction

My own business bores me to death. I prefer other people's.

Oscar Wilde

Sooner or later every organization looks at strategic deals like mergers or acquisitions. But while the rewards of making the right deal can be tremendous, the cost of getting it wrong can be even greater. And most acquisitions fail. Study after study suggests that 50–80 per cent of all acquisitions are unsuccessful, because they:

- do not generate the expected benefits;
- cost more than was anticipated;
- take longer and were more problematic to implement than was foreseen.

And this is usually down to:

- lack of clarity at the outset over what is to be achieved and why;

- lack of experience in the acquisition process so that the amount of time, work, resource and cost involved in any deal is underestimated (with the result that the deal itself is poorly executed or – worse – the wrong deal is secured);
- lack of forward planning of how the underlying commercial objectives will be achieved in practice – the deal itself is after all only a means towards an end, rather than the end in itself;
- poor implementation, so that even when the deal is finally done, the new business is not properly integrated and the benefits that underpinned the deal are not realized.

In addition, the ongoing business often suffers in the process because:

- management, which already has its hands full running the business, becomes distracted;
- employees become demoralized by the uncertainty created by the proposed deal;
- competitors target the business.

Four key objectives to getting it right

In spite of these pitfalls however, it is perfectly possible to increase your chances of making a successful acquisition or merger – and maybe even save time, effort and money in the process. When viewed at its most basic, the acquisition process can be reduced to just four fundamental objectives:

- Do the right deal.
- Do it efficiently.
- Generate value.
- Do this efficiently.

Do the right deal

In other words, buy what you think you are buying, for the right reasons, on the right terms. To do this you need:

- A *clear strategy*. Clarity over what you are trying to achieve, and why, is fundamental to the entire process. Once you have your strategy in place you will be able to assess which targets you should approach to enable you to achieve it. Similarly, a clear strategy will give you the foundation on which to base your offer and a yardstick against which to measure progress in negotiations, deal structure and even final documentation.
- A *post-acquisition/merger plan*. You must be very clear precisely how you will achieve your strategic objectives once you have acquired your target, and you need to plan from the outset what you are going to do post-completion. The

post-acquisition/merger plan should be constantly updated as new information comes to light, and ideally (where circumstances permit) it should be prepared in consultation with existing management who know the business and can therefore ensure the plan is grounded in reality.

∎ *Valuation of the proposed deal.* You need to be clear what the value of the deal is to you, and this needs to be realistic. It is not enough to say that a particular deal is strategically important: you need to be able to quantify this importance. How much is it going to affect your bottom line? As part of this exercise you will need to distinguish between value that can be achieved in practice (such as cost savings made when two head offices are combined, for example) and that which is more aspirational (such as 'the two plus two equals five' syndrome where, for example, the combined entity's sales are expected to be higher than they were for the two companies pre-merger). Once you are clear on the value of the deal, you will be in a position to calculate the maximum price that you are prepared to pay.

∎ *Good legal documentation.* Finally you need legal documentation that fairly reflects the deal you have agreed – and nothing else!

Do it efficiently

That is, do it as quickly and as cheaply as possible.

∎ *Treat the deal as a project.* The most efficient way to navigate your way through the acquisition process is to treat your deal as a project and adopt a formal project management structure. In particular, you should ensure you have:
  – *Adequate resources*: both financial and human (in terms of numbers and expertise). This will usually involve a combination of your own employees and outside professionals. Do use professional advisers. They will have done it all before and can advise you on the technical aspects of the deal and generally help you through the process.
  – *Proper organization*: in other words a project team, with a project manager, where everyone's roles are clearly defined. In this way you can ensure that your team not only works together but also that everything that needs to be done is done.
  – *Milestones*: against which progress can be measured.
  – *Good internal communication*: so that you (and your project team) are kept fully informed of progress.
  – *An approvals process*: to allow you to keep control of the project.
∎ *Prepare a communication plan.* In any deal you will have to balance a commercial desire for secrecy with a legal/regulatory/commercial need to go public. You should at the outset, therefore, produce a communication plan to manage the flow of information so that you are in control of what is said to whom, by whom and when.
∎ *But don't underestimate:*
  – *The commitment required to do a deal.* You somehow have to balance the demands of running your existing business with those of making an

acquisition. Managing the deal as a project will help, but you must accept that you will have a significant involvement in the transaction, and be the one to make the important decisions.

– *The disruption a deal will involve*. Acquisitions can be very disruptive. Apart from the increased workload they generate, they are also distracting. And if news leaks out they can unsettle your employees, customers and suppliers while giving your competitors the opportunity to target your business. You need to recognize this from the outset and work out how you can minimize the disruption to your existing business.

– *'Deal momentum'*. Deals develop an almost irresistible and potentially dangerous momentum of their own as they progress. After months of hard work, late nights and expense it can become very easy in the final stages to want to do the deal at any cost. You must be aware of this momentum and control it – by being absolutely clear at all times about what you are trying to do and why. And if the deal is not the right deal, you must be prepared to walk away. This is obviously easier said than done, but it is infinitely better than doing the wrong deal.

Generate value

Once the deal is completed, the real work begins. The objective after all is not to acquire or merge for the sake of it, but to generate value. Now you have to achieve the objectives that made you want to do the deal in the first place. Exactly how you do so will depend on the underlying rationale for the deal, but the key issues here are:

■ *Degree of integration*. You will need to decide whether you want the new business to become a seamless part of your own, or whether you wish to keep it separate. Even if this is to be a purely passive investment, there will usually be some degree of integration involved – if only to enable you to track performance. Mergers or major acquisitions on the other hand can involve complete integration of every aspect of the two businesses, transforming them in the process.

■ *Timing*. The issue here is how quickly you move, and there are two conflicting schools of thought on this:

– Strike while the iron is hot and do as much as possible as quickly as possible – full integration in 90 days, for example. The advantage of this approach is that introducing change should be easier immediately after an acquisition because everyone is expecting it. The disadvantage is that you may make mistakes since you cannot yet really know what you have acquired. You will also need an experienced integration team if you want to move fast and avoid chaos.

– Wait, often for as much as a year, until you have full knowledge of the acquired company, and then integrate. The advantage with this approach is that you should know and understand your acquisition and be able to make better decisions – albeit at the cost of slower momentum and increased likelihood of resistance to change.

Whichever overall approach is adopted, in practice you will usually end up with some combination of the two – reporting and personnel integrated quickly, for example, with operational changes made over time.

■ *Avoiding value destruction*. This is one of the hardest issues to address. You must balance the need to integrate the new business into your own without destroying whatever it had of value that made you want to buy it in the first place. If you absorb the new business at the cost of losing key employees or customers. for example, your acquisition will have been a waste of time and money.

Do this efficiently

That is, do it as quickly, cheaply and as painlessly as possible. To do so you need to:

■ *Plan in advance*. Integration requires careful thought and detailed planning of what you are trying to achieve and precisely how you are going to do it. You will not have the time to do this after the deal is signed, but must plan in advance so that you will know what you are going to do next even as the ink dries on the legal agreements. With your post-acquisition/merger plan already prepared, you should be in good shape.

■ *Treat the post-acquisition/merger plan as a project and manage it as such*. Just as the chances of making a successful acquisition are much improved when the process is properly managed, the same also holds true when it comes to integration. In particular you will need:

  – *Adequate resources, properly organized*. Post-acquisition integration is arguably the most important part of the entire acquisition process. As with the pre-acquisition process, it needs a dedicated team with a dedicated integration manager to carry it out. This is unlikely to be the same team as the one that made the acquisition/merger, since the skill sets are different, but it is helpful to have some links with the pre-acquisition team for continuity. Again, outside specialist help can greatly ease the whole process.

  – *Measurement criteria for success*. The post-acquisition/merger plan is in effect a change management programme which, in the case of full integration, can reach into every part of both the new and existing businesses. In order to be able to implement the plan you will not only need to identify the detailed steps required to do so, you will also have to establish how you will know whether you have been successful. It is, for example, one thing to have the integration of the two businesses' IT systems as a goal; it is another to know what this actually means in practice. Measurement criteria for success are therefore a must.

■ *Don't underestimate the trauma factor*. An acquisition or merger is by its very nature a traumatic experience for everyone involved. It will generate huge demand for information and reassurance, particularly from employees but also from customers and suppliers. It is extremely important that you recognize this and deal with it. This is often cited as the single most important post-acquisition action. If you can persuade your stakeholders that your vision is worth pursuing and that they should therefore back you, the whole process of integration will become much easier. If, on the other hand, you fail to deal with people's fear and suspicion, integration is unlikely to succeed. Just as you need a communication plan for the pre-acquisition process therefore, you also need an active and ongoing communication plan post-acquisition to explain how the deal is going to affect each employee or other stakeholder, why they should follow you and how well you are succeeding in integrating the two businesses. And finally …

■ *Don't forget your core business!* In all the excitement of making an acquisition or merger it is all too easy to become distracted from your existing core business. If you take your eye off the ball you may succeed in integrating the new business but then find that your business has suffered in the process. Despite the demands of integration you must continue to run your business through all the upheaval. And once you have finished integration, your core business will of course have changed – you will have new customers, products, employees, markets and so on. It will be time to start working out how you are going to capitalize on this going forward, and continue generating real value into the future.

Success is a science; if you have the conditions, you get the result.

Oscar Wilde

If you do the right deal, do it efficiently, generate value and do this efficiently, you will have the conditions for success and you will get the result.

Financial public relations in M&A environments

Peter Reilly, Aquila Financial

The role of financial public relations in M&A transactions

In an age of growing investor sophistication, near-infinite sources of instantaneous business information, and competition from other publicly listed companies for 'share of voice', financial public relations plays a crucial role in the daily operations of a public company. The sheer volume of public companies across global stock markets means that a strategic financial public relations programme must be followed to ensure that the long-term share price reflects the company's true value.

Ensuring the investment community and industry at large understands the company's 'story' is the key focus of financial PR: broadly speaking, managing the company's long-term 'financial reputation'. Any financial PR campaign should have as its objectives:

- communicating the company's business strategy, operations and management strengths;
- delivering a regular flow and consistent story to the financial media;
- ensuring the financial media give an accurate, and more importantly favourable, portrayal of the company;
- maintaining long-term awareness and support from the investment community.

Financial PR should support the company throughout its entire lifetime, from pre-listing through to the long term. Companies should consider every shareholder as a long-term relationship. Even though some shareholders may trade in and out of stocks, just having their interest and understanding is important.

Within an M&A environment, where a variety of factors drive the M&A agenda and success is dependent on any number of factors, the broad goals of financial PR do not change. However, with multiple competing business agendas, friends and foes in the media, and differing opinions in the investment community, a strategic approach to the financial PR is vital to improve the chances of success for the M&A transaction.

The reasons for communicating during a M&A are no different from a non-M&A environment: managing the expectations of stakeholders, communicating a regular news flow, and ensuring an accurate portrayal of 'your side' of the story. Above all else, you want the awareness and support of the investment community to carry on post-transaction, and that all other stakeholder groups support the M&A decision. Poor communication is regularly cited as a reason why many M&A transactions fail.

Similar to a crisis situation, a lack of communication will result in somebody else filling the communication void. Companies need to keep relevant stakeholders informed (employees – to retain staff; customers – to keep them loyal; community leaders – to keep their support, for example) and in particular the investment community, for it to understand the corporate story and support it through the M&A environment.

As a general rule, M&A financial PR efforts can be grouped into three phases: pre-, mid-, and post-M&A.

Pre-M&A phase

- Announce intent (triggered by regulatory requirements, rumour, 'buzz' in the industry, due diligence process).
- Media outreach – ensure they understand your 'story'.
- Investor outreach – explain the rationale clearly and consistently.

Mid-M&A phase

- Keep the flow of information constant.
- Give regular briefings.
- Explain the details.
- Outline the post-transaction actions and deliverables.

Post-M&A phase

- Communicate the new 'story'.
- Follow up – communicate the long-term results of the transaction.
- Explain any differences from the original plan.

Two types of M&A environments deserve special attention: they are 'mergers of equals' and 'hostile takeovers'.

Mergers of equals

Despite the term, in a 'merger of equals' transaction, there is always one dominant company. Poor financial PR from the dominant company regarding future plans, the new vision, and the value as a result of the acquisition can derail the transaction. While both companies should have individual plans in place, a coordinated financial PR effort by both parties will ensure consistent and timely delivery of the same message and make the story more believable.

Hostile takeovers

In a hostile situation, financial PR takes on a support role to defend or attack. The basic needs are the same: consistent, credible communication. The temptation to snipe is high, but leads to further acrimony and dirt-digging. Of course, the media love this and the hedge funds will be ecstatic as they will be able to trade on the ebb and flow of the fight.

The rules of financial PR

As a checklist, there are several broad financial PR rules that should be followed in a M&A environment:

∎ *Know your audiences/stakeholders.* As with any communication programme, ensure a good understanding of your financial PR audiences during an M&A environment. During the M&A situation it is too late to be creating lists of key financial editors, trade journalists, analysts or even key corporate investor contacts. These all need to be in place in advance of the transaction.

Financial audiences in order of importance will vary from industry to industry. Groups to consider include:
- tipsheet journalists;
- bulletin boards;
- industry newsletters;
- newspaper journalists/editors;
- trade magazine journalists.

With each of the audiences, it is crucial to know the individual needs. That is, what element of the transaction will be of more interest to them, and can that interest be leveraged into getting the key elements of the story across to a wider audience?

- *Plan.* Ahead of the transaction, companies should develop a plan for the financial PR, incorporating such elements as:
  - mapping out the M&A rationale and strategy;
  - developing positioning messaging for investor audiences;
  - identifying key influencers in the financial media (online and print);
  - setting financial PR objectives;
  - identifying tactical steps through the M&A process;
  - incorporating regular feedback to ensure financial PR is 'on track'.
- *Maximum impact.* Maximum impact on announcement of a transaction is desirable but often difficult to achieve. Too often negotiations are leaked, then holding statements are issued, and control of the agenda is taken away from the companies. 'X & Y companies are talking, no guarantee of a deal being done, further information in due course' is the usual statement, and in the absence of further information, the media will ask everyone else all about it. The pros and cons of a deal are discussed in a vacuum, and opinion is formed without a heap of input from the companies. If it is at all possible, to achieve maximum impact keep the deal absolutely quiet until it is ready to be announced.
- *Control the message.* Effective coordination of communications enables the release of information in a controlled, strategic method. Messaging should focus on the corporate 'story' – that is, deliver messages around such topics as:
  - an increased market share;
  - expanded technology expertise;
  - spread in geographic reach;
  - established economies of scale.
- *Communicate regularly.* Since a lack of communication will increase uncertainty and give rumours a reason to start, regular communication with the investor community is very important. Make your CEO or financial director available, with proper media training, to speak to the financial press regarding the transaction at regular intervals. Any reluctance to explain the deal will be taken negatively, and as a possible sign that the spokesperson is either out of the loop or not confident about the rationale. Remember, by not communicating you *are* communicating. In any M&A environment, the investment community will take even more notice where there is a lack of communication, and 'fill in the holes' regarding plans and strategies.
- *Explain the deal.* The financial community will want to know why the deal makes sense as soon as it is announced. Do not give any room for interpretation or inference; instead, map out the rationale and benefits, the structure, the process and consequences. Your investors can't support a transaction they don't know about or understand; you need to communicate about the deal to gain their support.
- *Maintain the momentum.* After the transaction has closed, it is important to maintain the flow of communications to investor audiences; indeed it is even more important than ever to provide periodic updates on the transaction progress, so that the business reputation around the transaction is preserved.

Post-M&A change management: taking charge of change

Norrie Johnston, Executives Online

Any merger or acquisition, be it large or small, inevitably entails a great degree of change, as disparate workforces, technology and administrative infrastructures have to be smoothly and effectively integrated. In fact, according to Executives Online's new *Challenge of Change Report 2006*, M&A is the fourth largest driver for change, on a par with the introduction of new technology, both of which account for 13 per cent of all change initiatives planned over the next 12 months. And the top three reasons for change programmes in 2006 deal with restructuring, improvement in efficiency and cost reductions, all of which are also necessary consequences of M&A activity.

So the state of change programmes in the UK is of crucial concern to any companies considering or undergoing M&A. And, worryingly, it seems there is much to be concerned about. An alarming number of change programmes are not well thought out, are poorly executed and are ultimately unsuccessful in meeting their stated aims. Unfortunately, according to our latest report, the blame lies predominantly at the door of the board and senior management.

Crucial to any business success is keeping staff motivated, yet post-M&A change programmes in particular will have a direct and possibly negative impact on employees, probably resulting in job losses. Therefore, they will be viewed with suspicion and concern across the organization, which means that if such change programmes are not well handled, the chance of failure is greater and they could actually cause more damage to the morale and culture of the company.

Recruiting the right executive is a full-time job.

Aren't you glad it's not yours?

Managing a business is tough enough. When a key executive role stands vacant, it's even harder.

An unfilled executive position represents huge opportunity costs for your organisation, and a tremendous burden on other executives who must cover for the role.

Now imagine an executive recruitment agency which delivers a great short list matching your brief in under 2 weeks – not in months like other executive placement agencies. Hard to fathom, but true: In just days Executives Online can provide fully briefed, interviewed candidates who are an excellent match to your executive resourcing requirement.

And with no up-front costs. You pay only when the right executive starts work with you.

We can do it this fast because our approach to executive recruitment is dramatically different from traditional executive headhunting. Starting with our 10,000-strong Talent Bank of pre-screened executive job seekers, and maximising the effective use of online channels, we find success with even the most difficult of briefs.

Today, 60% of companies are now struggling with even the most basic elements of sourcing executive talent, despite 80% having established relationships with search firms. Long delays in filling executive positions and the frequency of bad hires have made traditional recruitment methods less and less satisfactory. Request our *Executive Talent 2006* report for further information on organisations' struggles with executive recruitment.

And when your next critical vacancy arises, give us a call and see how our fast, effective permanent recruitment services deliver for you.

---

eol ExecutivesOnline Executive Recruitment

Executives Online for Fast-Track Executive Resourcing

Interim Management ■ Change Management ■ Project Management ■ Permanent Recruitment

Tel: +44 (0)1962 829 705 Fax: +44 (0)1962 866 116
enquiries@ExecutivesOnline.co.uk www.ExecutivesOnline.co.uk

By their own admission, more than a third of British businesses are performing poorly when it comes to managing change, and the problems lie with the vision of senior management. Although just over half of those surveyed believe UK companies are 'average' in their management of business change, almost two in five (39 per cent) believe management is 'poor' to a greater or lesser degree. Only one in 10 thought change was well managed. The majority of companies believe that 50 per cent or more of their change programmes actually deliver the expected benefits, but only one in five put the success rate as high as 70 per cent or above.

Yet it seems that even with such a poor perception of change management, the internal view is much rosier than that of outsiders who have worked on transformation programmes in the UK. We asked interim consultants, many of whom have handled change programmes, how they rated the management of change in British companies. They were much more critical than businesses themselves, with two-thirds saying that change was poorly handled. When it came to delivery of benefits, just over a third of interim managers felt that 50 per cent or more of initiatives actually delivered their intended business benefits. This fell to just 14 per cent of those who thought the success rate was 70 per cent and above.

Why is the success rate for business change programmes in the UK so low?

Staff issues

The biggest mistakes, accounting for 30 per cent, were concerned with staff issues. Poor management of staff during change is a common fault in UK businesses. Decisions come from the top and everyone else is supposed to agree to them; there is little consideration given to winning hearts and minds. All too often the workforce pays lip service to change programmes, but there is still deep-rooted resistance.

This view was echoed by our survey of interim managers and their experiences of change programmes. They also feel that an inability to get staff buy-in, cited by 23 per cent, is a major flaw of change programmes. Other problems include not allowing enough time (20 per cent), shortage of skills within the team (16 per cent) and lack of leadership (14 per cent).

When interim managers are drafted in to help with change programmes they usually have a better overview of the project and normally have a direct report to senior management. They usually have previous experiences of change programmes for comparison, so this means that they are uniquely placed to see where management deficiencies lie.

Management problems

Problems with management also dominate the list of most common problems faced by companies trying to implement change, creating an image of change programmes being half-hearted or ill thought out. Although a lack of management resource is the most often-cited problem, issues relating to management style and skills are also prevalent, such as a reluctance to take decisions or a lack of vision.

Although change has the potential to deliver massive benefits – as well as cause major problems – the day-to-day responsibility for such programmes seems to have been somewhat devolved down the organization. This adds to the whole picture of change being poorly managed as senior directors give over the handling of vital projects to middle managers and heads of function who, although perfectly capable at their own jobs, may not have the influence or the skills to push such important initiatives through an organization. The majority of change programmes (60 per cent) are handled by middle managers and function heads. Only 27 per cent are dealt with by director-level executives.

Even more worrying is the fact that the respondents feel that this is having a negative impact on the 'day jobs' of people who have been given the responsibility of overseeing change. The nightmare scenario is that not only are change programmes suffering because of deficiencies in their management, with responsibility being passed down the ladder to the middle ranks who do not have adequate skills, resources and support, other parts of the business are also being neglected because managers are overstretched. Over half of respondents said managing change programmes was a distraction.

Senior management ownership

The problems are further compounded by the fact that senior managers are not taking ownership of programmes. When we asked our respondents what they felt senior executives were particularly poor at, yet again the issue of staff management came top. Twenty-one per cent said senior management is not good at inspiring the workforce; 18 per cent and 16 per cent respectively identified managing change and effective leadership as problems.

Leadership skills

In 2002 the leadership skills displayed by senior managers were also found wanting. Areas where they could do better included effective change leadership (82 per cent), communicating the news of change to the workforce (78 per cent) and identifying the most appropriate individuals to manage change (78 per cent). Sadly, it seems that senior management is lacking in many of the core skills expected of leaders and that are vital for the implementation of change.

The poor opinion of the role of senior management in the change process is all the more worrying considering the importance that many people attach to executive sponsorship for nurturing and shepherding change programmes through an organization.

Expectations versus outcomes

We asked a small sample of companies to give their views on what they expected from executive sponsorship and what they felt they actually received. The majority of respondents were negative in their assessment of the role senior management had played in change projects in helping to achieve the end goals. If top executives have no clear vision of what those goals should be, the failure rate is quite understandable.

The problem, it would seem, lies with a lack of understanding or appreciation of what senior executives can and should actually bring to the business change process. Almost two-thirds of companies (64 per cent) said that executive sponsors did not understand their role in change programmes or the impact they could have on the end results. This is a recurring theme throughout the *Challenge of Change Report 2006* – senior managers, from the board down, seem to have taken their eye off the ball when it comes to change.

The change industry is a multi-billion pound business with a raft of consultancies ready to tell companies why and how they should change. Some even offer the means to deliver change, but the tide seems to have finally turned against the major blue-chip management consultancies, at least in terms of perception of value for money. The majority of businesses planning a major change programme prefer to use their own internal resource, drafting in experts to either fill knowledge gaps or manage the entire process if required.

The majority of change programmes (54 per cent) were handled exclusively by internal teams, with a further 24 per cent using external interims or managers to deliver all or part of a change programme. Only 20 per cent used an external agency, of which less than half turned to the blue-chip brands such as Accenture. Obviously most companies feel that internal teams understand the culture of their business best, a stance that is borne out by the number of firms that rate their internal resources as the most effective. Belief in internal teams obviously pays off, as almost two-thirds said this was the most effective approach, with a significant one in five citing the use of independent change managers as being the most effective.

Many businesses know what they want to achieve as the end result, but they do not know how to go about it. An independent change manager will have the expertise or experience to show the way it should be done. Organizations that need to transform themselves are logical candidates for the temporary addition of additional senior management talent – and an experienced change management professional can often be of great help in integrating companies post-M&A.

Indeed, Executives Online finds that a huge proportion of interim assignments that it and its candidates conduct have some element of change management about them. More than 600 of Executives Online's registered candidates are independent change managers. When we asked our candidates what proportion of their work as interim managers had been part of a larger corporate change programme, the average answer was a resounding majority at 64 per cent.

There still seems to be a feeling that the major consultancy brands have their place, particularly in the bigger global corporations and high-profile public sector jobs, with the sentiment being that 'nobody ever got fired for using a top five consultancy – even if the programme failed'. There is a lot to be said for turning to a known practitioner when planning change, whether it is well-respected consultancy or a particular methodology such as Six Sigma. But the disparity between usage and satisfaction when it comes to consultancies (whether boutique or global) and interim or contract workers is striking. Consultancies (boutique and global) were mentioned by 20 per cent of respondents, even more than those mentioning dedicated internal teams, but very few rated them the most effective way to deliver change. By contrast, although they comprise only 9 per cent of the mentions, independent change managers engaged to lead and support a company through change are rated the most effective resource by fully 22 per cent of respondents.

We conclude from this that although the concept of independent change managers is not well understood by the market – there being low awareness of them as an option – they deliver excellent value and results for the few organizations who employ them. Given interim/contract workers fared more poorly in clients' ratings, it appears the independent change managers' effectiveness is a result of their focused expertise and ability, rather than simply due to their 'separateness' from the organization. It appears there is a substantial opportunity for UK businesses and organizations which need to successfully transform themselves to enhance their success by engaging independent change managers.

The challenge of change is best met when a skilled and experienced manager takes charge of that change, and change is often best achieved from without rather than from within.

Note

The Challenge of Change Report 2006 was compiled using research conducted among almost 200 UK businesses from across the UK, questioning senior managers and those responsible for change or business transformation programmes. Nearly three-quarters of all Executives Online's respondents have been responsible for a programme of change or business transformation. The vast majority of respondents hailed from the area of HR, although there was a significant number of replies from people who were department heads, directors or in charge of project teams. A good cross-section of industries was represented, with notable sectors including the public sector (20 per cent), professional services (15 per cent) and manufacturing (9 per cent).

Taxation issues

Hurst & Company

Introduction

The tax implications and planning opportunities for acquisitions and mergers are similar in most respects. Where there are differences these are highlighted. It is usual for the tax consequences for the purchaser and seller to conflict. An important aspect of any deal can therefore be to strike a balance. Indeed, careful tax planning can often help the two to agree on a basis which improves their respective post-tax positions. Both parties to the transaction will wish to minimize the tax costs to themselves. This chapter considers how this can be achieved.

Deal structure

Shares versus assets

One of the first decisions facing both vendor and purchaser is whether the transaction should be in the form of assets or shares. The preferences of the purchaser and the vendor will generally differ here. An assets deal will generally be more beneficial to purchasers, as they can obtain tax relief on the goodwill (Finance Act (FA) 2002, Sch 29) and fixed assets acquired. On the other hand, a share deal is likely to be more attractive for the vendor because of the availability of reliefs (see section 'Key shareholder relief', below). Input from advisers at the negotiation stage facilitates a mutual agreement of the best tax position for both parties.

An acquisition of shares/assets of the target may be made by individuals, companies or by a partnership/limited liability partnership (LLP). While there is no immediate tax impact of the choice of purchase vehicle, it is important to think ahead as it will in time affect the availability of reliefs on any future sale by the purchaser, as well as the tax treatment of profits and their extraction.

Acquisition of assets

From a commercial perspective, the purchaser can choose the assets it wants and avoid taking on liabilities. As a result, legal/professional costs on the deal may be lower as there will be less due diligence requirements. The purchaser will acquire the assets at a base cost equivalent to the relevant allocation of consideration, which must be on a 'reasonable basis'. With this in mind, the purchaser can also seek to optimize its tax position by assigning as much value as is practical to depreciable goodwill and fixed assets that attract capital allowances. Setting out allocations in the sale and purchase agreement provides valuable documentation if HMRC queries the amounts later. On the other hand, where the vendor is a company there will be a corporation tax (CT) charge on the asset sale and a further tax charge on any extraction of the proceeds received to individual shareholders (so there is effectively double tax charged).

Acquisition of shares

If the vendor shareholders are individuals, a single tax (capital gains tax, CGT) charge will arise on the sale. However, if the shareholders are corporates, then either the substantial shareholding exemption (SSE) will exempt any gain from tax or a CT charge will arise. The assets within the target company will be unaffected by a sale of the company's shares, so their base cost and so on remains the same, and the plant pool for capital allowances continues. However, there may be restrictions in the offset of future gains/losses made on assets owned by the target company prior to the sale (pre-entry gains/losses).

In addition, where the target company has trading losses on being acquired, then the Income and Corporation Tax Act (ICTA) 1988, s 768 (change in ownership of company: disallowance of trading losses) would only prevent those being carried forward to offset against future profits from the same trade, if within a period of three years before and after the change in ownership there is a major change in the nature/conduct of its trade. Going forward, current year losses in the target could be surrendered to other companies within the purchaser group provided necessary conditions are satisfied.

Key shareholder relief

Qualification for reliefs (Taxation of Chargeable Gains Act (TCGA) 1992, Sch A1, Sch 7AC, ss 152 onwards)

The most significant reliefs for the vendor are taper relief for individuals and SSE for corporates.

Sale by individuals

'Qualifying' individual shareholders will be entitled to taper relief to reduce the taxable gain on the sale of their shares, resulting in a possible effective tax rate of just 10 per cent where the target company has been a 'qualifying' trading company.

Sale by companies

Where a 'substantial' shareholding – 10 per cent or more – has been held for at least 12 months, SSE should be available to exempt the gain entirely from tax provided both the vendor and target company are trading companies (or members of a trading group) immediately before and after the sale. Rollover or holdover relief is available for asset sales by the company to defer chargeable gains arising where proceeds are reinvested in qualifying group assets within a specified timescale. This can be of equal importance to both vendor and purchaser.

Pre/post sale planning

Pre-sale planning

Debt restructuring prior to sale can reduce capital gains on a share disposal by a company (should SSE not apply). Care should be taken in advance of loan waivers to avoid creating a taxable credit with no corresponding tax deduction, or generating a value shift adjustment (this is a complex area). Pre-sale restructuring by the vendor through demerger or transfers of businesses can provide significant benefits. Tax breaks exist so this restructuring can often be done free of tax, but detailed anti-avoidance provisions should be considered (see ICTA 1988, s 703; TCGA 1992, ss 135 and 179).

On a share purchase, disclaiming capital allowances claimed by the target company can provide choice regarding the utilization of tax losses against future profits, particularly where, for instance, there is a concern about the anti-avoidance provisions of ICTA 1988, s 768 (see the notes on acquisition of shares above). This could also help an otherwise brought-forward loss to be converted into a current-year loss available for group relief purposes post-acquisition. Disclaimers can be done either by the purchaser or the vendor, but you need to ensure provision for this within the sale and purchase agreement.

Similarly, a dividend could be paid pre-sale to a corporate vendor (if SSE does not apply) and the purchase price reduced accordingly. This may result in a lower overall tax bill for the vendor and reduce the burden of financing the acquisition for the purchaser. This may also be relevant where the sale is by an individual and capital gains business assets taper relief is not available.

Post-acquisition planning (ICTA 1988, s 13; TCGA 1992, Sch 7AC; ITEPA 2003, s 404)

To improve the rate of corporation tax, so far as the small companies rate is concerned, consideration should be given to transferring acquired businesses into existing/similar subsidiaries, thereby reducing the number of associated companies for following accounting periods. But you should retain the option to sell distinct subsidiaries tax free where SSE applies. Where inter-company balances are created by such planning these can be subject to transfer pricing rules (after April 2004).

For shareholders/directors of the target companies, structuring exit packages with occupational pension payments can provide income tax and NIC (employer and employee) savings additional to the £30,000 tax-free payment. How to extract profits will depend on the specific tax circumstances of the company and the shareholder. Dividend, salary/bonus, debt finance or management charges require specific calculations to assess the appropriate mix.

Funding the acquisition (TCGA 1992, ss 150A–D, Sch 5B, s 151B, Sch 5C; ICTA 1988, Sch 28AA, s 842AA, Sch 15B, Sch 28B; FA 2000, Sch 15; FA 2006, Sch 14)

The acquirer will have its own considerations when choosing the method of funding the purchase. The key tax consideration for the purchaser will normally be to ensure that any interest costs are tax deductible. Loan interest is tax deductible, subject to anti-avoidance provisions, meeting the tests for allowable purpose and commercial levels of funding. Planning opportunities arise here with offshore subsidiaries to manage the overall rate of tax for the group through location of any acquisition borrowing. However, loan interest between UK and foreign group companies may be subject to both transfer pricing and thin capitalization rules. A review of the level of debt relative to equity and the market rate of interest will be crucial to avoid tax deduction restrictions.

In addition, an investment in certain qualifying shares (generally those of unquoted 'trading' companies) can attract beneficial tax relief for the investor. These reliefs come under the following:

■ enterprise investment scheme (EIS);
■ venture capital trust relief;
■ corporate venturing scheme.

Form of consideration planning (TCGA 1992, s 48, s 280)

The vendor will wish to ensure that its tax position follows the form that the sales consideration takes, the alternative forms being:

■ cash;
■ paper;
■ deferred consideration.

For the purchaser, consideration will generally be around access to cash to fund the purchase and a clause to postpone payment, either because of a shortage of immediately available cash or so that payments are contingent upon proven performance post-acquisition. To do this the purchase would normally offer paper, deferred consideration or an earn-out, or some combination of these.

Forms of consideration

Cash

Where a vendor receives cash, a capital gain arises immediately and, subject to reliefs, a tax liability becomes due for payment by the relevant date for individuals or company vendors as appropriate. This is the case even where all, or part of, the consideration is to be deferred. For individuals, where the consideration is payable by instalments over a period exceeding 18 months, HMRC may also allow the total liability to be paid in instalments. If a conditional contract containing a substantive condition ('condition precedent') is entered into, then the tax trigger point is delayed until that condition is satisfied.

Where the total monies to be received are 'unascertainable' at the date of disposal – being contingent on future events – then the 'right to receive' this 'unascertainable consideration' is deemed to be a separate asset which must be valued at the date of disposal and CGT paid accordingly. If subsequent monies received are less than the attributed value, a capital loss may arise which can be offset against the original gain.

The tax liability of an individual vendor could be deferred by reinvesting the proceeds in qualifying assets, for example shares in an EIS company. The position for a corporate vendor has already been addressed.

Paper

Where the purchaser issues shares/debentures to the vendors in exchange for their shares in the target, then, provided the conditions in TCGA 1992, ss 135–138 are met, the vendor is not treated as making a disposal of its target shares. Instead, the new shares/debentures are treated for CGT purposes as the 'old' shares – acquired on the same date and for the same price. Any chargeable gain is in effect rolled over into the new shares and will arise on the subsequent disposal of the new shares.

If a vendor receives an earn-out right (a right to receive), provided that right is to be satisfied in shares/debentures, then it can be treated as if it is itself a security and the same deferral applies. Care must be taken when drafting earn-out clauses in sale and purchase agreements to avoid capital payments being treated as remuneration. Advance clearance can and normally should be obtained under TCGA 1992, s 138 and ICTA 1988, s 707 to provide confirmation that the conditions are satisfied.

Where a loan note is to be issued, the taper relief position will vary depending on whether this is a 'qualifying' or 'non-qualifying' corporate bond. Where an individual vendor needs to extend his or her period of ownership in order to maximize taper relief entitlement, the 'paper' should be in the form of 'non-qualifying' corporate bonds. In either case, the loan note should not be capable of being redeemed within six months of issue, otherwise HMRC may see this as effectively being deferred cash consideration.

Consideration received in the form of the issue of shares/debentures of the purchasing company may fall under the employment-related securities provisions, therefore care is required when advising vendors who are also directors/employees.

Other matters

Finally, the following other matters will also need to be considered when giving tax advice in this area.

Tax due diligence

With a share purchase, as the purchaser will be taking on liabilities inherent in the target company, the tax due diligence process is undertaken to identify where a tax liability could potentially arise later as a result of transactions which took place before the acquisition. As a general guide the due diligence process would focus on reviewing:

■ HMRC enquiries and correspondence;
■ intra-group asset transfers in the previous six years;
■ reliefs claimed previously (holdover, rollover, stamp duty);
■ details of earlier reorganizations/reconstructions including clearances obtained.

Where the acquisition is to be of the assets (not shares) of the target company, the risk of taking on liabilities is much lower.

The outcome of the due diligence process may affect the extent of the warranties and indemnities sought by the purchaser, and extreme care should be taken by the adviser to think through the relevance of these matters to the case in hand.

VAT/stamp duty land tax (SDLT)/foreign taxes

The involvement of land and buildings requires care (and specialist input) regarding VAT and SDLT issues, particularly in terms of prior elections (option to tax) or tax-free transfers. The issues can affect both share and asset deals.

Overseas taxes

Taxes involved can vary significantly between countries, and therefore early local input to review the overseas issues is crucial.

Employment issues

Opportunities arise to review tax efficiency as part of aligning remuneration packages. Should the target operate share incentive schemes, care should be taken as these are subject to strict qualifying criteria.

Deal costs

Deal costs generally do not attract an immediate tax deduction in a trading company; however, certain costs, such as due diligence and fees for raising loan finance are more likely to qualify as a management expense of a holding company. Otherwise, acquisition costs are tax deductible on future disposal.

Conclusion

Mergers and acquisitions involve complex tax issues. Consequently, care is needed when giving advice in this area. However, with imagination these issues provide an opportunity to bring real value to both vendors and purchasers. It is fair to say that tax could even be the 'deal maker'.

Insurance issues in M&As

Alan Pratten, Heath Lambert Group

The last few years have seen an unprecedented increase in mergers, acquisitions and disposals activity. With increased activity, more complex structures and ever shorter timescales come increased levels of risk and exposure. Indeed, there are considerable risks to both purchasers and vendors in the negotiation of a sale and purchase contract.

Broadly speaking, insurance features in the M&A process in two distinct areas. First, it is increasingly commonplace for an adviser to be appointed to undertake insurance due diligence and /or for the vendor to produce a vendor's insurance due diligence report. The other area is that of transactional insurances, such as warranties and indemnities, which are designed to smooth the transaction taking place.

Insurance due diligence

The insurance due diligence process is applicable to companies throughout the world, no matter where they are domiciled or where their subsidiaries are located. It addresses issues such as:

- asset and liability protection;
- revenue exposures;
- corporate liabilities (including corporate governance);
- warranty and indemnity insurances;
- environmental liabilities (both first and third parties);
- historical liabilities;

- key-person issues;
- credit insurance and bonding;
- transfer of undertaking (TUPE) regulations, including ancillary benefits;
- risk management/health and safety.

In obtaining an insurance due diligence report, private equity houses and/or banks are seeking to gain clarity about the following areas.

What is the total cost of risk?

- premium/brokers fees;
- self-insured retentions;
- uninsured areas.

It is important to understand exactly what an insurance programme costs, both in terms of premium expenditure and those areas that are either self-insured or uninsured and could therefore cost the new company (Newco) in the future. It is also important to look at the whole package. While the premium expenditure of a company may seem low, on further examination it may be that it is self-insuring considerable amounts of risk that could arise in the future. There may also be areas of cover that the company has traditionally not insured at all. Insurance due diligence will examine these areas and recommend whether cover should be purchased in the future.

An insurance due diligence report would comment on the anticipated total cost of an insurance programme for Newco going forward.

Are there any historical liabilities?

If the transaction is one of shares, liabilities will transfer to Newco. It is important to establish what reserves have been made for such liabilities, and how these liabilities will be reserved for in the future. Insurance due diligence will comment on whether insurance policies are in place, or could be in place, to mitigate any of these historical liabilities.

What are the risks associated with the business?

Insurance due diligence will often involve comment and/or benchmarking against similar businesses. While obtaining a full claims experience gives an indication of risk, interviews with management and comparisons with peers in the industry provide a much clearer picture. They also give a useful guide to the risk management practice of the target company.

Leaders in the Field

nsurance is necessary for every business, but only becomes critical when things go wrong. Don't you want to know that your insurance partners are leaders in their field?

Our Mergers, Acquisitions and Disposals Practice is a dominant force in the market. Our success is based on our detailed knowledge and understanding of the sector. We are focused on the real needs of your business and developing meaningful partnerships.

We're looking forward to showing you how we could help you.

For more information contact Alan Pratten

+44 (0)20 7560 3000

Email: apratten@heathlambert.com

Heath Lambert Limited is authorised and regulated by the Financial Services Authority.

 Heath Lambert Group   *Surprisingly different*

Are there any specific transaction issues relating to the deal?

The report will seek to clarify the position with regard to directors' and officers' liability cover, where one policy is likely to be forced into run-off at completion date with another policy needing to be put in place at completion date. There are also issues of key-person cover relating to any key personnel who are to be involved in Newco going forward. This is often a requirement of the banks or other debt/equity providers.

Carve-out issues

Insurance due diligence is especially important for a carve-out from a larger organization. As will often be the case, a new insurance programme will be required from completion date as the parent company divests itself of all responsibility. It is also likely that the smaller company going forward has in the past relied on the parent company's insurance or risk management department to organize, place and manage the insurance issues. Going forward, Newco will need external advice to fulfil this function.

Other carve-out issues include maintaining access to parent company historical policies. Historical policies may have significant self-insured retentions and/or the involvement of a captive that need to be reserved for in the future. If historic aggregates are eroded, Newco will be uninsured and have to bear the cost of future claims.

The due diligence process

The typical insurance due diligence process is as follows:

Preliminary stage

- Agree letter of engagement.
- Sign letter of confidentiality.
- Obtain information from the data room, management and other advisers.
- Agree an action plan with scope and timescale.
- Obtain a copy of the information memorandum or business plan.
- Meetings with management/financiers (as appropriate).
- Undertake risk management surveys (as required).
- Undertake a confidential marketing exercise (if allowed).
- Discuss sale and purchase provisions with lawyers in regard to warranties that relate to insurance.

Delivery stage

Typical deliveries are a:

- report;
- letter of appropriateness;
- insurance programme.

Warranties and indemnities

Warranties and indemnities insurance is designed to pay defence costs and damages if there is a breach of warranty or indemnity given by the vendor in the sale and purchase agreement. The period of cover would be structured to mirror the period of contractual indemnity.

Cover is particularly useful for the avoidance of or reduction in escrow requirements, deferred considerations, or taking loan notes when minority shareholders or offshore shareholders cannot (or will not) make warranties or where the purchaser seeks a higher indemnity than a vendor can or will provide.

Both vendor and purchaser cover is available, as well as a hybrid format of the two.

Threats to the business

During the often lengthy discussions over the disposal of a business, the purchaser will use a number of 'weapons' in risk allocation, such as negotiation on price, completion accounts, and warranties and indemnities. The vendor can assume contractual liabilities for the business activities prior to the sale. These could impact the vendor for the whole period of the contractual liability – normally from 18 months to seven years.

The purchaser will want some form of recourse if the company turns out to be something other than the vendor represented it to be. Issues such as net asset value, key customers, fraud, non-disclosure, misrepresentation and environmental matters introduce a range of potential claim events to both parties. The purchaser may be unable to recover its full 'loss of economic value' from the vendor as a result of the warranty breach.

Solutions

Insurance can be used as an additional negotiating instrument in the risks that the purchaser may try to impose on the vendor. For example, the vendor has the option of accepting a reduced price or trying to lay-off or cap such risks via insurance. Insurance can provide comfort to the purchaser, as it does not have to rely on the ability of the previous owners of a company to meet pre-sale liabilities. This can be particularly effective where the previous owners of a business are not likely to be (or do not want to be) accessible.

The vendor is able to walk away from the company knowing that past liabilities have been ring-fenced. This can also achieve a reduction in escrow, deferred consideration or loan note provision. The purchaser can insure the full loss of economic value that may follow a warranty breach by the vendor, where the quantum of the breach is capped by the vendor.

What benefits will be gained from insuring?

Insurance:

- enables private equity houses to limit warranties;
- affords protection to the assets of either the corporation or individuals involved;
- facilitates the deal by removing potential sticking points over liability;
- avoids or greatly reduces the need for escrow, delayed payments or loan notes;
- credit enhances a deal by providing A+ paper to back up the warranties.

Differences in liability transfer

The main difference between a vendor policy and a purchaser policy is the same as the difference between a first and third-party loss. Under a vendor policy, legal liability must be established in order for the policy to respond. Under a purchaser policy, loss under the terms as defined in the policy must be established for the policy to respond. Therefore, it could be argued that the process of establishing a legitimate claim is less onerous for a purchaser policy than a vendor policy, which is reflected by the indemnity criteria.

What are the exclusions?

Exclusions vary from policy to policy but fall broadly into the following categories:

- fraud/dishonesty;
- warranties to future events;
- pollution/environmental;
- property (both tangible and intellectual);
- insured versus insured;
- adequacy of pension provision;
- adequacy of bad debt provision.

Although these exclusions are normally in the base wording, underwriters may be willing to consider offering cover in appropriate circumstances.

What is the period of cover?

The periods follow those in the sale and purchase agreement, and are typically for up to seven years for tax.

What are the policy limits?

Limits of between £5 million and £100 million are available, and can potentially be higher, depending on market capacity and the structure of the transaction.

Other transactional insurance products

There are a number of other insurances that may come into play.

Tax liability insurance

This provides protection against the failure of a transaction to qualify for its intended tax treatment. This solution is applicable for outstanding tax issues attached to a target company, which make it less attractive.

Litigation buy-outs/litigation caps

These involve the transfer or capping of known and/or potential litigation. This solution is applicable for an otherwise sound target for whom the outcome of a single piece or group of outstanding pieces of litigation is unknown, in terms of time to completion of litigation or likely costs. It is useful for an outstanding piece of litigation that is affecting the attractiveness or pricing structure of a transaction.

Environmental insurance

Environmental insurance provides cover for first and third-party legal liability, on-site/off-site clean-up, bodily injury/property damage to the extent required by statutory authorities, business interruption, legal defence costs, operational/manufacturing environmental risks going forward and a 'cost cap' to limit known liability costs. This area of insurance has been extensively developed over the last few years, providing a broader coverage than is available on standard liability policies.

Note

Warranty and indemnity insurance is not always available or appropriate for environmental liabilities transferring as a result of a transaction. This more specific policy format is often a better solution.

Credit and political risk insurance

This is for insolvency or default of customers and/or political risk resulting in frustration of contract, foreign exchange transfer delay and/or loss of assets held overseas. Traditionally credit insurance protects short-term cashflow and longer-term profit against the impact of bad debt. Credit insurance can now be used to secure the debtor asset, allowing access to more flexible funding options. It is often used during an acquisition or disposal to give finality to debt provisions in the sale and purchase agreement.

Contingent insurance

This type of policy indemnifies against a specific event or basket of events occurring in sequence: for example, a required event (such as completion of construction) not happening because of another specified event, such as labour strikes. A parent company may wish to divest one of its subsidiaries. The legal ramifications of liability between subsidiaries of the same parent post-divestment differ between various European countries. Potential buyers may have concerns that problems of other subsidiaries could create a chain of liability to their new acquisition, as it was once also linked to that parent. Insurance can potentially transfer this risk, providing peace of mind for the purchaser and removal of a potential balance sheet liability for the vendor.

Public offering of securities

Directors and officers liability programmes commonly exclude claims arising from the public offering of securities and issuing any prospectus. A specialist stand-alone cover not only ensures the directors and officers are covered but can also address other areas such as the higher limits required, broader jurisdiction and the periods of contractual liability. Cover can also be extended to indemnify the company and its sponsors.

Defective title and lease indemnity

Traditionally purchased on a location-specific basis, cover is now available for portfolio transfers. Recognizing that the timescales on many deals do not allow for full due diligence on all leases and title deeds, insurers will provide cover on a portfolio transfer basis. Cover includes restrictive covenants, incorrect use, boundary and access disputes, planning consent issues, lease transfer issues and disputes over ownership of title.

The importance of being earnest

The importance of ensuring that all the potential risks and exposures to both purchaser and vendor are identified and managed cannot be overestimated. For example, in a recent transaction involving a cash-in-transit business, time was a factor and an insurance due diligence report was critical in order to anticipate the risk and insurance issues that Newco was likely to face upon completion. Risk and insurance is extremely important to this sector for a number of reasons:

- It is not possible to trade without cover.
- The cost of insurance is high and will determine the competitiveness of the end service.
- The levels of self-insurance required by insurers are likely to be significant – these must be reserved for.
- Capital expenditure is very relevant – the cost of security can be large and ongoing as systems become more sophisticated. This will in turn impact on both the premium cost and self-insured retention.
- The breadth of cover must be wide and among other things should include infidelity of employees.

Before embarking on any merger, acquisition or disposal activity, it is vital that the expertise of a professional insurance adviser be brought to bear.

Service agreements and pension provisions

Richard Jones, Punter Southall & Co

Background to service agreements

Service agreements are effectively the contracts of employment for senior management and in particular the directors of a business. As with a contract of employment, the service agreement sets out the details of the role and the terms and conditions that will apply to that individual's employment with the company. The scope of a service agreement, which is too wide to cover in detail in this chapter, includes, but is not limited to, the following items:

- The role and the responsibilities that are part of that role.
- Any restrictions upon the individual on taking on concurrent roles with other parties.
- The hours of work and the location in which the work will be completed.
- The basic salary to be provided and arrangements for future reviews of the basic salary.
- Bonus arrangements and any other profit-related pay arrangements such as options schemes and long-term incentive plans.
- The pension benefits that will be provided.
- Any insurance benefits, such as death in service, private medical and permanent health insurance, that will be provided.
- The procedures for reclaiming out of pocket expenses incurred as a result of the employment and procedures for the approval of senior management expense claims.

- Holiday entitlements and the procedures for booking holidays and accounting for holiday days not exercised in the relevant period.
- Sick pay entitlements and the procedures for sick leave.
- Contractual agreement to comply with various pieces of legislation while undertaking the role (for example, the Data Protection Act or health and safety legislation).
- A contractual agreement on confidentiality and agreement to retain proprietary information within the company.
- Termination procedures and in particular notice periods and entitlements.
- Disciplinary and grievance procedures.
- Protections for intellectual property that will be created by the individual while in service with the company.
- Restrictive covenants and non-compete arrangements that will come into effect if service with the company is terminated.

A specialist employment lawyer can provide advice on service agreements and draft the necessary documentation. However, the provisions in respect of pension benefits are often a neglected area of consideration in determining the service agreement, and it is the specific pension provisions on which this chapter is focused.

For senior management, pension arrangements are often designed to provide them with an income equal to two-thirds of their full remuneration before retirement at a relatively early age (the 60th birthday is the latest age at which senior management benefits typically become payable). Such a pension benefit can, at retirement, be equal in value to 15 or even 20 times the annual remuneration of the senior manager, with the impact that their pension benefits make up a very substantial proportion of these individuals' net worth.

Types of senior management pensions

Senior management pensions can be divided into two main categories, those which operate on a defined contribution (DC) basis and those that operate on a defined benefit (DB) basis.

In a DC arrangement, the sponsoring employer pays a set level of contributions each year, usually expressed as a percentage of salary, into each member's individual fund. The pension a member receives depends on the amount of contributions paid in respect of that member by both the employer and the member, the level of investment returns generated on those contributions and annuity rates at the time the member retires.

A DB arrangement presents much greater risks to the sponsoring employer as the benefits are fixed by reference to a formula typically based on salary and service. The employer remains responsible for ensuring that sufficient funds are available to meet the benefits. The sponsoring employer is exposed to fluctuations in costs because of investment returns, mortality experience and other experience such as salary increases, inflation and the exercise of member options.

Historically, senior managers in the UK were provided with a DB arrangement that aimed to provide a fully inflation-protected pension of two-thirds of their remuneration in the final year of working (with some averaging features to protect those who reduced their workload in the years before retirement), payable from age 60. Such a benefit would add 20 per cent to 60 per cent to an individual's remuneration each year, depending on the person's age and benefit structure, and quickly accumulate to a capital value of many times the senior manager's remuneration.

More recently DC arrangements have become more popular as these provide a greater degree of clarity on pension costs and are of lower risk for the employer to provide. However DC arrangements only provide a small advantage for the employer (through savings in National Insurance costs) over paying greater cash remuneration and allowing senior managers to decide what amount of pension saving they require. Therefore many remuneration packages these days are constructed on the basis that no pensions will be provided but, should senior manager(s) wish, the employer will pay a proportion of the remuneration to a DC arrangement and share the saving in National Insurance with the senior manager(s). This provides senior managers with greater flexibility on remuneration, whereby they can choose to take cash if they wish or alternatively have some of their remuneration paid into their pensions (known as a 'salary sacrifice' or a 'flexible benefit' arrangement).

DC arrangements and flexible benefit arrangements are quite transparent and easily understood, and thus do not present significant difficulties for service agreements. DB arrangements are much less transparent, and present significant issues when putting together service agreements with senior management.

Point of transaction as a trigger for change

Most companies recognize that in their employment market the presence of a DB pension arrangement provides little competitive recruitment advantage and generally is undervalued relative to its potential cost to the employer. Therefore, a more attractive remuneration package can usually be provided at the same cost by providing more cash in the remuneration package at the expense of pension benefits.

For this reason a merger or acquisition will often be used as a trigger event for changing from a DB pension arrangement to a DC pension arrangement or even a flexible arrangement. Such changes add to shareholder value even if they have the same cash cost, as there is a reduction in risk and the addition of transparency in remuneration packages.

Although there can be difficulties in making such a change for current employees, these difficulties are often exaggerated and, from a shareholder perspective, there are significant gains in making such a change. Even where the difficulties are unmanageable (typically this is because of trade union involvement, contractual issues or the provisions of the DB arrangement governing documents) such a change should be made for new employees, and in particular any new senior management appointed as a result of the transaction.

Agency costs and DB pensions

The opacity of DB arrangements presents significant issues for shareholders in attempting to align the interests of senior managers with their own focus on shareholder value. This problem can be particularly acute in a merger or acquisition, where the existing senior managers are currently members of a DB arrangement and they will be retained following completion. In particular:

- Management often reports the costs of the benefits being granted each year in a DB arrangement as a percentage of salary calculated across the scheme as a whole. While this is a good estimate for the overall cost of the DB arrangement, it masks the costs of senior management benefits. It would not be atypical for the average cost to be around 15 per cent of remuneration per annum, but the cost of individual senior manager benefits to be significantly in excess of 30 per cent of remuneration per annum.
- Where management are receiving such generous benefits each year and the cost is under-reported (whether consciously or just as a result of the very technical nature of DB arrangements), an incentive is created to continue with the DB arrangement for all staff to mask this extra remuneration being granted to senior managers. In most cases it is clearly in shareholders' interests for a DB arrangement to be shut off to new benefits and replaced by a DC arrangement. Where management are gaining extra remuneration, the incentive to undertake what is a time-consuming project is much reduced.
- Most companies are no longer providing DB arrangements for new employees, including senior managers, and thus where such an arrangement is provided, its generosity can prevent senior management from moving on even where they have reached the limit of their ability to add to shareholder value.
- A DB arrangement is completely separate from the employer and managed by a different set of individuals – the trustees. The Pensions Regulator in the UK has increasingly been encouraging trustees to act like material unsecured creditors of the company, and to conduct negotiations robustly with the company. Where a senior manager has to negotiate over an arrangement that in effect provides a substantial part of his/her net worth, it becomes difficult for that senior manager to make hard decisions that might add to shareholder value or to negotiate robustly with the trustees.

For these reasons alone we strongly recommend that, even if there is no possibility of closing the DB arrangement to all employees, senior management employees are taken out of the arrangement at or shortly after completion of an acquisition. This may require a degree of individual negotiation with the senior management, but the benefits from the removal of agency costs can be significant.

Annual pay reviews and promotions

The opacity of DB arrangements presents additional problems for remuneration committees and other decision makers in setting pay packages for senior management individuals who are beneficiaries of such arrangements. This can be a particular problem where promotions or redesigns of remuneration packages are involved as a result of merger and acquisition activity.

Most DB arrangements provide benefits that are linked to 'final salary' at retirement but based on total company service. For an individual with a number of years of service already, a significant increase in remuneration not only increases the monetary value of the additional benefit to be granted over the coming year, but has the effect of increasing in value the prior benefits that were granted in respect of previous years of service.

A simple example will illustrate this point clearly. Imagine a 50-year-old senior manager with 30 years' service with the employer and membership of the DB arrangement. He currently earns £60,000 per annum, and as a result of a promotion where he is taking on a more senior role, he will receive a 20 per cent pay rise. The senior manager's accrued pension has a valuation of around eight times his current earnings, and thus the impact on the value of his current accrued pension of the 20 per cent pay rise is to increase it by around £100,000 – not bad for an increase in future earnings of £12,000 per annum. The real impact of this increase in value will be seen in the year-end accounting numbers as well as future cash contributions, as the benefits have increased faster than reserved for in the valuation(s).

Remuneration committees need to be aware of the 'windfall' gains created inadvertently by pay rises, and also when comparing the remuneration packages provided to senior managers against median market remuneration packages from surveys. Making adjustments to packages on the basis of market medians, without taking account of the value of accrued DB benefits, is not comparing like with like.

The purpose of comparing against the market median is to provide an analysis of what the senior manager could earn were he or she to change jobs. In order to make this comparison fair it should be assumed, for the purposes of calculating the value of DB benefits, that the senior manager has already left employment. The increase in the value of DB benefits over the coming year therefore needs to take account of two different elements: the increases in the value of the past service benefits granted as a result of remuneration increasing faster than inflation (the statutory required increase for former employees' pensions), plus the cost of an additional year of service being granted within the DB arrangement.

While this may sound quite complex, actuaries have been calculating numbers on what is known as the 'current unit method' for many years, and this does not present them with any difficulties. Remuneration committees should already have their actuary calculating the cost of each senior manager's pension costs – taking account of individual benefit packages and the individual's age – rather than using average rates across the whole scheme. To extend this analysis from the usual 'projected unit method' calculation to the 'current unit method' is straightforward.

Other pension issues with service agreements

There are two other aspects of pension that should be considered when dealing with senior management service agreements. The first is the definition of 'pensionable' remuneration, being the remuneration upon which the pension benefits are based, which needs careful consideration for both DB and DC arrangements. This is particularly the case when considering termination packages and long-term incentive plans – generally one would not want these elements of remuneration to be 'pensionable'. Second, generous early retirement benefits present a double-edged sword to some extent, and should be considered carefully. While such benefits can allow an under-performing senior manager to be moved on without significant impediment, they also encourage good managers to leave. Ideally, the company would like to retain discretion over whether to allow a senior manager to take early retirement.

Summary

Senior management service agreements set out the terms and conditions that apply for their employment. Pension provisions are often neglected but can be crucial, especially where DB pension arrangements are in place.

Preparing for admission to the Alternative Investment Market (AIM)

Andrew Millington, Mazars

Since its launch in 1995, the AIM market has established itself as one of the world's most successful markets for small and medium-sized growth companies. In that time, over 2,000 companies from more than 30 business sectors have joined the market, in the process raising more that £20 billion.

The benefits of joining AIM

Often companies view listing on a public market primarily as a way of raising funds for investment in further growth. However, there are many other reasons that companies should consider AIM as an attractive market, including to:

- determine an objective market value for the company's shares;
- enhance the company's status with customers and suppliers;
- raise the company's profile;
- improved ability to complete acquisitions with the option of offering shares as part of the consideration;
- enable greater employee participation and commitment.

AIM is particularly attractive when compared with other stock markets for the following reasons:

- A simplified regulatory regime: so long as there is no offer to the public (for instance, a placing to less than 100 investors), the impact of the admission document directive is significantly reduced.
- The criteria for entry are focused on meeting the requirements of smaller companies: for instance no track record is required, and there is no minimum market capitalization.
- There are tax advantages for both the company and investors.
- There are fewer requirements for shareholder approvals, for example when making acquisitions.

The admission process

Once the decision to seek an admission to AIM has been taken, the process requires careful planning, and is often considered in three distinct phases:

- pre-admission phase;
- admission process;
- post-admission issues and ongoing requirements.

Each phase requires different considerations, information requirements and outputs.

Pre-admission phase

As company owners/directors may not have previously been through an AIM admission or other stock market flotation, they often look to advisers to assist them in a number of areas during the pre-admission phase. As much as anything the admission requires very careful organization of internal resources, the gathering of information and overall planning of the project. A highly structured approach can also help to save both time and cost.

Each company should give careful consideration to key issues well in advance of the run-up to admission. Doing so allows the company time to put into place any significant pre-admission objectives. The key areas that should be considered in detail include the following.

Corporate and financing structure

It is important that personal and corporate objectives are aligned. This includes a detailed review of the corporate and financing structures of the business, and consideration of issues such as:

- simplifying the financing structure and reviewing the likely ongoing post-admission finance requirements;
- cleaning up the ownership structure by consolidating and simplifying shareholdings;
- deciding whether to use an existing holding company (in the case of a group) or to establish a new holding company to undertake the admission;
- reviewing post-admission dividend requirements and removing dividend blocks in the existing structure.

Tax planning

Effective and careful tax planning should ensure that all those affected by the float process gain maximum tax advantage. This includes considering the tax position of:

- *the company*: impact of any pre-admission reorganizations;
- *the shareholders*: considering taxable gains on disposals and reliefs available under EIS or VCT to individuals or venture capital trusts;
- *the management and key employees*: taxing of share-based payment schemes.

Financial reporting

Information included in the admission documents needs to show a 'true and fair' view. If companies have previously not been subject to audit, the reporting accountants will need to perform their own procedures to audit standard. This can be difficult if financial information from prior years is not readily available.

The information also needs to be presented in a form that is consistent with that which the company will use when preparing its next set of published accounts. Any changes to accounting standards, policies and legislation should be borne in mind. Other key considerations include:

- In group situations, the preparation of consolidated accounts is required.
- Whether accounts have been prepared under UK, US or international financial reporting standards and, if not, an assessment of the procedures required to convert to one of these generally accepted accounting procedures. From 1 January 2007, all AIM companies will need to prepare accounts that conform to IFRS.
- A review of existing accounting policies to ensure they are in line with industry best practice.
- Looking at changes in the group structure, particularly as a result of acquisitions and disposals.
- Considering the impact of any qualifications made to auditors' reports.

Control systems

Management must be able to demonstrate that the appropriate control systems are in place to monitor the key business activities. This should also cover significant IT-based systems. Assessment at an early stage should identify any systems deficiencies that need to be rectified before the admission process starts. In particular, investors will want to be reassured that systems in operation are sufficiently robust to enable the accurate reporting of data to management, while also safeguarding against the occurrence of fraud and error.

Management and governance

A stock market listing frequently requires the 'beefing-up' of the board. In particular, corporate governance good practice requires the appointment of non-executive directors. Non-execs often bring a great wealth of experience through having worked in the market in which the business operates, or through their experience of dealing with stock market rules and meeting with institutional investors. The role of each of the directors should be clearly defined, and their remuneration determined.

At the same time a strong management team should be built around the core directors. This will help to inspire investor confidence, and provide an element of continuity to the team should any of the key directors decide to exit the business shortly after the admission.

Marketing

Prior to admission, the directors and their advisors will try to determine who may be the target investors, as well as the likely market appetite for their flotation. These discussions should also help to determine the timing, nature and extent of financing. For example, it will be necessary to consider what proportion of the company's shares should be floated. There is no minimum for companies listed on AIM. However, a lower float percentage can affect the liquidity and turnover in trading of a company's shares.

This is also a good time to consider the operating structure of the business and evaluate any non-core activities. These may ultimately be sold prior to the listing to assist with raising funds for investment in core activities or to simplify the business for presentation to investors. The directors should also consider how best to build the business's corporate image, and review its relations with the media.

Appointment of advisers

The appointment of good advisers should help to maximize the likelihood of the admission being successful. The principal advisers for an AIM listing are the following.

Nominated adviser (NOMAD)

Each company needs to appoint a NOMAD who is required to confirm to the London Stock Exchange that the company is complying with AIM rules on entry and that the directors are aware of their obligations and responsibilities. The NOMAD coordinates and leads the admission process.

Broker

The broker is responsible for attracting funds and the placing of the shares. AIM rules require that a company retains a broker at all times. Frequently the NOMAD and the broker are from the same organization.

Reporting accountant

The role of reporting accountant is principally focused on reviewing and reporting on historical and forecast financial information, together with performing detailed due diligence on the business.

Lawyers

The lawyers are responsible for performing due diligence on the company's litigation position and for reviewing significant contracts that the company needs to disclose as part of the admission process. They are also involved in ensuring that statements in the AIM admission document are properly supported and verified.

Public relations

The appointment of a public relations company is made principally to assist with raising the profile of the business within the marketplace.

All of the advisers work closely with the management team to ensure that information is collated in a structured way and in line with the admission timetable.

Admission process

The process of listing on AIM usually takes three to four months. This is often a period of high activity, and requires significant involvement from the board, key management and the company's advisers. The admission process itself follows are fairly well-set pattern, with the requirements being largely similar from one admission to another.

Stage 1: planning

Stage 1 of the admission process involves the NOMAD taking an initial view as to the company's suitability for admission. During this phase the NOMAD will perform a number of tasks including:

- reviewing the business and the issues it faces in moving to a plc;
- drawing up an initial timetable based on the quality and availability of historic figures and reliability of forecasts;
- appointing the advisers – reporting accountant, lawyer and public relations company;
- agreeing engagement terms;
- outlining all documents required;
- preparing a list of all parties involved in the process.

Stage 2: due diligence

The due diligence phase involves work by the reporting accountant and lawyers to assess the suitability of the company to proceed towards admission. The reports prepared by the advisers follow a set pattern and include the following:

- *long form report*: includes an overview of the company's business, its history, and a review of financials, including review of internal controls and accounting policies/procedures;
- *short form report*: summary of the audited accounts for the last three years, for inclusion in the admission document;
- *working capital report*: review of profit forecasts to be included in the admission document for supporting the future working capital adequacy statement made in the admission document.

Once these are complete, the NOMAD assesses the results from the reports and considers any areas that need to be addressed, such as deficiencies in internal controls. When satisfied with the due diligence work, the NOMAD will confirm to prospective investors that due diligence has not indicated factors that would call into question the suitability of the company for admission.

Stage 3: broker research

The next stage of the process involves the broker's analyst performing an assessment of the state of the market in which the company operates and the overall prospects of the company. The research is carried out independently from the company and all the parties involved in the due diligence process. This ensures that elements of potential bias are eliminated. The results of the research are not included in the admission document.

Stage 4: drafting process

The admission document is a public document, and the responsibility for its preparation rests with directors. The document explains in detail:

- reasons for seeking admission and details of the fundraising;
- the business;
- its prospects;
- details of the board and management, remuneration arrangements and corporate governance procedures;
- financial information – historic and projections;
- risk factors;
- 'lock in' arrangements – requirements for key existing shareholders not to sell their shares within a specified period after flotation;
- other information to support the admission or as required by the AIM rules in order to comply with selected parts of the admission document rules.

The drafting process is controlled by the NOMAD, and frequent meetings are held with all advisers to discuss content and presentation of information. A detailed verification of information in the admission document is conducted by the lawyers. This represents the ability of the company to support all statements made in the admission document.

Stage 5: marketing

The broker arranges for management to meet with potential investors typically in 'road shows'. These meetings are usually attended by the managing director and finance director, and are based around pre-prepared presentations and the draft admission document ('pathfinder'). The meetings may need to be arranged at several locations if the company has overseas operations – this is common for international companies seeking admission to AIM.

The marketing process frequently involves significant activity over a short time-frame – typically two weeks. As there are many back-to-back meetings, management need to be energetic and highly motivated.

Stage 6: placing and placing agreement

Following the presentations with potential investors, the sales team of the broker assesses feedback from investor meetings. The broker then builds a 'book' of shares that that investors would be willing to buy at a range of prices. On completion of this process, the final share price is set and shares are allocated to investors. Placing letters confirming allocations are distributed to investors, and the broker considers whether it needs to underwrite any shares not placed or reduce the level of funds to be raised. Finally, the placing agreement is signed between the brokers, directors and the company.

Stage 7: admission to AIM

In the run-up to admission, letters sent to investors are signed and returned to the broker. This is followed by 'impact' day when the:

- flotation is made public;
- admission document is issued in final form;
- placing agreement is signed by respective parties;
- application is made for admission.

Funds are collected by the broker from investors, and after three days, trading in shares commences and net proceeds of funds raised are paid to the company. Finally, the shareholders' register is updated to reflect all new shareholders.

Post-float issues and ongoing requirements

Once the admission process is complete there are many ongoing requirements that the company and the directors need to fulfil.

Financial and other information

Companies trading on AIM must provide regular updates on the financial performance and developments to shareholders and other stakeholders. It is therefore important that companies continue to have robust and reliable accounting systems and internal controls. In particular it is important to monitor performance against budget and market expectations.

Ownership

The ownership structure of the company will have been considered in detail as part of the pre-admission process. However, circumstances may change following flotation, and this calls for careful monitoring of shareholdings, for example for signs of share sell-offs or unusual trading activity. Being a listed company also increases the risk of potentially hostile activity from predators or key competitors. It is helpful to build action plans which consider how the directors will react to such situations should they arise.

Investors will often look towards growth in share price and dividend distributions as key indicators of success for the business. It is important to review the dividend policy, to balance the demands of returning funds to shareholders with retaining funds within the business to assist with future growth opportunities.

Strategic plans

Funds raised from the admission are frequently used to invest in future growth strategies for the business. These strategies should be focused on building and sustaining the performance of the company, thereby increasing enterprise and shareholder value. They should also be closely aligned with tax planning opportunities available to the company.

At the same time as refining the business's strategies for growth, these strategies should also be clearly communicated to shareholders. This will help to improve market perception.

Management and governance

The structure of the management team following admission requires careful consideration. While much thought is put into the structure of boards pre-admission, often the structure will only be finalized shortly before the admission process starts. Allowance must be made for such issues as the evolution of the board and making best use of the non-executive directors' contacts and experience. In addition, the remuneration and audit committees require implementation to comply with best practice corporate governance requirements.

Marketing and communication

The ongoing marketing of the business takes on further significance once a company is listed. It is helpful to have a person or team responsible for investor relations, to answer questions and queries from shareholders as well as to send out key information, such as annual reports and interim statements of financial performance. In addition, the increased scrutiny placed on the company means that relations with the media need to be carefully handled. Building the corporate image and enhancing market perception can best be achieved through a well-constructed PR programme.

Regulatory issues

Being listed on AIM brings many more regulatory considerations and requirements. For example, companies must comply at all times with the AIM Rules, which provide detailed guidance on the requirements for disclosure and other continuing obligations. Certain aspects of the Companies Act and EU Directives also increase the regulatory burden placed on listed companies and their directors.

How to choose your professional advisers for an AIM flotation

David Massey, Athanor Capital Partners

At some point in their development most companies consider growth by way of acquisition. While this can be financed either out of cashflow or debt, the other obvious route is by using paper. Most vendors will not take unquoted paper, and this means the company has to consider a flotation. The most successful smaller companies market in the world is the Alternative Investment Market (AIM) of the London Stock Exchange. If your company is at too early a stage to contemplate AIM, there is increasing interest in Ofex (now renamed PLUS Markets). If your company is larger than this and contemplating a full listing, you already have too many advisers.

The chief executive of a small company contemplating a first AIM admission could be forgiven for throwing in the towel and going for a trade sale when confronted by a first 'all parties' meeting. This generally comprises principals plus actual work doers from at least six professional advisers jockeying for control over the process while charging the client in aggregate several thousand pounds an hour. So how is this to be avoided, what if anything do all these professionals actually do, and how do you choose appropriate advisers?

The first item to realize is that while the client is paying, it is in large part paying for other people to cover its back. In theory the professional advisers are there to undertake due diligence enquiries to ensure that the company is suitable for listing, put together the appropriate documentation, and assist the company in fulfilling its continuing obligations. In practice very little of this contributes to the company's objectives of raising money and getting a listing.

For an AIM admission, the dramatis personae are:

- nominated adviser (NOMAD);
- nominated broker;
- lawyers to company;
- lawyers to NOMAD;
- reporting accountants;
- financial PR.

NOMAD

If you are doing an AIM admission, then the company must have a NOMAD. Note that a company does not 'list' its shares on AIM (only the full list is 'listed'), it has them admitted to trading, as any number of people will be pleased to point out. City jargon fulfils the same purpose as any other: to make outsiders feel excluded and uncertain, and therefore more easy to control.

The requirement for a NOMAD is absolute; if your NOMAD resigns and you do not have another one, the company's shares will be suspended until it does. The role of the NOMAD is that of primary adviser to the company, but in reality it is the gate-keeper to AIM. The highly successful delegated regulation of AIM means that the stock exchange passes no opinion on whether any individual company is suitable for admission. It delegates this role to the NOMAD, with the sanction being that if a NOMAD is associated with too many unsuitable companies it could have its status withdrawn.

To be a NOMAD a firm must have a minimum of four appropriately qualified individuals with experience of smaller company flotations. At the time of writing there are nearly 100 NOMAD firms, ranging from the largest investment banks though corporate finance practices of accounting firms and stockbrokers to corporate finance boutiques with only a handful of staff.

The NOMAD must be satisfied that appropriate due diligence enquiries have been made, and that the document (prospectus in the case of money being raised) is not misleading, has appropriate risk warnings and contains all the material facts. As a rule of thumb, if you do not wish to disclose something it is probably material. The document ultimately produced is in most cases completely anodyne and does not operate as a marketing document for the company.

The criteria to consider when choosing a NOMAD are:

- size of firm;
- its normal deal size;
- its area of expertise;
- whether it is solely a NOMAD or also acts as broker.

Many NOMADs will not take on very small companies (market capitalization less than £10 million), because these companies are seen, correctly, to have a higher risk of failure. But some firms specialize in this area and are adept at raising money in the sub-£1 million range. It is very important for your deal to be in the range within which the NOMAD (and other advisers) is comfortable.

There is a preponderance of certain types of company on AIM, in particular mining and other natural resource stocks. This is not just because the AIM rules are accommodating to these types of company (which they are), but also because from an investor perspective the risk/reward balance is perceived to be attractive. If they work, natural resources stocks can be very profitable, which balances the inherent higher risks of small companies.

Natural resources stocks require special expertise, in particular the preparation of what is known as a 'competent person report', an additional expert report. If your company is active in a sector such as these, there are a handful of specialist firms to which it is best to go. Similarly, if your company has exposure to China or Russia, or specialist technology/biotech intellectual property, it is best to select a NOMAD which has done similar deals before. It will save time and effort in terms of due diligence enquiries.

Many firms are integrated, and offer to be both NOMAD and nominated broker to the company. This may result in a small saving on fees (and they may insist that they provide both services), but the downside of this is that you are more dependent for advice on just one source.

Broker

The least vocal participant in meetings is often the broker to the company. This is strange because everyone else at the table is engaged in spending money, but only the broker is raising it. If the broker cannot sell the deal to the investor base nothing will happen. The average AIM flotation raises considerably less than £10 million. It is easy to talk about raising money, but a large proportion of firms you will meet will not actually be able to raise more than £1 million. Very few can raise over £10 million. So how do you choose?

While institutional investors (pension funds, specials situations funds, venture capital trusts and so on) do now routinely invest in AIM stocks, be aware that the definition of a smaller company by most institutional standards is anything less than £100 million, and some will say less than £250 million. Relatively few institutions invest in stocks with a capitalization of £10 million or less. Also, the smallest holding a unit trust or similar institutional investor will hold in a company is probably £250,000. Funds have routine clear-outs, and holdings of say £100,000 are often considered a nuisance and simply sold out, perhaps with negative effects on the share price. So if you are looking to raise single-figure millions on a market capitalization of a few tens of millions or less, then most of your investor base, although hopefully with a couple of funds as cornerstones, will come from private clients.

So ask whether your broker has:

- an extensive private client network;
- a smaller number of high net worth individuals;
- an institutional base.

Lawyers to the company

As with any other professionals, law firms are increasingly specialized, and there is no value in appointing the local firm that does your conveyancing to handle a major corporate transaction. In any listing, as in any corporate finance transaction, the lawyers are there to write all the bits of the document that nobody wants to read at the time but will be sure to scrutinize at length later if it all goes wrong.

Legal costs are the least easily controlled in any transaction, as the various firms involved engage in a daily exchange of versions of the contracts and other documents in an increasingly arcane process. The sheer weight of paper produced is daunting, but not so much as the bills (at £350+ per hour for partners) for producing it.

The appointment of legal advisers suffers more than any category from the 'my daddy is bigger than your daddy' syndrome, and small firms making acquisitions often end up appointing big-name law firms to handle their business, presumably on the assumption that it will intimidate the other side. Actually it might, but at great cost. It is also fair to say that the other advisers involved will want to see that that the lawyers have handled such transactions in the past, and may even insist on your using one of a certain number of firms nominated by them. But unless you enjoy the process of going to see big London firms, the size of the firm should be in proportion to the size and complexity of the deal. Indeed, there are a large number of smaller firms whose partners have been involved in many larger transactions but have split off from big firms to form their own firm. By using one of these you will pay lower rates and probably get a more senior person handling your case.

If you have a cross-border deal then it would be suicidal not to appoint established specialists in this area. Similarly, property and media/intellectual property requires specialist knowledge. The most important piece of advice is to agree fixed fees for the work rather than paying on the clock. The latter is almost certain to result in a painful billing experience. Finally, it is quite common for you to have to appoint two sets of lawyers, as the NOMAD may wish to appoint its own firm, at your expense of course, to review the work done by the company's lawyers at your expense.

Accountants

Any firm of the size that can contemplate an AIM admission will already have auditors. What it needs for AIM is to have a firm of reporting accountants which produces the long form working capital report (which is not published, but seen by the advisers and increasingly by institutional investors) and the short form report (which is published).

The point about the working capital report is that it is in nobody's interest for a company to list on AIM and then run out of money in short order. It is embarrassing for the advisers, does not do the reputation of the stock exchange any good, and the investors who will have lost virtually all their money are not that happy either. AIM rules require that a company have enough working capital for a year following listing. In practice this is interpreted as 18 months.

The crucial point is that the working capital requirement can become a huge hurdle which can only be crossed by the company raising enough new money. If the brokers prove to be unable to raise quite as much as they originally intimated, the listing might have to be aborted. So it is important to work with a firm of accountants that really understands your business and does not build in unnecessary contingencies in its working capital projections which could ultimately scupper the deal.

Big firms do give some investors comfort, but below a certain deal size the vast majority of investors are unconcerned about the absence of a 'Big Four' accounting firm on the document. However, other advisers will want to know that the accountants have done AIM listing work before.

Financial PR

Financial PR firms can be divided up into two types. The first, and increasingly the model for the industry, is made up of hard-working PR professionals who will make an effort to understand your company and make sure it is always presented in the best light. The second, and waning, type is small firms of older but well-preserved (in alcohol) former journalists who operate solely from a contact book. Both have their advantages.

You must identify your objectives from financial PR. Note that if you have an existing industry or consumer PR firm and it offers to do the financial PR, decline politely but firmly. Financial PR is a niche business relying on specialist contacts. The objective of financial PR is not to get your name (or preferably photo) in the national press. It is there to focus potential investor interest on your flotation and help maintain an interested investor base in the future. You have in most cases come to the market to raise money in the future, so you need to build a relationship with your investors.

A company is not required to have a financial PR, but at the time of writing there are over 1,500 companies on AIM. Each of these will have many announcements every year including profits, annual meetings, trading updates, placings, acquisitions and so on, so the relatively small number of journalists covering financial stories is faced with literally thousands of items a year. Thursday is the busiest day for financial news and Monday the quietest – PRs don't like working weekends either.

Check out the *Financial Times*, the paper of record. Its coverage of smaller companies is limited to about a dozen one-paragraph summaries on the back page of the 'companies and markets' section, and about a half-page inside. The only way you are likely to get a bigger piece is by being arrested for fraud. You may think that the mere fact that your company is coming to market is worthy of coverage but it is not, and PRs have to work hard to get coverage.

Look for PRs who can demonstrate which journalists they actually know personally, and show you evidence of campaigns for companies similar to yours. It is also worth bearing in mind, as with NOMADs and brokers, that you may well get better service as a relatively large client of a small firm rather than the other way around.

Note, by the way, that investor relations is different from financial PR. Smaller companies usually only have investor relations functions when their corporate broker is not doing its job.

Ofex (PLUS Market) instead of AIM

If your company is not yet big enough or sufficiently evolved to consider an AIM listing, there is increasing interest in listing on the even more junior market PLUS Markets, formerly known as Ofex. The advantages of such a listing are that the company has a valuation put on its shares, and gains a degree of credibility from having gone through the due diligence process of obtaining a listing. It is also considerably cheaper, in some cases by an order of magnitude.

The downside is that there is for most stocks considerably less liquidity than on AIM, although there is a degree of overlap: the more liquid stocks on PLUS Markets see considerably more trading in their shares than the bottom end of AIM. This means that in most cases your shares will have less value as acquisition currency on this market, but there are many investors who like to see a market quote for their investment, however illiquid. You can always go on to an AIM listing later as the company develops, and if you have gone through the process once, it is a lot easier all round.

It is considerably harder to raise money for PLUS Markets stocks than for AIM ones, and raisings in the few hundred thousand pounds range are the norm. Many stocks go on to PLUS Markets without raising any money at all. But if you *are* looking to raise money, make this very clear from the outset – many advisers will not undertake to do it because there can be no guarantees of success.

The advantage of PLUS Markets in cost terms is that the company needs only to have a corporate adviser that is a member of PLUS Markets. This keeps cost down but concentrates your sources of advice. So, it means that it is even more essential to choose an adviser with whom you can work, and whose advice you respect. The actual process of obtaining a listing is less onerous and more transparent – you can download the PLUS Markets rules from its website.

Are you paying by the hour?

You don't pay NOMADs and brokers by the hour. If you are paying any of the others in this way, stop it. The reason is that you cannot control and will not even see the flow of documents between the parties, and can be faced with a life-threatening bill if three lawyers have been working on your document at hourly rates of between £150 (juniors) and £350+ (partners). Get all the professionals to agree a fee for the job, and an abort fee in the event that for some reason it does not happen. A deal can fall apart for any number of completely unforeseen reasons.

Summary

- If your company operates in a specialist area (mining, technology, media and so on), or has significant overseas operations, choose advisers who have worked on deals in these areas before.
- Pick a firm where you matter as much to them as they do to you. The largest NOMADs on AIM have over 50 clients. There is little advantage to being the smallest.
- As your company grows its investor base will evolve, and so will its list of advisers. Pick the ones that are right for now.
- If you are looking to raise money, check that the amount you are looking to raise is within the placing power (that is, the ability to raise funds) of the broker.
- Depending on the size and complexity of the deal there is no need to go for big names.
- Pay accountants and lawyers on a fixed-fee basis, not by the clock.
- If the costs (not just financial but in terms of your time as well) of all the above look to be very high compared with the rewards of a listing, consider PLUS Markets instead of AIM.

Contributors' contact list

Acquisitions International
First Floor, Redheugh House
Thornaby Place
Thornaby on Tees TS17 6SG
Tel: +44 (0) 870 199 4056
Fax: +44 (0) 1642 671 749
Contact: Dr Mike Sweeting
Email: drsweeting@aol.com
www.acquisitionsinternational.com

Alliotts Chartered Accountants and Business Advisers
Congress House
14 Lyon Road
Harrow
Middlesex HA1 1DN
Tel: +44 (0) 20 8861 1771
Fax: +44 (0) 20 8861 3759
Contact: Mary Clancy
Email: maryc@alliotts.com
Website: www.alliotts.com

Aquila Financial Ltd
181 Union Street
London SE1 0LN
Tel: +44 (0) 20 7202 2600
Fax: +44 (0) 20 7202 2608
Contact: Peter Reilly
Direct line: +44 (0) 20 7202 2601

Email: peterreilly@aquila-financial.com
Website: www. aquila-financial.com

Athanor Capital Partners Ltd
55–56 Queens House
Lincoln's Inn Fields
London WC2A 3LJ
Tel: +44 (0) 20 7430 1991
Fax: +44 (0) 20 7430 1992
Contact: Graham Brown
Email: gbrown@athanor capital.com
Website: www.athanorcapital.com

BCMS Corporate
Kingsclere Park
Kingsclere
Newbury
Berkshire RG20 4SW
Tel: +44 (0) 1635 299 616
Fax: +44 (0) 1635 299 502
Contact: David Rebbettes
Email: david.rebettes@bcmscorporate.com
Website: www.bcmscorporate.com

B P Collins
Collins House
32–38 Station Road
Gerrards Cross SL9 8EL
Tel: +44 (0) 1753 889995

Fax: +44 (0) 1753 880851 + 889857
Contact: David Stanning
Email: david.stanning@bpcollins.co.uk
Website: www.bpcollins.co.uk

Bureau van Dijk Electronic Publishing
Zephus Limited
5th Floor, Croxley House
14 Lloyd Street
Manchester M2 5ND
Tel: +44 (0) 161 838 9555
Fax: +44 (0) 161 8389550
Contact: Lisa Wright
Direct line: +44 (0) 161 838 9551
Email: Lisa.Wright@zephus.com
Website: www.zephyr.bvdep.com

Cavendish Corporate Finance Ltd
40 Portland Place
London W1B 1 NB
Tel: +44 (0) 20 7908 6000
Fax: +44 (0) 20 7908 6006
Contact: Peter Gray
Email: pgray@cavendish.com
Website: www.cavendish.com

Cobalt Corporate Finance Ltd
Greybrook House
28 Brook Street
London W1K 5DH
Tel: +44 (0) 20 7491 1271
Fax: +44 (0) 20 7491 1272
Contact: Paul Rivers-Latham
Email: prl@cobaltcf.com
Website: www.cobaltcf.com

Conybeare Solicitors
Clearwater House
4–7 Manchester Street
London W1U 3AE
Tel: +44 (0) 870 753 0925
Fax : +44 (0) 870 762 7925
Contact: steven@conybeare.com
Email: steven@conybeare.com
Website: www.conybeare.com

Executives Online Ltd
Dolphin House
St. Peter Street, Winchester
Hampshire SO23 8BW
Tel: +44 (0) 1962 829 705
Fax: +44 (0) 1962 866 116
Contact: Norrie Johnston
Email: norrie@executives.online.co.uk
Website: www.executivesonline.co.uk

Faegre & Benson LLP
7 Pilgrim Street
London EC4V 6LB
Tel: +44 (0) 20 7450 4500
Fax: +44 (0) 20 7450 4545
Contact: Edward Hoare
Email: ehoare@faegre.com
Website: www.faegre.co.uk

Field Fisher Waterhouse
35 Vine Street
London EC3N 2AA
Tel: +44 (0) 20 7861 4000
Fax: +44 (0) 20 7488 0084
Contact: David Wilkinson
Email: david.wilkinson@ffw.com
Website: www.ffw.com

Heath Lambert Group
Friary Court
65 Crutched Friars
London EC3N 2NP
Tel: +44 (0) 20 7560 3000
Fax: +44 (0) 20 7560 3540
Contact: Alan Pratten
Email: apratten@heathlambert.com
Website: www.heathlambert.com

Horsey Lightly Fynn
20, West Mills
Newbury
Berkshire RG14 5HG
Tel: +44 (0) 1635 528122
Fax: +44 (0) 1635 517140
Contact: Simon Arthur

Direct line: +44 (0) 1635 517136
Email: sarthur@hlf.uk.com
Website: www.hlf.uk.com

Howles & Co Ltd
95 Hampstead Way
London NW11 7LR
Tel: +44 (0) 20 8731 7182
Fax: +44 (0) 20 8731 7633
Contact: Geoff Howles
Email: geoff@howles.co.uk
Website: www.howles.co.uk

Hurst & Co Accountants LLP
Lancashire Gate
21 Tiviot Dale
Stockport
Cheshire SK1 1TD
Tel: +44 (0) 161 477 2474
Fax: +44 (0) 161 476 4423
Contact: Rachel Murphy
Email: rachel.murphy@hurst.co.uk
Website: www.hurst.co.uk

Kerman & Co
7 Savoy Court
Strand
London WC2R 0ER
Tel: +44 (0) 20 7539 7272
Fax: +44 (0) 20 7240 5780
Contact: Daniel O'Connell
Email: doc@kermanco.co.uk
Website: www.kermanco.com

Kidd Rapinet
14 & 15 Craven Street
London WC2N 5AD
Tel: +44 (0) 20 7925 0303
Fax: +44 (0) 20 7925 0334
Contact: Philip Wild
Direct line: +44 (0) 20 7024 8029
Email: pwild@kiddrapinet.co.uk
Website: www.kiddrapinet.co.uk

MacRoberts
Excel House, 30 Semple Street
Edinburgh EH3 8BL
Tel: +44 (0) 131 229 5046
Fax: +44 (0) 131 229 0849
Contact: Alan Kelly
Email: alan.kelly@macroberts.com
Website: www.macroberts.com

Mazars LLP
Sovereign Court
Witan Gate
Milton Keynes MK9 2HP
Tel: +44 (0) 1908 680737
Fax: +44 (0) 1908 690567
Contact: Paula Gurney
Email: paula.gurney@mazars.co.uk
Contact: Stephen Harris
Email: stephen.harris@mazars.co.uk
Tel: +44 (0) 1908 680747
Contact: Adrian Alexander
Email: adrian.alexander@mazars.co.uk
Tel: +44 (0) 1273 206788
Contact: Oliver Hoffman
Email: oliver.hoffman@mazars.co.uk
Tel: +44 (0) 113 387 8725
and
Lancaster House
67 Newhall Street
Birmingham
B3 1NG
Tel: +44 (0) 121 212 4579
Fax: +44 (0) 121 236 2779
Contact: Andrew Millington
Email: andrew.millington@mazars.co.uk
Website: www.mazars.co.uk

Mishcon de Reya
Summit House, 12 Red Lion Square
London WC1R 4QD
Tel: +44 (0) 20 7440 7000
Fax: +44 (0) 20 7404 5982
Contact: Kevin McCarthy

Tel: +44 (0) 20 7440 7465
Email: kevin.mccarthy@mishcon.com
Website: www.mishcon.com

NELLEN Solicitors
19 Albemarle Street
London W1S 4HS
Tel: +44 (0) 20 7499 8122
Fax: +44 (0) 20 7493 0146
Contact: Gideon Nellen
Email: gideon.nellen@nellen.co.uk
Website: www.nellen.co.uk

Nelsons
Pennine House, 8 Stanford Street
Nottingham NG1 7BQ
Tel: +44 (0) 115 958 6262
Fax: +44 (0) 115 958 8113
Contact: Duncan Taylor
Email:
duncan.taylor@nelsonslaw.co.uk
Website: www.nelsonslaw.co.uk

Pinsent Masons
1 Park Row
Leeds LS1 5AB
Tel: +44 (0) 113 244 5000
Fax: +44 (0) 113 244 8000
Contact: Peter Wood
Direct line: +44(0) 113 225 5437
Email:
peter.j.wood@pinsentmasons.com
Website: www.pinsentmasons.com

**PKF (UK) LLP Accountants and
Business Advisers**
Farringdon Place, 20 Farrindon Road
London EC1M 3AP
Tel: +44 (0) 20 7065 0000
Fax: +44 (0) 20 7065 0650
Contact: James A. Turner
Direct line: +44 (0) 113 228 4118
Email: james.turner@uk.pkf.com
Website: www.pkf.co.uk

Punter Southall & Co Ltd
126 Jermyn Street
London SW1Y 4UJ
Tel: +44 (0) 7839 8600
Fax: +44 (0) 7839 3343
Contact: Richard Jones
Email:
richard.jones@puntersouthall.com
Website: www.puntersouthall.com

Index

Index of advertisers